D1098726

Contents

The Methuen Drama Book of Royal Court Plays 2000–2010

Under the Blue Sky
David Eldridge

Fallout
Roy Williams

Motortown
Simon Stephens

My Child
Mike Bartlett

Enron
Lucy Prebble

Edited and with an introduction by
Ruth Little

Bloomsbury Methuen Drama
An imprint of Bloomsbury Publishing Plc

B L O O M S B U R Y
LONDON · OXFORD · NEW YORK · NEW DELHI · SYDNEY

Bloomsbury Methuen Drama
An imprint of Bloomsbury Publishing Plc

Imprint previously known as Methuen Drama

50 Bedford Square	1385 Broadway
London	New York
WC1B 3DP	NY 10018
UK	USA

www.bloomsbury.com

**BLOOMSBURY, METHUEN DRAMA and the Diana logo are trademarks
of Bloomsbury Publishing Plc**

This collection first published in Great Britain in 2010 by Methuen Drama
Reprinted by Bloomsbury Methuen Drama 2011, 2016

Under the Blue Sky first published by Methuen Publishing Ltd in 2000,
copyright © David Eldridge 2000
Fallout first published by Methuen Publishing Ltd in 2003,
copyright © Roy Williams 2003
Motortown first published by Methuen Drama in 2006,
copyright © Simon Stephens 2006
My Child first published by Methuen Drama in 2007,
copyright © Mike Bartlett 2007
Enron first published by Methuen Drama in 2009
Reprinted in this volume with amendments to the text
copyright © Lucy Prebble 2009, 2010

British Library Cataloguing-in-Publication Data
A catalogue record for this book is available from the British Library.

ISBN: PB: 978-1-4081-2393-5

Library of Congress Cataloging-in-Publication Data
A catalog record for this book is available from the Library of Congress

Series: Play Anthologies

Typeset by Country Setting, Kingsdown, Kent
Printed and bound in Great Britain

Introduction

This volume brings together five landmark British plays produced at the Royal Court Theatre in the first decade of the twenty-first century. Each has had a significant impact on contemporary theatre culture both nationally and internationally. The collection begins with a play rooted in the late twentieth century: David Eldridge's triptych about love, war and teaching (*Under the Blue Sky*, 2000). The later plays in the volume reach out to examine the clash of racial and cultural identities in contemporary Britain (Roy Williams' *Fallout*, 2003), the brutal and bitter legacy of the war in Iraq (Simon Stephens' *Motortown*, 2006), and the emotional consequences of divorce and child custody battles (Mike Bartlett's *My Child*, 2007). Towards the end of the decade, Lucy Prebble turns back to trace the current global financial crisis to its origins in America's hubristically overheated economy of the 1990s (*Enron*, 2009). Although disparate in form, theme and subject matter, they are all plays of concentrated reckoning characterised by vivid theatrical imagination, richly idiomatic dialogue and probing irony.

The Royal Court Theatre reopened in February 2000 following a major rebuild. In the same year the Boyden Report, commissioned by the Arts Council, and the Theatre Review of which it was part, led to the publication of a National Policy for theatre in England which argued for – and resulted in – the injection of £25 million into the industry by 2003. Some of the funding supported strategic initiatives aimed at increasing cultural diversity within the sector, and the shift in policy and practice invigorated the new writing industry in London and across the country.

This has been a decade of cataclysmic events and unpredictably evolving global phenomena: from the iconoclastic horror of 11 September 2001 to the devastation of the 'war on terror' in Iraq and Afghanistan; from the London bombings of 7 July 2005 to the global financial crisis of 2008/9 and the increasingly palpable evidence of planetary climate change, the major events of the new millennium have reminded us of our contingent lives and choices, our insatiable appetites and our frailty. Their consequences have propelled both emerging and maturing playwrights towards new paradigms and perspectives.

Throughout this period at the Royal Court a process of consolidation and expansion was under way. Ian Rickson developed a strategy of bringing playwrights from the small studio space in the Jerwood Theatre Upstairs to the Court's main stage. His aim was to expand their ambitions, skills and opportunities, and the status and profile of their work, ensuring, according to Michael Billington, 'that writers went on to deliver their second and third plays, the hardest thing in our impatient culture where people are always frantically seeking the next new thing, rather than admiring maturing talent'. [1] At the same time, the theatre began seeding relationships with the next generation of writers, a project which incoming artistic director Dominic Cooke intensified from 2007 with a renewed and strategic emphasis on the work of the Young Writers' Programme and its incorporation into the core activities and play development processes of the building. Simon Stephens, Leo Butler, Michael Wynne, Rebecca Gilman and Roy Williams all made the journey from Upstairs to Downstairs, where they joined senior play-wrights including Conor McPherson, Terry Johnson and Caryl Churchill. Upstairs, Laura Wade, Lucy Prebble, Christopher Shinn and rising international stars Marius von Mayenburg, Juan Mayorga, Vassily Sigarev and the Presnyakov Brothers (Oleg and Vladimir) were making their mark in a series of challenging and transformative productions.

Cooke encouraged an immediate and engaged response from young playwrights to world events and to the contra-dictions and complexities of our lives and cultures. His programming stimulated and reflected a burgeoning dramatic interest in the critical analysis of systems of power and their dysfunction, the rituals and taboos of the middle classes, and the relationship between faith and fundamentalism. He main-tained relationships with pioneering playwrights including Churchill, Martin Crimp, Mark Ravenhill and Wallace Shawn, while introducing new and previously unheard voices in the work of Alia Bano, Polly Stenham, D.C. Moore and Bola Agbaje.

David Eldridge's dramatic triptych *Under the Blue Sky* was presented at the Royal Court in the Jerwood Theatre Upstairs in September 2000, directed 'with cool precision' by Rufus Norris.[2] It won a *Time Out* Live Award for Best New Play in the West End in 2001. Described by critic Dominic Cavendish as 'an education in wit and compassion',[3] *Under the Blue Sky* is a study of three sets of relationships between school teachers in the late 1990s. It is a funny, painful and poignant play, infused by the grief of war, the unlearnt lessons of history and the fierce, mortal desire to seize the day. It was presented in a traverse staging with a bed at one end and a kitchen range at the other, and its action is based on 'a repeated pattern of unequal love',[4] finally broken in the closing moments when two middle-aged teachers tentatively acknowledge the deeper meaning of their platonic relation-ship. 'It's the end of the century,' argues Robert at the play's conclusion: 'People look back and try and make sense of who we are. It's natural. It's a moment. We're educated and used to explaining the world around us. We teach. We should know better than anyone else.' The fact that they do not is the source of the play's comedy and its darker tragic implications.

Under the Blue Sky was successfully revived in the West End in 2008, and has become a turn-of-the-century classic; its implications have shifted, according to Eldridge, and gained new resonance in the post-9/11 world: 'When *Under the Blue Sky* was first produced . . . boys in Union-Jack-draped coffins weren't being unloaded at Brize Norton . . . What sounded like a nostalgic memorial then, now sounds as much like a memento mori.'[5] Throughout the play Eldridge demonstrates his plural perspective on his characters, combining moments of joyous farce with astute social commentary and a poignant and sympathetic acknowledgement of human vulnerability.

Roy Williams is an acclaimed playwright who joined the Royal Court's Young Writers' Programme in the 1990s and

emerged as an astute chronicler of the social and cultural
pressures experienced by young people in multiracial Britain.
His plays, including *Lift Off* (which won the George Devine
Award in 2000) and *Clubland* (2001, which won an *Evening
Standard* Most Promising Playwright Award) chart the
loyalties, tensions and conflicts within urban peer groups
marginalised by race, class and social pressure. In *Fallout*, his
first play for the Downstairs stage metamorphosed in Ultz's
spare design into a wire-meshed basketball court, he portrays
black teenagers drawn into violence and mutual mistrust by
an absence of male role models. *Fallout* was commissioned by
Ian Rickson for the larger space specifically with the aim of
tackling urgent and resonant subject matter and encouraging
a 'mythic gesture' on the part of the playwright.[6] Charles
Spencer in *The Daily Telegraph* described the production as
'the moment when a promising dramatist spectacularly
achieves his full potential.'[7]

   Fallout opens with the killing of a schoolboy by a gang on
a troubled estate. The boy is a victim of a new internecine
racism between young people of African and Afro-Caribbean
backgrounds, 'like deh is two kinds of black'. But there is also,
the play points out, another kind of black, represented by Joe,
who grew up on the estate and now returns to police it. He
has been drafted into the community in the wake of the
McPherson Report highlighting institutional racism in the
police force. The scenario is not based, however, on a simple
opposition between those who stayed and those who got
away; Joe brings with him a host of assumptions about his
own culture. His behaviour is influenced by internalised and
displaced racism, and his unresolved anger contains the seeds
of his own downfall. 'What Williams pins down brilliantly,'
claimed Michael Billington in *The Guardian*, 'is the corrosive
envy that pervades a culture of limited opportunities.'[8] *Fallout*
is characterised by immediacy and energy; its compressed
structure, punchy dialogue and fluid scene shifts increase the
sense of tension in the crucible of the estate. In Rickson's
'bruising confrontational production', *Fallout* was hailed as 'a
thrillingly fine play'.[9]

Simon Stephens' first play, *Bluebird*, was produced during the Young Writers' Festival of 1998. Stephens later became resident dramatist at the Royal Court, where his plays *Herons* and *Country Music* were produced in the Jerwood Theatre Upstairs. *Motortown* resulted from a provocation by Ian Rickson to write a play that acknowledged and explored the playwright's dark side; to uncover something 'dissonant, aggressive, ugly, violent'.[10] Stephens wrote much of the play in four days, between the announcement of London's successful bid for the 2012 Olympics and the aftermath of the bombings that took place on 7 July 2005, and it was directed by Ramin Gray on a bare stage under exposed lights: 'If the euphoria of the Olympic success energised my writing then the terror of the attacks on London drove through my play like a train.'[11]

In Stephens' view, both the 'war on terror' and the war in Iraq demanded the urgent attention of playwrights, and *Motortown* deliberately destroys clear moral categories to shatter the comfort and complacency of its audiences. Danny has returned from Iraq to an England offering 'all the stinking attractions of a dog turd', according to critic Lyn Gardner.[12] His former girlfriend won't see him because his letters frighten her, and his parents too are in anxious retreat. Trained in violence and tainted by horrors he cannot articulate, Danny inevitably plays out at home the obscene gestures of the 'theatre' of war. The play combines deliberately banal dialogue and a shocking act of onstage violence, to which we, like Danny in Iraq, must bear witness. When it is over, the actors mop the bloodstained stage 'in a ritual that feels both like an absolution and a terrible punishment.'[13] Stephens gazes across the abyss separating the cosseted middle classes from suburban fringe-dwellers such as Danny and, beyond him, the abandoned urban underclass. Critic Michael Coveney pointed out that the play 'owes a debt of honour to the first European working-class tragedy, Georg Buchner's *Woyzeck*'.[14] *Motortown* also acknowledges the 'terrible state' of the planet, and our chronic inertia in response to it: 'There are too many people. There is not enough water. There is not enough oxygen. And nobody admits it . . . we'll continue to eat it all up and eat it all up and eat it all up until the only thing we've got left to fucking eat, Danny, the only thing we've got left to eat is each other.' Fluid scene changes, choreographed by Hofesh Schechter, involved the rhythmic, synchronised rearrangement of chairs. The workings of the play remained visible throughout; it was an act of deliberate, unavoidable moral provocation. Coveney described *Motortown* as 'an instant modern classic, the first major anti-war play of this era'.[15]

Mike Bartlett's *My Child* was directed by Sacha Wares in 2007 in a radically transformed Jerwood Theatre Downstairs as the first production under incoming artistic director Dominic Cooke. The forty-five-minute play was Bartlett's first for the stage, and introduced an influential new writer, whose work is characterised by economy and scene elision, social enquiry and intensely focused scenarios. *My Child* draws obliquely on the high profile media campaign of Fathers 4 Justice and considers the often painful marginalising of fathers in family breakdown. Denied access to his child by a hostile ex-wife and driven by anger, frustration, grief and love, a Man kidnaps his son and becomes a social outcast, compounding his isolation and impotence in the face of public opprobrium and an intractable legal system. He asks his mother why she counselled him 'to put others first . . . To try to be moral and good, and not selfish . . . To love.' 'Look at me', he says: 'It's not how the world is.'

  Written without stage directions in terse, compressed dialogue, *My Child* is a study of emotional disorientation, in which contested moral codes and gender roles lead to dysfunctional relationships and broken lines of communication. Miriam Buether's traverse design remodelled the theatre stalls to suggest a London Underground train carriage, with actors and audience compelled to share the same claustrophobic space: 'the climactic fight', according to Michael Billington, 'leaves the audience feeling endangered'.[16] 'I'd never have thought,' claimed John Peter in *The Times*, 'that so much life, anger and pain could be contained in such a short span.'[17] Bartlett has since premiered two plays at the Royal Court: *Contractions* (2008) and *Cock* (2009).

Lucy Prebble's first play, *The Sugar Syndrome* – a study of paedophilia and anorexia bulimia set in the world of internet chatrooms – was written at the age of twenty-two and produced in 2003 in the Jerwood Theatre Upstairs. Characterised by 'moral seriousness, suspense, compassion and topical interest',[18] the play won the Critics' Circle Drama Award for Most Promising Playwright, and established Prebble as a writer of moral intelligence and emotional insight. Her second play for the Court, *Enron*, was commissioned by Headlong Theatre Company and co-produced with the Royal Court and Chichester Festival Theatre in 2009 in the Jerwood Theatre Downstairs, directed by Rupert Goold. At once a case study and a universal allegory, the play charts the notorious rise and fall of energy giant Enron and its founding partners Kenneth Lay and Jeffrey Skilling, who, along with the company's CEO Andy Fastow, oversaw 'the corporate crime that defined the end of the twentieth century'. The play is an epic multimedia satire – a comedy with a tragic structure – which analyses the conditions and behaviours that led ultimately to the global financial meltdown of 2008/9. 'It's a time of little conflict internationally,' claims an Enron employee in the early 1990s, 'the fastest growing economy there *has ever been* . . . It feels – genuinely – like the most exciting time to be doing business.'

Enron is a 'gripping, shocking and strangely moving' play;[19] a brilliant and damning epitaph for the unbounded excesses and self-consuming rituals of 1990s capitalism. Punctuated by striking images and choreographed ensemble action, '*Enron* does for our era what Churchill's play [*Serious Money*] did for the 1980s, catching the lure, turbulence and brash excitement of high-voltage trade, but leaving you eager to see more traps for fat cats.'[20] Prebble fashions witty theatrical metaphors for the virtual markets and financial instruments designed to conceal Enron's growing debt; hungry raptors prowl Fastow's 'lair' while the blind mice of corporate leadership stagger in the dark and the voice of financial probity is replaced by the mouthings of a ventriloquist's dummy: 'Here is the blustering energy of capitalism, the illusion of being a delirious romp; and here too its narcissism and testosterone-fuelled nastiness.'[21] This is the world of the bubble, and the bubble must burst. But as Skilling himself continues to insist, even at the point of imprisonment, there will always be another: 'Don't part with your illusions. When they are gone you may still exist, but you have ceased to live.'

Each of the plays in this volume demands attention and merits inclusion for its originality, artistry, anger and compassion. Together they provide a map of the presiding concerns, social tensions and political upheavals of the last decade, and demonstrate vividly that playwriting can be a tool for excavating and interpreting the deepest, most complex and profound aspects of human experience.

Ruth Little
Royal Court Literary Manager, 2007–10

Notes

1 *The Guardian*, 15 January 2007
2 Michael Billington, *The Guardian*, 21 September 2000
3 *Daily Telegraph*, 21 September 2000
4 Paul Taylor, *The Independent*, 21 September 2000
5 *The Independent*, 17 July 2008
6 Ian Rickson, interview in *The Royal Court Theatre Inside Out* by Ruth Little and Emily McLaughlin (Oberon, 2007), p. 416
7 19 June 2003
8 18 June 2003
9 Charles Spencer, *Daily Telegraph*, 19 June 2003
10 *The Royal Court Theatre Inside Out*, p. 434
11 *The Royal Court Theatre Inside Out*, p. 437
12 *The Guardian*, 25 April 2006
13 Lyn Gardner, *The Guardian*, 25 April 2006
14 *What's On Stage*, 25 April 2006
15 *What's On Stage*, 25 April 2006
16 *The Guardian*, 10 May 2007
17 *Sunday Times*, 20 May 2007
18 Alistair Macauley, *Financial Times*, 23 October 2003
19 James Hall, *Daily Telegraph*, 22 September 2009
20 Benedict Nightingale, *The Times*, 24 September 2009
21 Henry Hitchings, *Evening Standard*, 23 January 2009

David Eldridge

Under the Blue Sky

For Ruth and Stevo

David Eldridge was born in Romford, Greater London. His full-length plays include *Serving it Up* (Bush Theatre, 1996); *A Week with Tony* (Finborough Theatre, 1996); *Summer Begins* (RNT Studio and Donmar Warehouse, 1997); *Falling* (Hampstead Theatre, 1999); *Under the Blue Sky* (Royal Court Theatre, 2000, awarded the *Time Out* Live Award for Best New Play in the West End in 2001); *Festen* (Almeida and Lyric Theatre, 2004); *M.A.D* (Bush Theatre, 2004); *Incomplete and Random Acts of Kindness* (Royal Court Theatre, 2005); a new version of Ibsen's *Wild Duck* (Donmar Warehouse, 2005); *Market Boy* (National Theatre, 2006); a new version of Ibsen's *John Gabriel Borkman* (Donmar Warehouse, 2007); *Under the Blue Sky* remounted starring Catherine Tate (Duke of York's Theatre, 2008); an adaptation of Jean-Marie Besset's *Babylone* (Belgrade Theatre, Coventry 2009); and *A Thousand Stars Explode in the Sky* (with Robert Holman and Simon Stephens; Lyric Hammersmith, 2010).

I am deeply indebted to all the teachers who talked to me about what they do and to Lyn MacDonald's brilliant books, *1915: The Death of Innocence*, *The Roses of No Man's Land* and *To the Last Man: Spring 1918*, which inspired aspects of the third act. As she says, 'In the end it is the people who matter.'

And special thanks to the Royal National Theatre Studio for time and space to work.

DE, August 2000

Under the Blue Sky was first performed at the Royal Court Jerwood Theatre Upstairs, Sloane Square, London, on 14 September 2000. The cast, in order of appearance, was as follows:

Nick	Justin Salinger
Helen	Samantha Edmonds
Michelle	Lisa Palfrey
Graham	Jonathan Cullen
Robert	Stanley Townsend
Anne	Sheila Hancock

Director Rufus Norris
Designer Katrina Lindsay
Lighting Design Johanna Town
Sound Design Rich Walsh

Characters

Nick, *aged twenty-eight*
Helen, *aged twenty-seven*
Michelle, *aged thirty-eight*
Graham, *aged thirty-six*
Anne, *aged fifty-eight*
Robert, *aged forty-two*

Setting
Leyton, east London; Hornchurch, Essex; and Tiverton, Devon.

Locations
A kitchen and living area; a bedroom; and a patio in a cottage garden.

Time
February 1996; May 1997; and August 1998.

Note
The play should be performed without an interval.

Act One

As the house lights dim, the long thunderous sound of a huge bomb exploding and police sirens wailing is audible.

February 1996. The kitchen and living area. A flat in Leyton, east London. Seven p.m.

Nick *crushes a clove of garlic in his crusher and empties the contents into a pan. He then peels and chops a large onion with a knife larger than he needs for the job.*

Nick *is twenty-eight.*

A slight pause.

Helen *enters. She is drinking a glass of red wine.*

Helen *is twenty-seven and looks good in her outfit.*

Helen   The ceasefire's over.

Nick   It was a bomb then?

Helen   Yeah. It's on the television.

Nick   Where?

Helen   They've bombed the Docklands. Canary Wharf, I think.

Nick   And you thought it was thunder?

Helen   D'you want any help?

Nick *tips the onion into the pan.*

Nick   You can chop up that green pepper.

Helen *puts down her wine and takes the knife* **Nick** *was using. She makes a start gutting the pepper.*

Nick   Cheers, Helen.

Nick *adds olive oil to his garlic and onion and switches on the hob. He gives it a stir with a wooden spoon.*

Helen   Your hair looks great short like that.

Nick   Thanks.

He watches **Helen** *as she chops the pepper. He pours himself a glass of red wine.*

Is that new?

Helen   Yeah. D'you like it? It's from Principles.

Nick   Yeah. It's very flattering.

Helen *smiles at* **Nick**.

Helen   Shall I put this in?

Nick   Not yet.

He drinks. The onion and garlic begin to sizzle.

I knew it was a bomb. The flat shook. It shook, didn't it?

Helen   It unnerves me to think we were close enough for that to happen.

Nick *stirs the onion and garlic and then hunts around in the fridge for the mincemeat. A slight pause.*

Nick   Stop looking at my arse, Helen.

Helen   Why would I be looking at your arse?

Nick   You know you're obsessed with my arse.

Helen   I'm not obsessed with anyone's arse. Let alone yours, my dear.

Nick *takes out the mincemeat and shuts the fridge door.*

Nick   Apparently Amanda Harrison's going to send me a valentine's card with 'sexy bum' on it.

Helen   Amanda Harrison?

Nick   In year eleven.

Helen   Lovely.

Nick   So the other girls tell me.

Helen   I've never had a card from a pupil.

Nick   You've never had a card full stop.

Helen   Yes I have.

Nick   What? You sent to yourself when you were thirteen?

Helen   You're such a git.

Nick   Didn't you ever fancy a teacher?

Helen   No.

Nick   Really? I thought everyone had an adolescent crush on one.

Helen   No. Not that I remember.

Nick   I think the reason people fall for teachers the way they do's because of that. I don't think it's any of that stuff about it being a noble profession. The person who puts his own ambitions and dreams to one side. That's all crap. That's the sort of thing people who don't know us say. No. I think it's because you remember that person who made school worth coming to. Like a first love. And then later on in life when you meet a teacher you fancy and you go out and you sleep together you can't help it. You're a devoted fourteen-year-old all over again.

Helen   You do talk complete rubbish, don't you?

Nick *laughs and takes the knife from* **Helen** *and slices open the packaging around the mincemeat.* **Helen** *takes her wine and drinks it.*

Nick   Are you going to Sarah's party?

Helen   I don't know. When is it?

Nick   Wednesday night.

Helen   Who's going?

Nick   The usual lot. Sort of sad single-people get-together. Drink tequila, get very pissed and reveal secrets and then stagger home at four in the morning, with some dim light in your brain saying 'Shit. Year seven first lesson.'

Helen *smiles.* **Nick** *empties the mincemeat into the pan and stirs it together with the onion and garlic.*

Helen   Well, this is about time.

Nick   What?

Helen   You've been in here a year and this is the first time you've invited me over.

Nick   It's not.

Helen   It is.

Nick   You've been over here?

Helen   You know I've not.

Nick   No?

Helen   And how many times have I cooked for you? Had you over for dinner parties and drinks?

Nick   Sorry.

A long pause.

Helen   So what's this thing you want to talk to me about?

Nick *looks at* **Helen** *and thinks.*

Nick   Let's wait until after dinner. Yeah? OK, darling?

Nick *smiles.* **Helen** *drinks.*

Helen   You're such a flirt.

Nick   And you're so bloody serious. So boring. Why are you my friend?

Helen *smiles and pours herself some more wine.* **Nick** *stirs the meat and onions.*

Helen   Watch it, haircut one hundred.

Nick   Shit.

Helen   What?

Nick   I forgot to pick up fresh chillies.

Helen   Use powder.

Nick   Powder? Powder . . .

Helen   D'you want this wine all over your clean shirt?

Nick *laughs and raises his glass.*

Nick   To a good one.

Pause.

Helen   I put my bag in your room.

Nick   OK.

Helen   Is that OK?

Nick   You can sleep in my room if you like.

Helen *smiles and drinks.*

Helen   Can I?

Nick   If you want to you can.

Helen   Really?

Nick   Yeah. Course you can.

Helen   I might like that.

Nick   I haven't tried out the sofa bed yet. Perhaps tonight's the night I get my head down on there. Three hundred quid it cost me. I think it should be down to the PE department because they're the only ones who've had the benefit of it.

Helen   It's all right. I'll sleep on the sofa bed.

Nick   Whatever you fancy.

Helen *laughs.*

Helen   Yeah.

Nick   What?

He opens a cupboard and takes out the dried chillies.

I remember I overdid it once with the dried chillies and when I burped and farted it stang.

Helen   Nicholas . . .

Nick   Don't Nicholas me.

Helen   So what is it you want to talk about, Nicholas?

She drains her wine and pours herself another.

Because to be honest I think I'll be half cut by the time we've eaten that chilli.

Nick   Well, the future.

Helen *laughs and laughs.*

Nick   What?

Helen *downs the whole glass of red wine.*

Nick   Ding bloody dong.

Helen *puts down her glass, wipes her mouth and folds her arms.* **Nick** *looks at her and then shakes his head and begins to sprinkle the dried chillies over the meat and onions.*

Helen   I've got a pretty good idea what you want to talk about.

Nick   Have you?

Helen   Yeah.

Nick   What?

Helen   I think it's obvious.

Nick   Is it?

Helen   It's about us, isn't it?

Nick   What?

Helen   All the time we've been spending together. And going out. And all that. All that stuff.

Nick *stirs the meat and thinks.*

Nick   Look, Helen, I think you've got this . . .

Helen   I've noticed things have been changing. Things have been developing in a way they haven't before, haven't they?

Nick   No, Helen . . .

Helen   Admit it. They have, haven't they?

Nick   Helen, I wanted to talk to you because I'm thinking of leaving.

A pause.

I'm applying for another job.

He stirs the meat. A long pause.

Helen *is embarrassed and wounded.* **Nick** *goes over to hug her but* **Helen** *shies away.*

Nick   I wanted to talk to you first, Helen.

Helen   Yeah.

Nick   It's not far. Half-hour tops on the train from Stratford.

Helen   Yeah. Not far.

Nick   You can take those driving lessons you've been saying you're going to take. Pass your test. You're the only teacher I know who doesn't drive.

Helen   How stupid of me.

A pause.

Nick   Helen.

Helen   What school is it?

Nick   It's in Essex. To start in September. I drove up there at the weekend to have a proper nose around. It's a lovely school.

Helen   Is it?

Nick   The football team were playing at home and I watched the first half. Then I had a look at the dining halls and then I got talking to the chaplain. He showed me round the chapel. You should have seen it. There were these long rolls of honour. Of old boys who passed away in the two world wars.

Helen   It's an independent school, is it?

Nick   Yeah. So?

Helen   A public school?

Nick   It doesn't feel much like one but I suppose so.

Helen   Why do you want to go?

Nick   You know I've been feeling tired.

Helen   Of what?

Nick   Of the kids. I'm good at crowd control but I do want to actually teach at some point as well, Helen.

A slight pause.

He goes to the cupboard and takes out a tin of chopped tomatoes and a small tin of kidney beans.

You know teaching? I've had enough of being a bloody social worker, Helen.

He takes a tin-opener from the drawer.

And I want to teach A level again.

Helen   Well, there are plenty of colleges in the borough.

Nick   And I've been thinking I want a change from the East End. I want to move.

Helen   Well, I don't know about that.

A pause.

Nick *looks at* **Helen** *and takes the tin of chopped tomatoes which he starts to open. He tips the opened tin of chopped tomatoes into the pan, which he stirs.*

Nick   I'm tired of spending all day telling kids off. I want to be challenged. Intellectually. Every time I read a novel there I am fantasising an epic sixth-form discussion about it.

He smiles.

Now that is not normal. That is sad. That is very boring. Remember you're boring. I'm not boring.

Helen   Don't make fun of me.

Nick   Come on. I'm meant to be teaching them English and about half the bloody kids haven't even got it as their first language.

Helen   You're exaggerating.

A slight pause.

I think you'll be making a mistake.

Nick   Why?

Helen   I think you should stay.

Nick   Why? I want a career.

Helen   Things are going to get better.

Nick   I want a department of my own. I want a career. Not a slog.

Helen   Things are getting better. We were only saying last week how things have improved since the inspection?

Nick   Things have improved a little bit. No one's pulled a knife on you in six months. Big deal.

Helen   Don't make fun of that.

Nick   I'm sorry.

A slight pause.

Helen   Things are getting better at school. I wouldn't
have been in favour of it before but the kids wearing blazers
and a proper uniform has made a difference.

Nick   It's great. But it's not enough.

Helen   Well, I would rather be where I am than silver-
spooning a bunch of toffee-nosed brats from Essex.

Nick *studies* **Helen**. *A pause.*

Nick   Fine. OK. Fine.

A slight pause.

Helen *picks up the knife and points it at* **Nick**.

Helen   'Fuck off, Miss, I'll fucking kill you. I'll fucking stab
your heart, Miss. You bitch. You bitch-whore.'

Nick   I know what happened. I was there.

Helen   And have you seen me running away?

Nick *takes the tin of kidney beans which he opens with the tin-opener.*
Helen *puts the knife down. A pause.*

Nick   It isn't my duty to be unhappy. I owe it to myself to
be happy in my work and I'm not. Why are you trying to
put me on this huge guilt trip?

Helen   I'm not making you feel guilty. You feel guilty.
If you're feeling guilty don't blame your guilt on me.

Nick   Helen, you're being so hard on me.

Helen   Am I?

Nick   I thought I could talk to you about this?

Helen   Things will get better. I promise you, Nick.

Nick   I want a change . . .

Helen   And things will change.

Nick   Don't you see I need a change? This is like talking to a brick wall. I need to move on.

A slight pause.

I need to move on now. I've had enough. I know I've had enough. It's been hard but I've enjoyed it cutting my teeth here and that is it.

Helen   So having cut your teeth you can piss off and leave the kids that need good teachers like you?

Nick   Helen, I need to move on. And I think it's a terrific department.

Helen   You know the department?

Nick   Not really.

Helen   You've already been for an interview haven't you? You have haven't you? Last week. Last Tuesday. I thought it was strange.

Nick   Yeah.

Helen   You told me you had an inset? Why didn't you tell me? Why did you lie to me?

Nick   Stop it. Just stop it. Please. Stop this. It isn't fair. I wanted to talk to you. All I wanted to do was talk to you. Please. You're my friend. You're my friend, aren't you?

Helen   Yeah, I am.

Nick   Then let me go. Let me try and do this. Help me to do this. Be here for me. Understand please. Please try and understand. I'm so fond of you.

Helen   I know, but . . .

Nick   You must have been able to tell I've been unhappy? Why I've been needy. Spending time with you. Talking over and over things. And then I saw this job. And everything was clear.

Helen   But you've not been honest with me? You've not told me anything. I can't believe you didn't tell me about it. I can't believe you lied to me.

Nick *takes the kidney beans and tips them into the chilli which he stirs. A pause.*

Nick   You know I'm going to miss you, Helen.

Helen   Are you?

Nick   Yeah. I am really. I don't know if it's going to work out or not in this school.

Helen   I'm sure it will.

Nick   It's totally new to me. The only time I've ever been in a public school was when I was a lad. Our comp played them in a friendly. They gave us sausage, chips and beans beforehand and a cream cake and tea afterwards. It was like a dream.

A slight pause.

He smiles.

Can you imagine me getting up on a Saturday morning to teach year-seven boys?

Helen *shakes her head.*

Helen   First form. You'll have to get used to calling them first form.

Nick   See. You know more about it than I do. There's me getting all misty-eyed over the chapel on a guided tour. But can you see me in a front pew down on my knees with my hair parted?

Helen *laughs and shakes her head.*

Nick   I don't know whether I'll like it but I want to give it a go. If I get it.

A pause.

Helen   I'm going to miss you so much.

Nick   And so will I.

Nick *tips the pieces of chopped green pepper into the pan. He stirs the chilli. A slight pause.*

Helen   We're still going to see each other, aren't we?

Nick   Yeah. Course we are. You can come up and stay.

He studies **Helen**. *A pause.*

If I'm honest I guess I have been thinking about us as well.

Helen   Have you?

A pause.

Nick   Yeah. Well, we are close.

Helen   Yeah.

A pause.

Nick   Maybe it won't be a bad thing for us to see not quite so much of each other.

Helen   Why?

Nick   I don't know what us has been all about. I know I love us being friends.

Helen   So do I.

A pause.

Nick   Why can't you say what you feel?

Helen   Say what?

A pause.

Nick   I'm confused. You're clearly not. But you only ever meet me halfway emotionally. And I don't know if that's good. I don't know how I feel about it. Us. I feel really confused.

Helen   So am I.

Nick   I don't think you are. I am.

Helen   So what do you want me to do?

Nick   Just talk to me. Honestly. I wanted to talk to you about moving on. Going to another school. I admit it. Of course I wanted you to talk about your personal feelings.

Helen   Personal feelings?

She can't believe it. A slight pause.

So I can put my heart and guts on the floor in front of you? Sob and wail like a widow and hope it might change your mind? And in the process confirm your gut feeling it might be good for us to see less of each other. Good for you to see less of me. While you create a new life for yourself in Essex. Is that what you want? Well, you can get stuffed.

Helen *tries to leave.* **Nick** *stands in her way.*

Nick   Talk to me.

Helen   Piss off.

Nick   Come on.

Helen   Get lost. I mean it.

Nick   I'm sorry.

Helen   I can't tell you how I feel about you.

A long pause.

I could never.

Nick   Do you love me? Are you in love with me?

A long pause.

Helen   Why are you doing this? You've just been telling me you want to leave. You want to move away. This isn't fair and it isn't right.

Nick   You're the most important person to me in the world.

A slight pause.

But I don't know if I love you. I don't know if I can love you. If I'm capable of loving you.

Helen   You arsehole. You fucking arsehole.

A long pause.

Why are you torturing me like this?

A pause.

I can't talk any more. I feel so exposed.

A pause.

Nick   Sometimes I think it was a mistake I slept with you. I'm sorry.

Helen *looks at* **Nick**. *A slight pause.*

Helen   A mistake?

Nick   I don't know. Yeah. I think it was.

Helen   What, just that night or our whole friendship?

Nick   No . . .

Helen   I mean you wanted it. You wanted to sleep with me.

Nick   And you didn't?

Helen   I knew I thought a lot of you. That I was feeling like I liked you more than just fancying you.

Nick   We were both drunk.

Helen   No, you were drunk and you wanted it.

Nick   So are you saying I forced myself upon you?

Helen   No.

A pause.

This is so ugly. I don't want this. Why are you talking about this?

A pause.

To be honest I think it wasn't a fantastic thing that it happened when it happened but I know it did something.

A pause.

Like you cracked something. And it all leaked out.

A pause.

I felt different then.

A pause.

With every word I say I feel I'm betraying myself. I'm shrinking in front of you.

A pause.

The things you said to me.

Nick   When?

Helen   That time. Then.

Nick   I was drunk.

A slight pause.

I didn't know what I was saying.

Helen   You were heavy and pissed and you moved me around the bed like I was a prone body. But your words? The things you said. Your promises.

Nick   I don't know what to . . .

Helen   No.

Nick *stirs the chilli and turns the hob down. A slight pause.*

Helen   Your memory of it is that we were both drunk but I was sober. I remember every clumsy movement and every word you said like it's shot through my memory.

A slight pause.

I thought tonight would be my turn. You know that? To fall on you. Half cut.

A slight pause.

I feel so awful I wish the earth would swallow me up.

A long pause.

Nick   I reckon the chilli will be about another fifteen minutes. Perhaps I should boil the kettle and get the rice on? I got some lovely fresh bread from Sainsbury's.

Helen   Lovely. Really splendid. Lovely. I love chilli. And you make the best chilli, Nicholas.

She thinks. A pause.

I suppose if you're a terrorist. If you're proud of your culture. But you don't have any structure to fulfil or contain that sense of identity. Then that bomb isn't an unnatural response. Is it?

Nick   I don't know.

Helen   It's not enough believing in something. Having a passion. You have to have a voice to voice it.

Nick   That's why we do what we do, isn't it?

Helen   I was in the bar at university with some people and this Irish guy was talking about the 1916 uprising. The rebels were shot and martyred. The ringleader was a schoolteacher. Another bloody romantic, I suppose. Anyway, this girl joined in and said how she objected to these mythic pasts. It was like our Poppy Day. The myth of sacrifice. I didn't really understand what her objection was but I thought it's not your bloody history. Then this other bloke said Remembrance Sunday made him feel proud. He said he'd been on a school trip to the war cemeteries and heard the Last Post being played. And we were all quiet. Then the girl left and someone else said she was uptight and she needed a good nobbing and they all laughed. I hadn't said anything.

Nick   What are you talking about this for?

A slight pause.

Helen   I don't know.

A slight pause.

So really I should be booking up my driving lessons, shouldn't I?

Nick *studies* **Helen**.

Nick   Well, you need a car.

Helen   So hopefully even allowing for failing my test three times, or something hideous like that, I should have a car by the time you start work in Essex.

Nick   You'll pass first time, I'm sure. I haven't even got the job yet.

Helen   You'll get it.

A slight pause.

I could get a Clio or a Fiesta or something like that, couldn't I?

Nick   Yeah.

Helen   Can we talk about your school?

Nick   I don't know if I want to any more just now.

Helen   I'd like to talk about your school.

Nick   Can't we talk about something else?

Helen   What else have we got to talk about? Our friendship? Our relationship? Whether making love three years ago was a mistake?

Nick   Helen.

A slight pause.

You're making me feel edgy.

He takes a saucepan which he fills with water. He turns on the hob. When it boils neither of them take any notice.

Helen   You know, I just can't work it out? All the things we've done together. All the times we've got drunk and talked about what's important to us. All the times. Yet in three years. This is the first time. The fact that we spent a night together is mentioned.

Helen *fights back the tears. A long pause.*

How many kids are there? There. At your new school.

Nick   Over a thousand not including the prep.

Helen   What's the uniform like?

Nick   Blazer. Grey trousers. Not that much different from ours.

Helen   Have they got a swimming pool?

Nick   An open-air one.

Helen   An open-air one?

Nick   But they're thinking of rebuilding.

Helen   Is it a rugby or a football school?

Nick   Football.

Helen   That's right. You said earlier.

Nick   Stop this.

Helen   I want to know.

Nick   Please stop this.

Helen   I'm your friend. You're going. I'd like to know.

Nick   Then be my friend and try and understand. I'm sorry. I've messed things up. I've said things badly. Things have come out wrong. Don't you think I wish I didn't feel so confused?

Helen *starts to weep. A slight pause.*

Nick   I'm sorry. I'm sorry. I think the world of you.

Helen   Do you?

Nick   I've never gone out with anyone, have I?

Helen   What?

Nick   In the time we've known one another. There's been no other relationship. I've not wanted anyone.

Helen   You've gone out with people?

Nick   I've had dates. But who's there been?

Helen   No one that I know about.

Nick   No one.

Helen   I saw that guy for a month. We've never been going out. You don't have any right . . .

Nick   I know I don't.

A slight pause.

Perhaps I felt something about that?

Helen *really cries.*

Helen   I only saw him because I wanted you to . . .

Nick   What?

Helen   I don't know . . .

Nick   Fight over you?

Helen   No. I wanted you, not him.

Nick   But I didn't know how I felt. I still don't. But the longer it's gone on the more certain I've become that if I really wanted us. Us. In that way. Surely I would know? What am I holding back? What's holding me back?

Helen   Nothing.

Nick   There's something.

Helen   There's nothing stopping you. Just let it be . . .

Nick   All I know is I love you as a friend and this is ugly, Helen. It's hurt us both but all I wanted to try and do was talk to you. I want to leave and that is it.

Helen   I don't want you to go.

Nick   It's what I want.

Helen   Stay with me.

Nick   I can't . . .

Helen   Let me see you every day . . .

Nick   This is no good.

Helen   I know you're not sure how you feel but don't just . . .

Nick   What?

Helen   Leave me and go from me. Don't do that. Please.

A pause.

Nick   It's no good. I want this job. I don't know if our friendship can be any more than it is.

Helen *is heartbroken.*

Nick   Please don't cry any more.

Nick *goes to* **Helen** *but she picks up the knife. It is unclear whether she intends to hurt* **Nick** *or herself.*

Helen   You're not going.

Nick   Please . . .

Helen   You're not leaving me . . .

Nick   Give me that knife.

Helen   I'm not going to let you leave.

Nick   Helen. Just pass me the knife.

Helen   Tell me that you'll stay.

Nick   I can't say that.

Helen   Then I will do something . . .

Nick   No. Calm down and give it to me.

Helen   I think about you all the time . . .

Nick   I know . . .

Helen   I can't help it . . .

Nick   I know.

Helen   I think about the things we do . . .

Nick   Yeah?

Helen   And I think about all the things we're going to do . . .

Nick   We've had a right laugh, haven't we?

Helen   Like when we went to Warwick.

Nick   That's right.

Helen   To see your friends.

Nick   Billy and Susan. They thought you were great.

Helen   And I was embarrassed because they thought. They presumed I was your girlfriend.

She calms a little. A pause.

It was a lovely meal. And I was drinking Billy's Jim Beam by the end. You must have been ashamed of me?

Nick   No.

A pause.

Please. Give me the knife.

Helen   No.

Nick   You can't force me to stay. It's no good.

Helen *clearly threatens* **Nick** *with the knife.*

Helen   You're not leaving me. I'll kill you. I'll kill you right here and now.

Nick   No you won't.

Helen   I will. I'll put this right through your heart.

Nick   If you really loved me you wouldn't hurt me like this.

A slight pause.

Remember when that boy threatened you?

Helen *wipes away a tear and nods.*

Nick   How you felt?

Helen *nods and cries.*

Nick   You told me how scared you were.

Helen *nods and sobs.*

Nick   You're scaring me, Helen.

A slight pause.

You'd never hurt me. You'd never threaten me with that if you truly love me.

Helen   I do. I thought if I just waited.

Nick   I know. But this isn't helping anything, is it?

Helen   No.

She shakes her head and completely breaks down. **Nick** *embraces her as she cries and cries.*

I'm sorry, I'm sorry, I'm sorry, I'm sorry.

Nick   I'm sorry too.

Helen   I'd never hurt you.

Nick   I know you wouldn't.

Helen   I'd never ever hurt you.

Nick   You're just upset.

Helen   I can't stand the thought of not seeing you every day.

Nick *kisses her forehead as he comforts her.*

Helen   I can't stand it. I don't know what I'm going to do without you.

Nick   You're not losing me.

Helen   I want you, I want you, I want you.

Nick   Let's just be friends now, eh?

Helen   I am your friend.

Nick   Let's not analyse us. Let's just be. Let's just be us.

Helen *nods.*

Nick   I don't know. Maybe I'm just not ready yet.

Helen *nods.*

Nick   No more tears now. Eh?

Helen *nods.* **Nick** *roots around in the cupboard and takes out some rice and the bread.*

Nick   It's easy-cook rice. By the time it's done the chilli should be ready.

A pause.

He tips some rice into the pot on the hob.

Helen   It's awful, isn't it?

Nick   What?

Helen   The bomb.

Nick   Yeah. It is. They're psychopaths. And the other lot as well.

Helen *studies* **Nick**. *He takes the knife from her, wipes it with a cloth and uses it to slice the bread.*

Helen   When you go I'll come and visit.

Nick   If I go.

Helen   Of course you'll go.

A slight pause.

I'll learn to drive. I'll pass my test. I will.

Nick   You can do it. No problem.

Helen   I'll come and see you.

Nick   Whenever you want to.

Helen   We can go out for meals. And go to the cinema. Have days out like we always do?

Nick   Yeah. We can.

Helen   And Essex'll be nice, won't it? It'll make a nice change. I'll pass my test and I can drive us off out into the countryside and we'll find quiet pubs that do good food.

Nick   Yeah.

Helen   And we can make plans to do things together like we always do.

Nick *nods. A slight pause.*

Helen   Maybe we can book a holiday. It's something we've talked about loads of times but we've never got round to it.

A slight pause.

Somewhere hot. Away from this country.

Nick   Why don't we talk about it when I've got dinner dished up? We can talk about what I'm going to do and where we can go away. If we want to. Then, can't we?

Helen   What about the south of France, Nick? July. A farmhouse. Or a cottage or something. Maybe an apartment with a pool.

Nick   I'd like that.

A pause.

Helen   Just me and you. Somewhere we can be.

Nick *nods.*

Nick   I'd like that, Helen. The two of us on our own. We can spend proper time together and catch up on everything we've been doing.

Helen   Can we?

Nick   Come on, let's just have a good evening.

Helen   Yeah.

Nick   Let's have a good evening and put the last half-hour behind us.

Helen   Yeah.

A pause.

Nick   Water under the bridge. Yeah?

Helen   Water under the bridge.

A slight pause.

Nick   Promise?

Helen   Promise.

Helen *smiles. She walks towards* **Nick** *and they embrace. A slight pause.*

Slow fade.

Act Two

May 1997. The bedroom. A house in Hornchurch, Essex. One a.m.

Michelle *and* **Graham** *enter, snogging furiously. They are all over each other and through the next undress each other – not always successfully as they are both pissed.*

Michelle *is thirty-eight.* **Graham** *is thirty-six.*

Michelle   I want it.

Graham   Do you?

Michelle   I want it. Give it to me.

Graham   How do you want it?

Michelle   I want it inside me.

Graham   You can have it inside you.

Michelle   Can I? Tell me I can.

Graham   You can.

Michelle   I feel horny.

Graham   You can have it all.

Michelle   Give it all to me.

Graham   It's hard for you.

Michelle   It is. Isn't it?

Graham   Yes it is.

Michelle   I want to touch it.

Graham   No, don't touch it.

Michelle   I want to.

Graham   In a while.

Michelle   Now.

Graham   It's so tempting.

Michelle   Show me it.

Graham   Let me see your breasts first.

Michelle   Do you want to see them?

Graham   I want to see them.

Michelle   I want you to see them.

Graham   I've thought about seeing them so many times.

Michelle   Tell me.

Graham   So many times it's hard to pick.

Michelle   Tell me you've thought about my breasts.

Graham   Last week. On the athletics track. You were supervising second-form girls and you had a tight white polo shirt on.

Michelle   Did you want to rip it off?

Graham   I wanted to rip it off and clasp them.

Michelle   Clasp them.

Graham   Yes. Clasp them. Two huge balls of love fun.

Michelle   Go on. Clasp them now.

Graham   Yes I am.

Michelle   Do you love it?

Graham   Yes I love it.

Michelle   You're wearing your army uniform.

Graham   My CCF uniform.

Michelle   Tell me you're back from the war.

Graham   I'm back from the war.

Michelle   Tell me you've only got three hours.

Graham   I'm back from the war.

Michelle   A hero.

Graham   Battle-scarred.

Michelle   Battle-scarred. Yes.

Graham   I've only got an hour. God, your nipples are hard.

Michelle   An hour?

Graham   Yes, an hour. Sister.

Michelle   Sister. Sister?

Graham   You must remember last time I returned from the front? You nursed me and pleasured me.

Michelle   How did I pleasure you?

Graham   We only had an hour then but you did everything.

Michelle   I did everything, didn't I?

Graham   You were so naughty I wanted to put you over my knee and spank your bottom.

Michelle   But you couldn't, could you?

She pushes **Graham** *over on to the bed and sits astride him, pinning his arms down.*

Because you were weak from your wounds and I tended to you.

Graham   Yes you did.

Michelle *kisses* **Graham** *softly.*

Graham   Is this all right, Michelle? I mean, this is pretty wild.

Michelle   Shut up, Graham, you're spoiling it.

Michelle *rubs his chest.*

Graham　That's nice.

Michelle　This naughty little nurse wants to see your rifle.

Graham　No, don't.

Michelle　Your naughty little nurse wants to see your rifle.

Graham　No please don't . . .

Michelle　Let me see your bang bang.

Michelle *puts her hand inside* **Graham**'*s trousers.*

Graham　Michelle.

Michelle　Oh dear.

Graham　What?

Michelle *laughs.*

Graham　What are you laughing at?

Michelle　What? Look what you've done already? It's all sticky.

Graham　No it's not.

Michelle　Yes it is.

Graham *tries to kiss* **Michelle** *but she laughs and moves away to avoid the kiss.*

Graham　Why are you stopping?

Michelle　Why do you think, dimbo?

Graham　What?

Michelle　We can't carry on now, can we?

Graham　Yes we can. I want to. I want to feel your body.

Michelle　Of course we can't carry on.

Graham　Well, why don't we wait for a while?

Michelle   You've had a bottle and a half of wine. I don't think so, Graham.

Graham   It'll be all right.

Michelle   For God's sake, man, don't be so ridiculous.

Graham   Are you upset with me?

Michelle   No, Graham. I'm not.

Graham   Then why are you being like this?

Michelle   Do you want me to spell it out for you?

A pause.

Graham   I'm sorry. I'm drunk and I've made a complete fool of myself.

Michelle   I wouldn't worry. You're not the first one, Graham.

She gets up off **Graham** *and starts to rearrange her clothing.* **Graham** *starts to cry.*

For God's sake, don't be such a baby, Graham. All you did was come in your pants. You haven't got a terminal illness or anything.

Graham *cries some more.*

Michelle   Stop blubbing, Graham, and go and get me a drink if you want to do something useful.

Graham *wipes his eyes and starts to rearrange his clothing.*

Michelle   I knew this was a mistake.

Graham *watches* **Michelle**.

Graham   Can't we just lie together?

Michelle   Why?

Graham   On the bed.

Michelle   Now?

Graham   We've had a great laugh. Think of the years we've known each other. Tonight's the first time we've been out for a meal and it's been excellent. Until now.

Michelle   Yeah. Until now.

Graham   You're humiliating me, you know?

Michelle   Well, that never did anyone any harm every now and again.

Graham   Thank you.

A slight pause.

Michelle   I knew this was a mistake.

Graham   Was it that bad?

Michelle   What? That's my question. What? The only thing that happened was that you couldn't control yourself.

Graham *starts to cry again.*

Michelle   Stop crying.

She shakes **Graham**.

If you don't stop crying and behave like a man I'm going home. And I'll never speak to you again. Do you hear me, Mr Tibbotson?

Graham *nods.*

Please can you go and get me a drink before I yell.

Graham   I'm sorry.

Michelle   Don't be sorry. Just get me a Bacardi.

Graham   I've made a complete fool of myself.

Michelle   Let's just be friends. Let's just forget this silly part of the evening ever happened, shall we?

Graham   Yeah. That's right.

A slight pause.

Michelle. I have valued your friendship and good advice over the years we've been colleagues.

A slight pause.

Michelle   So have I, Graham. You've always listened to my problems.

Graham   When I first met you I did, didn't I? I listened.

Graham *turns and exits.* **Michelle** *tuts and looks around the room for her handbag. A slight pause.*

Michelle *spots it and takes it. She roots around inside and pulls out a packet of condoms. She shakes her head and puts them back in. Then she finds her cigarettes and lighter. She lights up a fag and puts her head in her hands. A slight pause.*

She looks around for something to flick her ash into. She checks in the drawer of the bedside cabinet. She takes out a copy of Modern History Review *and underneath it a copy of* Razzle *which she looks at. She hears* **Graham** *coming and quickly puts the magazines back in their drawer, spilling ash on the duvet as she goes.*

Graham *enters. He has a bottle of Bacardi and a bottle of Diet Coke and a tumbler. He spots* **Michelle** *smoking.*

Graham   Is it all right if you don't in my bedroom? It's my asthma.

Michelle   Sorry, Graham.

She stubs her cigarette out on her packet and puts the half cigarette in the packet.

Can we just forget about what happened?

Graham *nods.*

Michelle   It was a lovely Chinese meal and you didn't embarrass me at all. When you started leaping around the dance floor.

Graham   You said I looked like a demented baboon.

Michelle   Thank you for dinner.

A slight pause.

And you must show me the photographs you took down in Dorset. I didn't realise you were such a keen ornithologist.

Graham   I don't show them to anyone. Birding is a private thing.

Graham *passes* **Michelle** *the tumbler and pours her a large Bacardi and then adds some Coke.*

Michelle   Cheers.

Graham   Do you mind if I change? Put my dressing gown on.

Michelle   No.

Graham *takes his shirt off and puts on his dressing gown before taking off his trousers and socks.* **Michelle** *finishes her drink and pours another, which she has straight.*

I'm going to drink myself silly. And then I'm going to pass out on your bed. Is that all right?

Graham   If you want to.

Michelle   And do you know why? Because I have been dumped and had non-sexual intercourse with the least sought-after member of the common room in one day. And I feel like a drink. That's why.

Graham   What do you mean you've been dumped?

Graham *perks up.*

Michelle   Nick finished with me this morning.

Graham   Did he?

Michelle   You don't really think I would have cheated on Nick with you, do you?

A pause.

Nick said he can't be with anyone right now.

A pause.

And do you know what? That is bollocks. That is bollocks.
What's really gone on is that jumped-up little hamster he
taught with in Leytonstone has got in the way. I would like
to get hold of her prissy little head of hair and rip it all out.
Very slowly. Jumped-up bitch. She's obsessed.

A pause.

Every weekend she's been up visiting in her silly little green
car. Making herself at home. Cooking omelettes for him.
I said to Nick, don't you see what she's doing? She's
obsessed with you. She wants to break us up. But he won't
hear a word said against her. It's like she's his conscience or
something. And then this morning he drops the bombshell
that his conscience is coming to our school. I said I thought
she wouldn't teach in an independent school? But he said
she feels much more comfortable working in the private
sector now. I said what a load of crap. She wants you for
herself. And then he said they were just good friends and in
the same breath he confessed he'd slept with her twice.
Twice? I said you fucked her twice and you expect me not
to feel threatened? He said the last time was fifteen months
ago and the time before that three years. And both times
they were drunk. I said it's either me or her and that's when
he gives me the speech about commitment and not being
ready for a relationship. Wanker.

Pause.

Well, he was fantastic in bed, but that's all I'll miss. That
bitch can have him as far as I'm concerned.

She looks at **Graham**. *A pause.*

You know that is a complete lie? That is a complete fucking
lie.

Graham Is it?

Michelle I think I'm in love with him, Graham.

She downs her drink. A pause.

Fucking hell.

Graham   Lucky you, eh?

Michelle   What?

Graham   Who have I ever had?

Michelle   Probably no one.

Graham   No. No one. As you put it. The least sought-after member of the common room.

A pause.

Michelle   And you know the ridiculous thing, Graham? You were meant to make Nick jealous.

She is beside herself with laughter. **Graham** *is gutted and quiet.*

My oh my. I'm an embarrassment.

A slight pause.

You're a great pal, Graham. Where would sixth form trips be without you and me?

Michelle *drinks.* **Graham** *sits on the bed beside her.*

Graham   Yeah. That's right. So you can pour your heart out to me. Your problems and your adventures.

Michelle Don the schlong. He was the first one, wasn't he, Graham? And I fell for him like a silly teenage girl. Now when was that? When did I confide him in you? My first.

Graham   Riverside Studios. All the way round the North Circular to Chingford on the minibus. And I was driving.

Michelle   Well, let me tell you something about Donald?

Graham   You told me all about him. You tell me about all your sordid little affairs when we go to the theatre. Yes.

Michelle   Forty-two visits in all. Come on, Graham.

A slight pause.

I remember him clear as day sidling up to me in the
common room. I'd been at school precisely two days and
what did Don go and do? Brought me a coffee and a Jammy
Dodger, brushed my hand and asked me if I was a pianist.
He said I had delicate elegant fingers.

A slight pause.

And I fell for it. I fell for it, didn't I, Graham? You know,
when he got me into bed forty-eight hours later. And went
down on me. Which was heavenly. He even fed me some
crap about his expert technique and playing a wind
instrument.

A slight pause.

He even persuaded me to go to a soul weekender at Caister,
didn't he? Don was in full *Miami Vice* mode. New sparkling
white trainers, arms on his jacket rolled up eighties style. He
even brought his saxophone. And I met my nemesis.

A slight pause.

Lorraine. In the chalet next door. She invited us in for a
Malibu and pineapple and Lorraine and Don hit it off. Told
him all about crawling out of her window when she was
fifteen to go down the Lacy Lady in Ilford. To hear one of
the funk mafia play. Don had been to the Lacy Lady and he
layed it on thick.

A slight pause.

I was in a foul mood of course. Which confirmed Don's
feeling he'd be having a better time with Lorraine. Who was
a dog clipper. And my mood got worse when I spilt a glass
of Bacardi and Coke down the cozzie I hired for the toga
party. Don wasn't sympathetic. Said to get a sheet off of the
bed and get it round me as we had to meet Lorraine and
Karen. Her mousy friend. One minute I was Aphrodite.
The next a crap ghost at a Hallowe'en party.

A slight pause.

Karen, who worked for Barclays, turned out to be a marked improvement upon Lorraine and we got on like a house on fire. Had a laugh with two firemen and didn't even notice Lorraine and Don had slipped away.

A slight pause.

I opened the door of the chalet an hour later, jazz is blaring out and what do I see? Don having sex with Lorraine from behind. And she'd been sick all over my Bacardi-stained toga. What a slut.

Michelle *pours herself another Bacardi.*

Graham   I went to a soul weekender once.

Michelle *ignores him.*

Graham   Don't you want to hear about it?

Michelle   No.

A long pause.

Graham *takes the Bacardi and has a swig and nearly gags.*
A slight pause.

Graham   I don't know why you have to be so awful to me.

A slight pause.

Michelle   When we took the sixth form in that pub at Liverpool Street. That was another one, wasn't it, Graham? Your friend in the history department.

A slight pause.

We'd just started going out. He was lovely. I adored him. I don't know why I . . . He treated me so well. You know we didn't sleep together for six weeks? And for me that was a world record. He stroked my hair. Kissed the small of my back.

A pause.

He could cook too. And he was so funny. A great mimic.
Do you remember the impressions he used to do of all those
characters in the *Carry On* films? And the old sitcoms. Rigsby
in *Rising Damp*. The headmaster. That silly bitch who does
the catering. He had them all down to a T. I used to get
annoyed with him when he mimicked me. I was silly. So
silly. I don't know why I betrayed him. It was too easy
somehow. With him. I know you're going to hate me saying
this but he was too nice.

A slight pause.

I hate myself.

A slight pause.

I do. I hate myself when I think about him. It. All of it.
I hate it. He's up in Bishops Stortford now, isn't he? Head
of department.

Graham *nods.*

Michelle   Good for him. I was so very jealous when
I heard he'd married.

Graham   They've got a baby now. A little girl.

Michelle   I didn't know that?

A pause.

Graham   Chloe.

Michelle   I always wanted to call my little baby Chloe.
If I do. When I do. Perhaps I will. Still.

A slight pause.

Graham   Stephen was a good bloke. He still sends me
a Christmas card.

A slight pause.

Michelle   I was bored with Stephen. He bored me. But Colin . . .

Graham   Colin was a cunt.

Michelle   I didn't know that word was in your vocabulary?

A slight pause.

Colin. Christ.

A slight pause.

He was a thrilling lover. And an utter utter brute.

Graham *swigs from the bottle. A slight pause.*

Michelle *actions for* **Graham** *to pass the bottle to her. He does and she takes a swig too.*

Michelle   Do you know what he forced me to do?

Graham   I don't want to know that.

Michelle   A thousand humiliations behind closed doors and yet so, so pleasant on parents' evening.

A slight pause.

And yet he sometimes found a tenderness I can only describe as. Childlike.

Graham *covers his ears.*

Michelle   Listen to me. Listen. You wimp. You stupid wimpy man. Listen.

Graham *uncovers his ears.*

Michelle   I was pregnant by Colin. I was pregnant.

Graham   Were you?

He thinks. A pause.

Did he make you get rid of it?

Michelle   No. I miscarried. I had a miscarriage. There.
You didn't know that, did you, Graham?

A slight pause.

About a month later we were queuing for hamburgers in
Romford. And he asked me how I was. And he said he
thought maybe what had happened was for the best. And
I knew it was over.

A slight pause.

I made my excuses and I locked myself in the disabled toilet.
And I slid on to the floor and cried so hard it hurt. This
spotty teenage lad broke the door in for me.

A slight pause.

I laughed and lied. Said my mother had just passed away.
I got caught. Wanted to be alone. And the little lad gave me
a handful of napkins and a free Diet Coke. I asked him if he
was dropping a hint. He said he wasn't. Said I looked great.
And there I was in Burger King's disabled toilet. Mascara
all over the shop. Flirting with a boy who could have been
one of my fifth form. That was when I started playing again.
And there have been so many, haven't there, Graham?
Until Nick. Until my darling, darling Nick.

A slight pause.

And you've been my confidant. Thrilling you with my
stories. Another expedition for our theatre club. Another
snatched half-hour or so feeding your fantasies. Your
adolescent little fantasies.

Graham   Don't do this to me.

Michelle   So many. Disasters. Torrid affairs.

Graham   No . . .

Michelle   That sixth former I had in my car.

Graham   No more now . . .

Michelle   In the back of my car. All over his exciting lean body.

Graham   Please.

Michelle   The groundsman I had all weekend. Snogging him outside the tobacconist's for all to see.

Graham *shakes his head.*

Michelle   The biology teacher I met at the gym. He had a wife. I didn't care.

Graham   Please.

Michelle   The adultery thrilled me.

Graham   You're a slut.

Michelle   My next-door neighbour with bad breath and nasal hair.

Graham   You're just a slut . . .

Michelle   And the parent. The parent with the blue BMW and his set of golf clubs.

Graham *covers his ears again.*

Michelle   His endless unfunny quips. About his son getting a good school report after the extra I was getting.

Graham   You foul . . .

Michelle   And then my beautiful Nicholas. Oh, my Nicholas.

Graham *shakes his head.*

Michelle   The joy being weak-kneed and girly.

Graham   Stupid cow . . .

Michelle   That I might sacrifice my Nicholas? Nicholas that has been taken away from me for you?

Graham   I can't stand you any more.

Michelle   You. Pathetic. Limp-wristed. Silly. Bore.

Graham   Do you really hate me?

Michelle   When I see you shouting and screaming at the kids doing CCF I abhor you.

Graham   What?

Michelle   When I see you playing soldiers with the cadets. The public-school cadet force. Pretending you're a real man screaming and shouting at quivering fourteen-year-old boys. I despise you. Captain Tibbotson. Commando section. No longer the weak-willed ineffectual history teacher. Now leader of men. Soldier. I saw you no more than a month ago. I was with Nicholas. And you had some boy out of his line. You were humiliating him. Your snide little attempts at humour and your horrible vile temper. Why was it? Something pathetic? Like not having shining boots? Not snapping his foot down quick enough on parade?

A slight pause.

I wish that boy were here now. I wish I could tell him. And watch him laugh. Mr Tibbotson. Captain Graham Tibbotson CCF Commando section a come-in-his-pants sissy.

A slight pause.

I wanted to sleep with you to get revenge on Nick but to see you entertaining? Flirting with the idea? Really thinking I wanted you. Was going to cheat on Nicholas with you. Seeing the smug flicker of a shabby weak man. A man feeling empowered in the way humiliating teenage boys usually only fulfils. It makes me want to watch you tumble down flights of stairs. I've learned to despise you on our cosy little theatre trips, Graham, but not so much as this evening. I go home and snigger into my bathroom mirror when I remember you agonising. Trying to hide your erection. In some tatty theatre foyer or other. Your tortured attempts to flirt with me.

A slight pause.

Over the seven years I've known you, yes, I have grown to hate you. You're clearly the only the man who wants me and that's not something I admire.

She laughs and laughs to herself.

And to watch you try and dance this evening. A demented baboon complements the spectacle with humour. But it wasn't even funny watching you fling yourself around that tiny dance floor. All I could do was hide my face and think why build a Chinese restaurant with a dance floor?

Graham   I used to be a good dancer.

Michelle   I don't care what you used to be.

Graham   I went to discotheques when they were still discotheques.

Michelle   I really don't give a damn.

Graham   And I did go to a soul weekender once. I went with my cousin.

Michelle   Well, you would have got on well with Lorraine.

Graham   I used to do the stomp.

Michelle   Really?

Graham   And I can waltz.

A slight pause.

I can waltz. You couldn't manage anything half so graceful. Your slovenly frame couldn't move with the precision and charm of a waltz.

Michelle   I want my Nicholas. He belongs with me. I've waited too long for someone like him.

A slight pause.

I want his kisses to shower the nape of my neck. I want his fine hands to steady my spinning, spinning nature. That's what I want. That cow Helen's not having him. He's mine.

A slight pause.

Graham   You. You . . .

Graham *can't get what he wants to say out.*

Michelle   What, you coward?

Graham   You . . . maths teacher! You fucking maths teacher!

Graham *storms out of the bedroom. A pause.*

Michelle *purposefully takes out her cigarettes and lights one up. A slight pause.*

Graham *enters. He has a huge bouquet of flowers. They are embarrassing they are so huge and he tears open the cellophane and grasps a handful of stalks which he throws at* **Michelle**.

Graham   I got them for you! Have them, you bitch!

Michelle *is slightly taken aback even after everything else.* **Graham** *throws more flowers at her.*

Graham   I got them for you!

A slight pause.

I went to the high street at lunchtime and I got them for you. After dinner. A Chinese meal. Back here. I'd give them to you. And you would like them. And be delighted and happy. That there were such beautiful flowers. For you.

He throws more flowers at her and throws the bouquet on the floor. He stamps on the bouquet and kicks it.

You go on and on and on about me but who are you? You're just a selfish cow. You've been at the school seven years and you still haven't even got your own form. You never get involved with anything or anyone. You're just interested in drawing your salary and your sordid succession of men.

Michelle   Which you wank yourself silly over . . .

Graham   And the theatre club? You only do that so you can pour out your disgusting mind to me and to try and appear cultured at school. You're the only person I know who thought that teacher in the play with Michael Gambon was accurate! You don't care about anything. You don't know anything. You have a mind that connects with numbers and that is about it because you certainly have no soul!

A slight pause.

I'm a man, a man. Although I don't feel much like one sometimes!

A slight pause.

Yes. Sometimes I don't feel like a man. I haven't even managed to find myself a wife.

A slight pause.

I had one hope.

A slight pause.

From being a gawky shy twenty-eight-year-old who'd never kissed a girl. But you? You don't believe in a bloody thing, do you? I've been hiding away all these years but now I've had enough. I've followed you in my car and watched you go drinking with Don. Argue with him in Indian restaurants in Upminister. I watched Stephen leave in the morning and blow kisses at you. And that afternoon I heard Colin fucking you. I heard you whining he was hurting you. Your incessant whine. I saw you giving Adams a blow job in the back of your car. I saw that.

A slight pause.

I came into your room when you were asleep in Edinburgh.
I saw your breasts exposed. How I wanted you. How
wanted to just take you. Have you.

Michelle   You're sick.

Graham   No . . .

Michelle   You stalker.

Graham   No. You are.

Michelle   It's you, isn't it?

Graham   What?

Michelle   You've been opening my mail? In my
pigeon hole.

Graham   No I haven't . . .

Michelle   I knew someone was tampering with my mail.

Graham   I haven't been doing that.

Michelle   I'm going to report you to the second master
for this.

Graham   No you won't.

Michelle   I certainly will. Do you really think I want to
see your horrible face in the common room again?

Graham *walks around the bed and opens the drawer of the bedside
cabinet. He takes out the brown manila envelope.*

Michelle   What are you doing?

Graham *opens the manila envelope and passes* **Michelle**
photographs. At least twenty prints. **Michelle** *looks at them
and gasps.*

Graham   You and that sixth-form boy. The parent with
the golf clubs. On top of him in the park. That lab
technician you've been quietly bonking.

A slight pause.

That's right. I know about that.

A slight pause.

Your body. Beautiful. In the moonlight. In your room.
I thought it was my last chance. At the festival. My
last chance.

A slight pause.

Michelle   What do you want from me?

Graham   Teach me.

Michelle   What?

Graham   Do your duty to me. I've waited seven years.

Michelle   I don't understand?

Graham   Make me a man. Teach me. Show me. Show
me. Make me a man. Show me. Give yourself to me. Show
me how. Show me. Have me. Now. Have me.

A long pause.

Michelle   Don't make me do that.

Graham   I've waited so long.

Michelle   Please.

Graham   You were going to before. Weren't you? You
were. You wanted to take my cock in your hands. You
wanted me. You wanted to use me.

He moves towards **Michelle***. She flinches.*

I'm not going to force . . .

A slight pause.

Please.

Michelle   I can't.

Graham   You can. I want you to.

Michelle   What about the pictures?

Graham   What about them?

Michelle   You know what.

Graham   I like them. I feel close to you.

Michelle   Can I have them?

Graham   Let's see, shall we?

Michelle   You won't show them?

A long pause.

Let's just forget any of this happened.

A slight pause.

Let's just pretend we've only been back ten minutes. We've had a drink. And you've put your dressing gown on.

A slight pause.

Graham   Touch my face. Tenderly.

Michelle *touches* **Graham**'s *face.*

Graham   Am I your soldier?

Michelle   You're my soldier.

Graham   And you're my nurse?

Michelle   Yes.

Graham *slips off his dressing gown.*

Graham   My shoulder's been bruised.

Michelle   Has it?

She looks.

Oh yes. I can see it. And there are bruises all over your back.

Graham   Will you kiss them better? Like the girl does on the ship. In *Raiders of the Lost Ark.*

Michelle   There, there.

Graham   That's nice.

Michelle   Does that make you feel nice?

Graham   Yes.

Michelle   What happened to you?

Graham   I escaped from the Gestapo. I was being tortured.

Michelle   You poor thing. You're brave.

A slight pause.

Graham   I've never kissed a girl before.

Michelle   Haven't you?

Graham   No.

Michelle   Why's that?

Graham   I'm shy. I'm very shy.

Michelle *sits next to* **Graham** *on the bed. She smiles at* **Graham**. *He is like a little boy.* **Michelle** *finds it very difficult through the next.*

Graham   Will you kiss me again, nurse?

Michelle   Yes.

Michelle *kisses all over* **Graham**'s *back.*

Graham   That's nice.

Michelle   It is, isn't it?

Graham   Will you kiss my lips?

Michelle   Yes.

Michelle *kisses* **Graham**'s *lips.*

Graham   That's lovely.

Michelle *kisses* **Graham**'s *neck and then his chest and his nipples.*

Graham   That's lovely. Really lovely.

Graham *kisses* **Michelle** *and her neck and then starts to unbutton her top.*

Michelle   Do you want to kiss me there?

Graham   Yes I do.

Michelle   Kiss me then.

Graham *kisses* **Michelle**'s *chest and neck again.*

Graham   When the war's over I'm going to marry my nurse and have a nice house.

Michelle   That's right . . .

Graham   We're going to have children and live in a nice street.

Michelle   Yes . . .

Graham   And after the war's over everything will be better, won't it?

Michelle   Of course it will . . .

Michelle *goes down on her knees and pulls at* **Graham**'s *underpants.*

Graham   The streets will be clean and we'll look after the sick people and the elderly people. And we'll educate the young properly. Show them how to behave. That's what we're fighting for, isn't it?

Michelle *looks at* **Graham** *genitals and then up at him.*
Graham *grabs* **Michelle**'s *hair.*

Graham   Is this what Colin did? Did he pull your hair? Did he grab it? When you laughed at him? I'm tired of you laughing at me. Of these games. These silly, silly games. I'm so tired.

Michelle *shakes her head. She is frightened.*

Graham   After the war we won't have to worry about anything, will we? We can stay in bed all day. When the war is over.

Michelle   Yes.

Graham   But now time is precious, my love. I've only got an hour and I have to be on a train to Portsmouth.

Michelle *nods*.

Graham   Mission behind lines. Top secret. I may be risking my life. Maybe I'll come back a hero.

Slow fade.

Act Three

August 1998. The patio. A cottage garden in Tiverton, Devon.
Ten a.m.

Anne *sits at the garden table with her feet up on another chair. The*
table is littered with the remnants of a barbecue and party from the
previous evening.

Anne *is fifty-eight.*

Robert *stands opposite* **Anne** *across the patio.* **Robert** *has*
a portable CD player in his hands with a long extension lead running
from it back into the cottage.

Robert *is forty-two.*

Anne   No.

Robert   You promised.

Anne   No, no, no.

Robert   You promised me.

Anne   Robert, if you think I'm dancing with you now
you've got another thing coming.

Robert   Now you made a deal.

Anne   I don't care what I said last night.

Robert   I know you didn't want to dance to Spandau
Ballet but this is Neil Sedaka.

Anne   No.

Robert *puts down the CD player and folds his arms. A slight pause.*

Anne   Are you sulking?

Robert   No.

Anne   What are you doing standing like that then?

Robert   I'm waiting.

Anne   Well, you better get some sunblock on your nose because you're going to have a long wait standing there.

Robert   You know, sometimes you're no fun at all.

Anne *laughs*.

Anne   That's not what my sixth form think.

Robert   Well, compared to my lot they're a pretty shabby bunch. On results day mine got me an inflatable sheep and a bottle of Dom Perignon. Now, correct me if I'm wrong but your lot brought you a packet of Celebrations and half a litre of Sainsbury's gin. Pathetic.

Anne   That's not what you said last night. When you were busy bonding with them. Anyway, they're normal kids. They haven't got Mummy or Daddy to buy champagne for teacher.

Robert   I thought one or two of them needed taking under my wing. A bit of pre-university guidance.

Anne *laughs*.

Robert   What?

Anne   From you? Robert, you started out on dramatic societies and ended up telling them to shag anything and watch out for modern languages students called Helen.

Robert   Which in retrospect does seem unwise.

Anne   Given that there are two Helens in my sixth-form set. One of whom's doing Spanish and law and the other who's doing German.

Robert   Proves my point.

Anne   What?

Robert   Find a university modern languages department and you will find the biggest concentration of Helens in the country.

Anne *laughs*.

Robert   See. You know it's true.

Anne   I don't think it was the association of their name and modern languages that offended them. More to the point that they should be steered clear of.

A slight pause.

Kids from Devon are more sensitive than they are in Essex.

Robert   I took them under my wing. They loved me.

Anne *laughs. A slight pause.*

Anne   The teacher who died. The geography teacher. She was called Helen, wasn't she?

Robert   Yeah. Very sad that.

Anne   Helen. I like that name.

A pause.

Robert   Will you dance with me? You'll make my day.

Anne   Will I?

Robert *picks up the CD player and grins.*

Anne   Don't make me. Please.

Robert   OK.

A slight pause.

As long as you promise me next time you have a party you'll dance with me. Even if it's 'True' by Spandau Ballet.

Anne   Even if it's not 'True' by Spandau Ballet.

Robert *feels funny and rubs his head.*

Anne   Are you all right, Robert?

Robert   Nave of wausea.

Anne   Wave of nausea?

Robert   Nave of wausea. Not good.

Anne   Have you had a Resolve?

Robert   No. Not yet.

Anne   There's a sachet in the bathroom cabinet. Or I've got some co-codamol?

Robert   Yeah. Resolve. I think I need Resolve.

Anne   I thought you seemed uncharacteristically energetic. What time did you get to bed?

Robert   Four.

Anne   Four?

Robert   Ish. We were listening to Nina Simone.

Robert *holds his head.*

Anne   What is it?

Robert   I'm sweating. I feel like shit.

Anne   It's hot already.

Robert   No. That's better. My stomach just did something gymnastic.

Anne   What were you drinking?

Robert   Stella. Red wine. Most of that Sainsbury's gin. Oh and the brandy we brought back from France last year.

Anne   Robert . . .

Robert   But your sixth formers did love me, didn't they?

Anne   You were the entertainment down from Essex. There's no one like you in Tiverton. That's for sure.

Robert   You watch. When they go to university you'll be going through me to keep in touch.

Robert *studies* **Anne**. *A slight pause.*

Robert   All your sixth form were asking what was going on between us.

Anne Were they?

Robert They said you're always going on about me in class.

Anne Did they? What did you say?

Robert We're mates.

A slight pause.

When you showed them the pictures. From Mexico. One of the Helens asked me about the sleeping arrangements.

Anne Cheeky little cow. What did you say?

Robert I told her the truth. We had a twin.

Anne What did she say?

Robert Nothing. I said we get on well and we always share a room when we go on holiday. To save money.

Anne What did she say to that?

Robert She said she thought it was a shame. She said she thought it was romantic. Holidaying together. She couldn't believe we've been going away together for six years. I said we were good friends for two or three years before that. When we first taught together. In Essex.

A pause.

She asked me if I'd been married. And I said no but I told her you had been. Was that all right?

Anne Yeah. My sixth form know that anyway.

A pause.

Robert I said we once shared a kiss but never a bed.

Anne You didn't say that, did you?

Robert No. And what if I had?

Anne Then you would have been bloody silly.

Robert   Why?

Anne   You know perfectly well why.

A pause.

Anne   Do you want some toast? Do you want something to eat?

Robert   I don't know.

Anne   I can make you scrambled eggs on toast?

Robert   I'm actually not that hungry. I finished off the tuna pasta before I went to bed.

Anne   Did you see I had the spare room painted?

Robert   Yeah. By the way. One of your students was sick in your stockpot. I covered it over with tinfoil.

Anne   Thanks.

A slight pause.

Robert   What time are we going to lunch?

Anne   I didn't know if you had to go?

Robert   No. We always have lunch before I go.

Anne   OK. Well, we can have a pub lunch.

Robert   I'll drop you off here and then I'll get on my way. Is that all right?

Anne   Yeah.

Robert   When I'm over we always have lunch and . . .

Anne   Then we'll have lunch.

Robert   Though I don't know if I can stomach a roast. Will you take the piss out of me if I have a salad? Tossed.

Anne   No, Robert. I won't.

Robert   And we need to talk about half-term.

A slight pause.

I don't know about you but I fancy Italy.

Anne   OK.

Robert   Tuscany might be nice. Late October.

Anne   Lovely.

Robert   Now, do you know the dates because I've got two weeks off?

Anne   Yeah . . .

Robert   I loved Mexico.

Anne   I loved Mexico. I didn't expect to like it as much I did. I don't know why. I felt uneasy about it.

A slight pause.

I felt uneasy about going away.

Robert   Did you?

A slight pause.

Anne   I did feel uneasy about us going away this summer.

Robert   Why?

Anne   I don't know.

A long pause.

Robert   We've had some wonderful holidays.

Anne   I know.

Robert   Remember our Scandinavian cruise?

Anne *smiles.*

Robert   We read *The Wild Duck* by the fjord in those plastic Viking helmets I got. And those Americans took pictures. It was so funny. And Mexico was splendid, wasn't it?

Anne Yes it was.

A slight pause.

Robert *smiles.*

Robert I wouldn't mind a sachet of that Resolve now, Anne.

Anne Robert, I'm not sure about half-term.

Robert Why?

Anne I've been thinking about it since we got back. I think I'd like to go to Belgium.

Robert Belgium?

Anne To Flanders.

Robert Why?

Anne I'd like to go to visit the war cemeteries at half-term. With my Auntie May. She asked me to take her. And I want to go. I've never seen them. She can't go on her own.

A slight pause.

Can she?

Robert No.

Anne Since I've been down here we've become close.

Robert I know that. So I'll see you at Christmas.

Anne She wants to go there before she dies. I can't refuse her that, can I?

A slight pause.

Anne She's so bloody difficult though. You know what the weather's been like. First sun in weeks and she wouldn't even let me run her into Taunton.

A slight pause.

I want to go. I'd like to see those cemeteries for myself. Apparently the silence is humbling.

Robert   What does she want to go now for?

Anne   She has a ghost she wants to lay.

A slight pause.

When we came back from Mexico I went over to see her. And she told me a story I never heard before.

A slight pause.

My Auntie May was fourteen when the First World War broke out. On occasion her father allowed her to attend tennis parties. To field the balls for the adults. And it was on one afternoon like that just after the war broke out my great-aunt met this young man. Arthur

A slight pause.

He was eighteen and Auntie May said he was hopeless at tennis. Everyone kept falling about laughing at him but he was so good-humoured he just laughed along with everyone else. But in the end he gave up and instead he amused himself fetching the tennis balls with May.

A slight pause.

Apparently, they hadn't been fielding long when the ball went into the ornamental part of the garden at the end and Arthur and May went chasing after it. She was light on her feet and located it quite quickly but Arthur, seeing she'd got hold of it, yells out to everyone: 'Lost ball. Carry on with another till we can find it.' And then he came over to her sitting in a little hideaway. With the lost ball. May said he was very handsome and although he was afflicted with some acne he had golden curls of hair. And bright blue eyes like the sea, she said. Arthur told he he expected to go overseas and he began to stammer. She said he was trying to pluck up the courage to ask her permission to write to her. She said she got goose pimples all the way up her arms and legs. And Arthur went to the front line and saw action at Ypres.

A slight pause.

She showed me the letters. There were six in all. And they were the most beautiful letters I have ever read in my life.

A slight pause.

When Auntie May showed me them I held them so delicately. They were almost brown and they felt like they might crumble. This treasure might crumble in my fingertips.

A slight pause.

I feel I spoil his writing trying to paraphrase his words. Précis those delicate love letters. But I had this powerful feeling reading them. The feeling of being young and in love, I suppose. My aunt never received another letter from him.

Robert Didn't she?

Anne No. No news at all. Then in 1916 May went to France with her mother and the Yeovil Red Cross Ambulance. She said she never stopped loving Arthur. Then in August 1917, when May had been at the front eighteen months, she saw him.

A slight pause.

Those thought likely to die were assembled in a great marquee tent. The surgeons had to concentrate their efforts on the ones they might be able to save. And consequently May never came across Arthur for some time after he arrived.

A slight pause.

There was one surgeon serving there who prided himself upon choosing one of the men from the marquee. Bringing one of the men everyone else had given up on back from the dead. And he settled upon a chap whose legs had been shattered and turned septic already. But May heard a voice from the stretcher beside him call her name.

A slight pause.

He was covered in mud and across his stomach was a rough dressing soaked in blood. Although it was all matted and muddy May recognised his blond curls and his blue eyes. And he said 'My angel.'

A slight pause.

The surgeon asked May what was going on. May asked him if he'd consider attending to Arthur but he said he'd chosen for that day. He allowed her five minutes to wash Arthur and change his dressings. May said she noticed he'd matured and she could see his acne had disappeared. He said that he loved her.

A slight pause.

Then Matron marched through the tent. Like a dreadnought. When she saw May crouched at the side of a tommy in the marquee she was furious and sent her to the surgeon's side straight away. They hacked off this poor man's legs and May said he vomited blood and screamed. He died on the table as May held his arms. But she said she was happy his suffering was over and she could return to Arthur. But he was gone. May went out towards the lines of bodies covered with blankets and great coats. She said she hesitated pulling them back but eventually she found him. The face she'd washed was smeared with mud again, she said, but his sightless blue eyes still shone in the sun.

A slight pause.

She clenched her fist around the thermometer still in her hand and splintered glass deep into her palm. May showed me her scarred hand.

A slight pause.

That's it. The story she told me.

A slight pause.

Robert   Did she stay at the front?

Anne   She served out the rest of the war. Then she returned to Yeovil and led a fairly solitary life. She only married for a very brief spell in her twenties.

Robert *nods. A pause.*

Anne   She says Arthur was her one and only true love. Innocent and unconsummated as she accepts it was. She wants to visit his grave. She says it's haunted her her whole life she wasn't able to tell him she loved him.

Robert *nods. A very long pause.*

Robert   What time are we going to lunch?

A slight pause.

Anne   Is that all you've got to say? In response to her story?

Robert   I'm sorry.

A pause.

I don't know what to say. I don't know why you've told me it.

Anne   I don't think my auntie and Arthur were in love. Really. She met Arthur and in a moment he was gone and there was a gap. With nothing but the imagination to fill it. She created this love of her life. From a sunny afternoon and half a dozen beautiful letters.

A slight pause.

They needed each other. She created this romantic love and it got them through the horrors they faced.

A slight pause.

I think what really haunts my auntie is guilt. That she never provided him with any more comfort in those conditions. That she didn't plead, beg the surgeon. She has this enormous guilt that she couldn't do more.

A slight pause.

No. I don't believe they were in love. They were only kids.
Think of a sixth former of mine or yours going out with a
third-form girl. It happens occasionally, doesn't it? They
might seem smitten. They might even be good friends, but
would you say they were in love?

Robert   I don't know. Probably not.

Anne   Romance is born out of innocence. And we all need
little fantasies sometimes. To get us through. May's story
has preoccupied me.

A slight pause.

It touched something very deep inside me. I wanted to tell
you about it. I've woken at night thinking . . .

Robert   About your own life.

Anne   When I was a sixth former I was so madly in love
with my English teacher. I adored him. It was the fifties.
That awful decade. And there was this embodiment of
everything the fifties weren't. He was relaxed and
compassionate. Daring. And he seemed fond of me as well.
I expect he was gay. How I loved him and how I missed him
when I went to university. My husband never came near
him. And then when I least expected it. After years of
disastrous marriage and divorce, another English teacher
appeared in my life. And I discovered feelings I'd long since
given up on unlocking.

A slight pause.

It's been much easier since I've been down here, us still
being friends but I've not been entirely happy. And then
May's story triggered something. This idea I've had of us.
Of a sort of. Compromise. On both our parts. Being friends.
It's a sham.

Robert   I agree.

Anne *studies* **Robert**. *A pause.*

Anne   In the time we've been friends I've loved us holidaying together.

Robert   So have I.

Anne   But I don't know if we should continue.

Robert   What? But why?

Anne   Robert, surely you should be doing other things in the holidays?

Robert   Like what?

Anne   You're nearly twenty years younger than me.

Robert   What difference does that make?

Anne   When you meet people. Don't they think it's strange we go off holidaying together?

Robert   No. Why should they?

Anne   It's not even like we're teaching at the same school any more.

Robert   So we can't be pals because we're no longer strictly speaking colleagues?

Anne   No. But you're often saying to me you don't have enough friends of your own age. People in a similar position.

Robert   What do you mean?

Anne   We can both feel lonely. I certainly can feel lonely down here. I know you can. You need to make other friends you see regularly. Who aren't married. Or haven't got kids.

Robert   What's that got to do with us?

Anne   And what about girlfriends?

A pause.

Robert   What about girlfriends?

Anne   Well, it's no wonder you have trouble dating when you're booked up to go on holiday with me all the time.

Robert   I don't understand this . . .

Anne   If I was dating you and you were booked up three months in advance to go on holiday with a female friend I probably wouldn't like it . . .

Robert   Who cares? I don't want to date anyone else . . . .

Anne   But Robert?

Robert   What? Tell me. Tell me please.

A long pause.

Anne   I know you want a family. I know you want to get married.

A long pause.

I'm holding you back. I know I am. Why do you think I moved down to Devon in the first place?

Robert   You said you were tired of a six-day week.

A very long pause.

Anne   I've been thinking about it since we got back from Mexico. I don't think we should go on holiday together any more.

A pause.

Robert   When we started teaching together you gave me confidence. I was shattered teaching in state schools. You built me back up.

A slight pause.

You know all of this talk about your aunt. About us. About phantom relationships crushed under the sheer weight of their circumstances. It's bollocks. It's such an evasion. Such a cop-out. You're not taking proper responsibility for your feelings and your actions. For us. You talk about history? Sell me a bloody story instead of talking honestly about me and you? *A slight pause.* I've grown up thinking most of what's happened the last eighty years has been because of

that dreadful war your aunt lived through. The Easter
Rising. That endlessly long fuck-up that is the Balkans.
Adolf. That aberration in the middle. At the heart of it.
Now I keep hearing this conclusion, that the reason he did
what he did was because the man was sexually frustrated.
But don't you see, Anne, even talking about what he got up
to with his niece or Eva Braun seems to offer him an
explanation. An excuse for what he did. But he was
responsible. And when he put a bullet through his brain it
was his way of not taking the can.

Pause.

It's the end of the century. People look back and try and
make sense of who we are. It's natural. It's a moment.
We're educated and used to explaining the world around us.
We teach. We should know better than anyone else.

Silence.

It's about us. What have I done and what haven't I done?
What I do and what I don't do and then how I choose to
remember it. Do you understand me? What I'm saying?
Anything else is the biggest abrogation of responsibility.
It's shit. And I believe that.

A pause.

Anne   The teacher who died. It was an accident, wasn't it?
Helen. How did she die?

A slight pause.

Please tell me.

Robert   I never really knew her but a bloke in the English
department was good friends with her. In fact they taught
together at a comprehensive in Leytonstone. In the East
End. Well, they were good mates and she followed him out
into Essex. Started last September. He was really popular
with the kids but I never liked him very much. Bit of a lad
out boozing with the PE department. Anyway, Helen

joining caused some trouble because he'd been going out
with Michelle Didsbury.

Anne   Slapper.

Robert   Yeah.

Anne   Is Graham Tibbotson still in love with her?

Robert   I don't think so. They fell out May before last.

Anne   Why?

Robert   No one knows. Anyway, the English department
has been lumbered with running sixth-form theatre
trips now. Anne why won't you . . .

Anne   But what about this girl?

Robert   Michelle was jealous of Helen's friendship with
Nick and they broke up over it a few times. But then it
comes out Michelle had been having an affair with one of
the lab assistants and Nick was in pieces about it. Anyway,
Michelle left Nick's place and he rang Helen. It was raining
hard but Helen said she was getting straight in her car.

A slight pause.

She lost control of her car. I think there's going to be a
memorial service for her in the chapel at the start of term.
For some reason the Rev's asked me to read a poem.

A slight pause.

Of course Michelle's dumped her lab technician and she's
been trying to get back with Nick. But I don't know if he's
even going to make it back to school.

Anne   Why?

Robert   I saw him in the pub last week. He was on his
own. A bit of a mess. As I said I've always thought he was
an arsehole but I felt sorry for him and I talked to him. He
said it was his fault but I said it wasn't. He said he asked her

to come over. He said he knew she'd always do what
he wanted.

A slight pause.

He said he's thinking of going back to Leytonstone to teach
in the comp again. It has no meaning. Teaching in a private
school. Helen would have wanted him to go back but I said
that was bollocks. That wherever you teach you're doing the
most important job there is. He said he thought teaching
should be a calling. It was for Helen. He only ever wanted
to be a professional footballer. I said very few of us are
doing it as a first choice and it's not a mission. It's a job.
And as it happens I think it's one of the best jobs you can
do. And you know what? He cried. Wept like a child. So
I gave him a hug. And then my mate turned up and took
the piss.

Anne *smiles.*

Anne   I think you're wonderful.

A slight pause.

Was she in love with him? Helen?

Robert   Yeah. Obviously. You know this Nick guy was
your replacement.

Anne   Was he?

Robert *nods.*

Robert   Nick knew Helen loved him and he didn't want
her but he wouldn't let her have anyone else. Selfish, eh?

A slight pause.

He accosted me when I was leaving the pub. He was saying
what a brilliant bloke I was. And then he said 'I loved her
you know. I really did.' And I don't know if it was because
I'd had a few beers or what but I said to him 'No you didn't,
Nick. You didn't love her. It was all about your fucking ego,
mate.' And it was like I'd gotten hold of his neck and

squeezed every ounce of blood up into his face. But I was that clear what I thought of him.

A pause.

What did you want to be, Anne?

Anne   What?

Robert   What did you want to be? Before you were married and took up teaching? Come on. What did you want to be?

Anne *thinks and smiles.*

Anne   I wanted to chef. You know I wanted to be a chef.

Robert *nods. A pause.*

Robert   I wanted to be a musician. A pianist.

A pause.

Anne   The thought of you sitting at a piano fills me with the most happy feeling.

A slight pause.

Robert   I want you to do something for me.

Anne   What?

Robert   If this is it. If as far as you're concerned we're not going to see each other in the holidays any more then I want you to dance with me now.

Anne   We'll still see each other in holidays . . .

Robert   We won't end up seeing each other. You know what it's like. If you don't make plans . . .

A slight pause.

You know what it's like. Dance with me.

Anne   It's half past ten in the morning.

Robert   Dance with me.

Anne   What about the music?

Robert   What about it?

Anne   It's Sunday.

Robert   Dance with me. Like you promised you would last night.

Anne   I was embarrassed last night. In front of my sixth form.

Robert   Please.

Anne *nods.* **Robert** *fiddles around with the CD player.*

Anne   Robert . . .

Robert   I want you to dance with me. If it's a slow one it's a slow one. If it's 'Oh Carol' I'll go mental.

'Breaking Up Is Hard To Do' by Neil Sedaka plays from the CD player.

Robert *laughs and shakes his head. He turns it up. He dances and is funny. He sings all the words.* **Anne** *laughs.*

Anne   Robert, the neighbours . . .

Robert   Fuck the neighbours . . .

He unbuttons his shirt and flashes his belly. He wobbles it.

Neighbours! You dour Devon bastards. I am from Essex and I am dancing!

Anne *laughs and shakes her head and* **Robert** *pulls her up to dance. They dance, singing all the words very loudly. They twist and twirl each other round. They do funny little movements and make each other laugh.*

Anne   I love this song . . .

Robert   It's a brilliant song . . .

They continue until the song finishes. **Robert** *turns the CD player off. They are breathless and laugh to themselves until they are silent.*

They look at each other. Very suddenly **Anne** *turns away as if she might cry but* **Robert** *approaches and kisses her on the lips. A slight pause.*

They kiss for a very long time. It is teenage and a joy to see. They stop and look at each other. A slight pause.

They kiss again. A slight pause.

They look at each other.

Robert   I'm sorry that I covered it over.

Anne   What?

Robert   The sick in your stockpot. But I didn't know what to do with it. And the tinfoil was handy.

Anne *smiles but is then serious.*

Anne   I don't know what this means? I came down here to Devon . . . I'm holding you back.

Robert   No.

Anne   I don't know where . . .

Robert   No. Listen to me.

Anne   But my age . . .

Robert   No.

Anne   I can't . . .

Robert   You can.

Anne   But what about what you want?

Robert   What?

Anne   We're at different stages in our lives.

Robert   I don't care . . .

Anne   We want different things . . .

Robert   I don't think we do.

A pause.

I want you.

A slight pause.

I don't know what love is but I do know that your face is the face I think about every morning.

A slight pause.

Your twinkling eyes and your hair. Your appalling bad manners in restaurants. Reading me favourite bits out of books you're reading. I think about your lined hands and kissing them. I think about the way you used to stand proudly in assembly. Then turn to me and catch my eye conspiratorially.

A slight pause.

All the places we've been in the world and the hung-over mornings we've had. The laughter, the endless laughter. Going out with our sixth formers because they're far more interesting than some of our fuck-shit boring colleagues. I don't know what. I can't say it. You know it all. Everything we've done. Everything we do. It's not just in my head. For God's sake, I'm completely in love with you. I've loved you for years and I love you now with a passion I never knew I had. I love you.

Anne   I know. I love you.

Robert *smiles and* **Anne** *laughs. They kiss.*

Anne   What are we going to do?

Robert   You're going to pack in teaching.

Anne   And do what?

Robert   And sell this place.

Anne   I can't . . .

Robert   You can . . .

Anne   And do what?

Robert   We're going to buy a little place. To eat and drink.

Anne   Robert, we can't do that. Where?

Robert   Somewhere in the middle. I don't know. Oxford. Anywhere. We'll serve food we like. Fish. Halibut and risotto. Monkfish on noodles. And fishcakes. Our place. I'll cork wine bottles and put a piano in the corner and I'll play.

Anne   Will you?

Robert   Every night of the week. We'll do it.

A slight pause.

And we will do it and it doesn't matter that we're starting out later in life because I've found you and it's not nine years too late because it's now and it's us and I love you and I know I'm just a fat English teacher who drinks too much and insults your students but I think you love me in fact you said a minute ago that you did so let's please do it and be happy because I know we can because you make me happy in a way no one else can and if it doesn't work out it doesn't work out and I'll bugger off back to Essex and play snooker but I think it will I know it will because I believe I make you happier than anyone else ever has or can. Am I right?

He is out of breath.

Anne   I think you need to start going to the gym.

Robert   Well, what do you think?

Anne   I think I'd like to. I'd love to.

Robert *grins. A slight pause.*

Robert   Now, what is my mother going to say about this?

Anne   What's my son going to make of this?

They both think and look at each other. **Anne** *seems worried.*

We can't just give up teaching. We've kids expecting us to see them right through their upper sixth.

A pause.

Robert   Anne, we've been teaching nearly all our adult lives. And I've loved most of it. But sometimes I feel like I'm watching from the sidelines. The times I've discussed kids and I've used the phrase 'This concerns the rest of their life.' Well, fine. But this is my life. We've done our bit. We've taught in state schools, grammar schools, private schools, the lot. We've got nothing to feel bad about. All right. Maybe we're not going to pack in teaching, but Anne . . .

Anne *thinks.*

Robert   And Anne. Please come to Italy with me at half-term.

Anne *laughs and shakes her head.*

Anne   What about May? My Auntie May. I'd love us to go too but I feel duty-bound. I made a promise I'd take her to see the cemeteries.

Robert   Did you fix up dates?

Anne   No.

Robert   Well, there you go then.

Anne   What?

Robert   You're not tied to a date or anything, are you?

Anne   But she's elderly. What if she passes away?

Robert *thinks and grins. A pause.*

Anne   What is it?

Robert   Anne, this November's the eightieth anniversary of the armistice. Why don't you go then? The head'll let you have two or three days off. I'm sure he will. There's bound to be a lot going on over there. It'll be a better time to visit. More poignant. There are probably going to be organisations for the old nurses represented. We could find out, couldn't we?

Anne   Yeah. We could.

Robert   Talk to the head. Your head's all right, isn't he?

Anne   Yeah. Great.

A slight pause.

Anne *nods. They don't know what to do. A pause.*

Robert *looks at his watch.*

Robert   Are we still going to lunch?

Anne   Yeah.

Robert   What are we going to do for a couple of hours?

Anne   I don't know, Robert.

Robert *looks at* **Anne** *hopefully.*

Robert   Sleep with me.

Anne *looks at* **Robert**.

Anne   I've got a video of my second-year production of *The Hobbit*. You haven't seen it yet, have you?

Robert   No.

Anne   I'm feeling quite hungry.

Robert   How do you fancy knocking up some scrambled eggs on toast?

Anne   Okay. You can load the dishwasher.

Robert   Have you got any bacon?

Anne   I'll defrost some.

Robert   Excellent.

He looks up. So does **Anne**.

Look at that sky, will you. Not a bloody cloud.

Anne   It's perfect.

Robert   I love it.

Anne   It is extraordinary. Not a cloud.

Robert   I wish every day could be like this.

They continue looking up.

Anne   Look, there's a plane!

Robert   Where?

Anne   There! It's trailing a sign.

She points.

What does it say?

They try to read the banner.

Robert   'B & Q Summer Sale. Ends Today.'

They both laugh.

Anne   I thought for a moment someone sent one up for us.

Robert   Sort of like – 'Rozza and Azza together for ever.'

Anne *looks at* **Robert**.

Anne   'Rozza and Azza together forever'?

Robert *nods.* **Anne** *laughs and looks back up at the sky.*

Anne   For a minute I thought the whole world knew.

Robert   Yeah. They will.

They look at each other.

They will.

Anne   Will they?

Robert   I promise you.

Anne   I don't know if I can . . .

Robert   You can. Don't spoil it. Not now.

They both look back up at the sky.

Anne   Just look at it, Robert.

Robert   Perfect.

Anne   Completely blue.

A slight pause.

The last post plays quietly as **Robert** *and* **Anne** *continue to look at the sky.*

When the last post ends, **Robert** *and* **Anne** *look at each other.* **Robert** *kisses* **Anne**'s *hand.*

Slow fade.

Roy Williams

Fallout

For Dona Daley

Roy Williams was born in Fulham and turned to writing full-time in 1990. He was awarded the OBE for Services to Drama in the 2008 Birthday Honours List. His plays include *The No-Boys Cricket Club* (Theatre Royal, Stratford East, 1996); *Josie's Boy* (Red Ladder Theatre Co, 1996); *Starstruck* (Tricycle Theatre, 1998, Winner of the John Whiting Award, Alfred Fagon Award and EMMA Award for Best Play); *Lift Off* (Royal Court Theater Upstairs, 1999); *Souls* (Theatre Centre, 1999); *Local Boy* (Hampstead Theatre, 2000); *The Gift* (Birmingham Rep/Tricycle Theatre, 2000); *Clubland* (Royal Court Theatre, 2001, winner of the *Evening Standard* Charles Wintour Award for the Most Promising Playwright); *Sing Yer Heart Out For The Lads* (National Theatre, 2002, 2004); *Fallout* (Royal Court Theatre, 2003); *Slow Time* (National Theatre Education Department tour, 2005); *Little Sweet Thing* (New Wolsey, Ipswich/Nottingham Playhouse/Birmingham Rep, 2005); *Absolute Beginners* (Lyric Theatre, Hammersmith, 2007); *Baby Girl* (National Theatre Connections, 2007); *There's Only One Wayne Matthews* (Polka Theatre, 2007); *Joe Guy* (Tiata Fahodzi, 2007); *Days of Significance* (Swan Theatre, Stratford-upon-Avon, 2007); *Angel House* (Eclipse Theatre, UK Tour, 2008); and *Category B* (Tricycle Theatre, 2009, part of their Not Black and White Season). His work for television includes *Let It Snow* (Endor Productions/Sky, 2009); *Fallout* (Company Pictures/Channel 4, 2008, Screen Nation Award for Achievement in Screenwriting); *Offside* (BBC, 2002, Winner of BAFTA Children's Film & TV Award for Best Schools Drama) and *Babyfather* (BBC2, 2001). For radio, his work includes adaptations of ER Braithwaite's *To Sir With Love* (BBC Radio 4, 2007) and *A Choice of Straws* (BBC Radio 4, 2009), and original plays, *Tell Tale* and *Homeboys* (both BBC Radio 4, 2007). His play *Sucker Punch* will open at the Royal Court in June 2010 and will be directed by Sacha Wares.

Fallout was first performed at the Royal Court Jerwood
Theatre Downstairs, London, on 12 June 2003. The cast
was as follows:

Fallout	Jason Frederick
Dwayne	Michael Obiora
Emile	Marcel McCalla
Perry	O-T Fagbenle
Joe	Lennie James
Matt	Daniel Ryan
Shanice	Ony Uhiara
Ronnie	Petra Letang
Manny	Clive Wedderburn
Miss Douglas/Inspector	Lorraine Brunning

Director Ian Rickson
Designer Ultz
Lighting Designer Nigel J. Edwards
Sound Designer Ian Dickinson
Music Stephen Warbeck

Characters

Shanice, *late teens, black*
Emile, *late teens, black*
Dwayne, *late teens, black*
Joe, *mid-thirties, black*
Matt, *mid-thirties, white*
Perry, *late teens, mixed race*
Ronnie, *late teens, black*
Clinton, *late teens, black*
Miss Douglas, *early forties, white*
Inspector, *early forties, white*
Manny, *late thirties, black*

The roles of Miss Douglas and the Inspector should be played by the same actor.

Time
Present

Setting
Various

Enter **Clinton, Dwayne, Emile** *and* **Perry**.

Clinton   Kick him in the head, kick him!

Dwayne   Yes!

Perry   My bwoi.

Clinton   Kick him.

Dwayne   Tek off him glasses and chuck dem.

Clinton   Chuck dem now, man.

Emile   Pass me de phone, yu fucker!

Clinton   Pass him de phone, yu fuck!

Emile   Pass it now.

Perry   Do it now.

Dwayne   My bwoi!

Emile   Trainers too.

Clinton   Gwan, Emile!

Perry   Walk barefoot, yu rass.

Clinton   Like yu do in Africa.

Emile   Trainers!

Clinton   Tell him, Emile.

Perry   Tell the fucker.

Dwayne   Bus his head.

Clinton   Bus him up.

Emile   Trainers!

Dwayne   Fuck dem over to us.

Clinton   Before yu dead.

Emile   Trainers!

Dwayne   Punch him.

Clinton   Kick him.

Perry   Bus him up.

Emile   Yu see yu! (*Kicks continuously.*)

Exit **Clinton**, **Dwayne**, **Perry** *and* **Emile**.

Enter **Shanice** *and* **Ronnie**, **Joe** *and* **Matt**.

Ronnie   Yer gonna love me, Shanice.

Shanice   I love yer awready, yu fool.

Ronnie   Well, yer gonna love me more, dread. See?
(*Shows a blouse.*)

Shanice   Nice.

Ronnie   Honestly?

Shanice   Honestly.

Ronnie   Yes.

Shanice   Bit small fer yu.

Ronnie   Got it fer yu.

Shanice   Ronnie!

Ronnie   It'll go nice wid yer black skirt, yer gonna look
the business, girl, no guy can refuse yu.

Shanice   Ronnie, wat am I doin right now?

Ronnie   Nuttin.

Shanice   I'm workin.

Ronnie   Shut up.

Shanice   Later.

Ronnie   Yeah, but I want see how well it fit.

Shanice   Why yu aways gettin me things, man?

Ronnie   It don't look right on me.

Shanice   So why buy it?

Ronnie   I didn't buy it.

Shanice   Ronnie, yu didn't?

Ronnie   I saw it in the shop.

Shanice   Oh man.

Ronnie   As soon as I lay my eye upon it, I thought of yu.

Shanice   Is it?

Ronnie   It was callin to me, Shanice.

Shanice   Shush.

Ronnie   I had to have it . . .

Shanice   Hold it down.

Ronnie   Why?

Shanice (*aside*)   Police.

Ronnie   Ware?

Shanice   Deh.

Ronnie   Wat, dem?

Shanice   Yes.

Ronnie   Yo!

Shanice   Ronnie!

Ronnie   Yo!

Matt   Yes?

Ronnie   Yu lot still here?

Matt   Can we help you?

Ronnie   Yu best go home. Ain't no criminals in here.

Matt   Is it written all over our foreheads or something?

Joe   How did you know?

Shanice   It's written all over yer foreheads.

Ronnie   Believe.

Shanice   Kwame?

Matt   That's right.

Ronnie   Don't yu lot get tired? Bin interviewin everyone, man. Over and over. How come yu Feds never come see me? Especially dat cute young one, wathimname. Oh man, yu should see him, Shanice. Not like these two. Bring him round, let him talk to me.

Joe   Who?

Matt   PC Adams, he has been getting this all month.

Ronnie   So yu like it den?

Shanice   It's awright.

Ronnie   Ca if yu don't like it . . .

Shanice   Wat, yu'll tek it back?

Ronnie   I'll get yu summin else.

Shanice   Yu stay ware yu are. Yeah, wat yu havin?

Joe   Two teas and a smile.

Shanice *feigns a smile.*

Joe   How big are dem chicken wings?

Shanice   I dunno, they're chicken wings.

Joe   Lemme have four.

Shanice   Comin wid yer tea.

Ronnie   No, try it on first.

Shanice   Shut up.

Ronnie   Come on.

Shanice   Awright! Love to go on. Keep an eye out.

Exit **Shanice**.

Ronnie   So, when are yu gonna send dat nice copper round to see me den?

Joe   What are you gonna tell him?

Ronnie   Watever he wants. Yu get me? (*Laughs.*)

Her phone rings.

(*Answers.*) Tracey! Wass up, girl? Hold up. (*To* **Joe** *and* **Matt**.) Keep an eye out.

Exit **Ronnie**.

Matt   Who let that out?

Joe   I like the other one.

Matt   Bit young for you.

Joe   Look me in the eye and tell me you wouldn't tap that.

Matt   I have a sister her age.

Joe   You've got a dick your age.

Matt   And a wife. What?

Joe   Something I heard.

Matt   Well, don't keep me hanging, Joe, let's have it.

Joe   A story I heard.

Matt   Yes?

Joe   When you were at Kilburn. PC Holmes was her name. Tits this big.

Matt   Nothing happened.

Joe   Oh yes?

Matt   We were friends.

Joe   No such thing.

Matt   I wasn't even married then.

Joe You were engaged.

Matt Are you always like this?

Joe You must have heard what they said about me.

Matt And they were right.

Joe You don't have to like me, Matt.

Matt Well, I do. Did you read the file?

Joe I flipped through it. All this must be kicking your arse by now.

Matt That's one way.

Joe Funeral's tomorrow.

Matt I know.

Joe You going?

Matt The super is.

Joe Royalty.

Matt You saw the Jubilee celebrations. We're all trying to be modern now. Shall we start?

Joe You're the boss.

Matt Kwame left the station at five forty-five. CCTV clocked him walking past the church towards the high street. Another one picked him up coming off the high, walking towards the swimming baths. He was inside for an hour. He went there, every Thursday. CCTV again, clocked him leaving the baths at 6.50 p.m. He bought a burger and chips from here at seven, left this place at seven ten. He was last seen walking towards the station, passing the church again. We assume he was going home. Seven fifteen. He was found at the bottom of the road.

Joe Seven twenty-five.

Matt It was like his head was used for a football. He died, two days later. There was another CCTV, but it wasn't working properly that evening. Typical. It kept getting jammed. All it got was a lamp post shining in its lens. We're bringing in a specialist, see if he can do anything, just like what we did for that missing girl. One witness says he saw a young man matching Kwame's description arguing with a group of boys earlier that evening. He also saw a silver BMW several times driving around the area playing really loud rap music. It was like the driver was lost or something. Whoever that driver was, he or she may have seen something, but so far, no one has come forward. Feel up to speed?

Enter **Ronnie**.

Joe   I wonder what the fight was about.

Matt   There was no fight.

Joe   Drugs. Phones.

Matt   That doesn't compute.

Joe   Why?

Matt   He was a straight-A student. On his way to university. He wasn't into gangs at all. We asked everyone, they all said the same thing, his nose was in the books.

Joe   He must have been fighting about something with them.

Matt   It wasn't a fight our witness saw, it was an argument.

Joe   So what was the argument about?

Matt   I don't know.

Enter **Clinton**, **Emile**, **Dwayne** *and* **Perry**.

Emile   Troll? Ware's Shanice?

Ronnie   Kiss my arse.

Dwayne   Shut up, troll, and tell him.

Ronnie   How am I supposed to do dat with my mouth shut? And I ain't no troll.

Dwayne   Sorry, Shrek.

Laughter.

Perry   My stomach is empty.

Emile   Troll. Food.

Ronnie   Yu'll have to wait.

Perry   Tower burger, large fries.

Clinton   Is dat wat yer gonna have?

Perry   Yes, Clinton, dass wat I'm gonna have, dass why I ordered it.

Clinton   Yu had a kebab an hour ago.

Perry   I'm still hungry.

Clinton   Don't see how.

Emile   Oh man, not again.

Dwayne   Shut up, Clinton.

Clinton   Tower cheeseburger is a lot to eat by yerself.

Perry   Clinton? Yu want me to order fer yu?

Clinton   I didn't say dat.

Perry   Dis bwoi drive me mad, yu know.

Clinton   But did I say dat?

Perry   Do yu want me to order fer yu? Why yu love to go round the block wid dis?

Clinton   Wid wat?

Perry   Now he's tekin the piss. Yer broke, yeah? Yu ain't got enuff dollars to buy a meal. Why yu can't ask?

Clinton   Don't get vex, P.

Perry   I don't know why yu can't say wat yu wanna say?

Clinton   Which is wat?

Perry   Does dis bwoi wanna die?

Clinton   If yu can't eat all dat by yerself, P, I'll help yu out.

Dwayne (*laughs*)   Bredren!

Emile   Oh juss help the college bwoi out, P. Can't you see, he's wastin away?

Perry   It's aways me he does dis to.

Emile   He's yer cousin.

Perry   Dat ain't my fault.

Clinton *stares.*

Perry   Wat?

Clinton   Nuttin.

Perry   Yu want sum?

Clinton   Yu don't have to.

Perry   I go ask yu again. Yu gimme more than yes or no, I go bus yer head. Yu want sum food?

Clinton   Yeah.

Perry   Gw'y.

Laughter.

Dwayne   Cold!

Clinton   I knew yu'd do dat.

Perry   Troll, give the bwoi sum food.

Clinton   Nice, cous.

Perry   Get a job, man.

Dwayne   Gimme a number-one meal.

Emile   Number two.

Perry   Wat yu want?

Clinton   Only if yer sure.

Perry   Pick a number before I kill yu.

Clinton   Two.

Perry   And a one fer me.

Ronnie   Yu lot mus be deaf.

Emile   Yu wan' die?

Matt (*gets up*)   Hey.

Emile   Yu want tek yer hand off my jacket please?

Matt   Take it easy, son.

Emile   Who dis fool?

Ronnie   Five 0.

Emile   Oh! So dass wat de smell was.

Enter **Shanice**.

Shanice   Yeah, I like dis one. Fits nice. Awright, Emile?

Emile   Ware yu bin?

Shanice   Out back.

Dwayne   Like yer top, Shanice.

Shanice   Go away, Dwayne.

Dwayne   But it look good.

Emile   I didn't get yu dat.

Shanice   Yu don't have to get me everythin, Emile, I bought it myself.

Ronnie   No yu didn't, I got it.

Emile   Tell it to shut up.

Ronnie   Shut up yerself.

Shanice   Ronnie! Yu like it?

Dwayne   Love it.

Clinton   Believe.

Shanice   Emile?

Emile   It's awright.

Dwayne   Dass it, awright? Yer gal look fine.

Shanice   He don't like it.

Ronnie   Shanice, don't, man, it look good.

Shanice   I'm changin.

Exit **Shanice**.

Dwayne (*mocks*)   It's awright!

Perry   Emile man, yer lucky yer my bredren. Ca if yu weren't, I woulda dived on yer gal from time.

Clinton   Not before me.

Perry   Yu go down on it, Emile?

Dwayne   Cold.

Perry   She give good shine?

Emile   Shut up.

Perry   Ease up, blood.

Emile   I'm tellin yer.

Clinton   Soff.

Perry   Go sit over deh, if yu go cry.

Ronnie   See, ain't juss me who tinks yer a pussy.

Emile   Yu don't shut yer mout, troll.

Ronnie   Wat?

Enter **Shanice**.

Shanice   Oh man, will yu two stop? Every time.

Dwayne   Put the other top back on.

Shanice   So yu can watch me all night?

Perry   Believe.

Emile   Rah, he's still starin.

Clinton   Who?

Emile   Mr White Man over deh. Yu like my friend, Mr
White Man? Yu want ask him out, get his number?

Joe *sucks his teeth.*

Emile   Sorry, brudda, we didn't quite catch dat. Wat, yu
can't speak till him tell yu to?

Joe   Bwoi.

Emile   Yer the bwoi.

Dwayne   So wat yu doin here, Mr Policeman?

Matt   Having a tea.

Clinton   They're here fer Kwame, innit?

Dwayne   Nuh, Clinton, really?

Emile   Wastin yer time, man, yu ain't gonna catch dem.

Joe   Them?

Emile   Wat?

Joe   You said them.

Emile   I know wat I said.

Joe   Them, as in more than one?

Clinton   Guy cussin yu, Emile.

Perry   He thinks yer stupid.

Emile   Yu tink I'm stupid?

Joe   What makes you think we're looking for more than one person?

Emile   I don't.

Joe   So why say it?

Emile   I say wat I like.

Joe   True, but why say that?

Emile   Ca I felt like it.

Dwayne   Easy, dread.

Joe   Choose your words carefully.

Emile   Yu my dad now?

Joe   Maybe, wass yer mudda's name?

Clinton   Oh shame.

Matt   Joe?

Emile   Wass he say?

Clinton   He's cussin yer mum.

Shanice   Sit down, Emile.

Joe   Yes, Emile, sit down.

Emile   Go chat wid yer gal deh.

Perry   I hate to break dis to yer, Dwayne. Yer dad's comin, dis way.

Dwayne   Oh man, wass he want? He bin stalkin me all day. Don't let him in.

Manny, **Dwayne**'s *dad, enters.*

Manny   Hey, son! Son? Ware yu going? Come here, son?

Dwayne   Wat yu want?

Manny   Lemme have one pound. Beg yu fer one pound.

Dwayne   Come outta my face, yeah.

Manny   Hey, bwoi.

Dwayne   Come outta my face!

Manny   Yer too rude, yer nuh.

Exit **Manny**.

Dwayne   Jesus, man, he's an itch I can't scratch, a pain in the arse.

Perry, *by the door, laughs.*

Dwayne   Wat yu laughin at now, yu baboon?

Perry   Jamal mek me laugh, man.

Dwayne   Jamal still in Feltham.

Perry   No, he come out lass month.

Dwayne   So wat yu laughin about?

Perry   Ca he's over deh, breakin into sumone's car. Have a look. The man love to steal cars, he muss have a hard-on fer it.

Dwayne   But he always get catch.

Perry   Exactly! The guy can't even drive properly. I was in a car wid him one time, half the time we were on the pavement. But deh's no tellin him. Guy tinks he's Formula One.

Clinton   Yo, policeman, I hope dat ain't yer car outside.

Matt   What car?

Clinton   Light blue Escort.

Matt   Oh what! (*Jumps up.*)

Dwayne   Oh yes, run, run!

Perry   Why yu tell him?

Clinton   I want see dis.

Dwayne   Come.

Exit **Matt** *and* **Joe**.

Dwayne   Yes, bwoi, run.

Perry   Bredren stole a police car! Deh gonna throw his arse in prison again and keep it deh. Fer trut.

Dwayne   He run fast.

Clinton   Too late, yu fool.

Dwayne   Come, let's go, I want see dis. Emile?

Emile   I catch up.

Dwayne   Yeah, go sex yer woman.

Exit **Dwayne**, **Clinton** *and* **Perry**.

Emile (*to* **Ronnie**)   Out.

Ronnie *sucks her teeth*.

Shanice   Ronnie.

Exit **Ronnie**.

Shanice *and* **Emile** *kiss*.

Shanice   Missed yu.

Emile   Missed yu too. I love yer hands. Did I ever tell yu dat? Yu got lovely hands.

Shanice *laughs*.

Emile   Wat? Yu think dat was funny?

Shanice   No.

Emile   So why laugh?

Shanice   Ca yu mek me smile.

Emile   Shut up, man.

Shanice   Yu do.

Emile   Yer tekin the piss.

Shanice   If yu don't like it, don't say it.

Emile   I won't.

Shanice   But I want yu to.

Emile   Look, don't wear dat top again.

Shanice   Oh man.

Emile   Juss don't.

Shanice   I knew yu didn't like it.

Emile   So why wear it?

Shanice   Ronnie got me it, yu know wat she's like.

Emile   Why yu still wid her?

Shanice   She's harmless, man. She ain't got nobody.

Emile   So?

Shanice   Can we not fight please?

Emile   Sorry, yeah.

Shanice   Yu will be.

Emile   Shut up, man.

Shanice and **Emile** *kiss again.*

Shanice   Yu ordered yet?

Emile   Yeah, number two.

Shanice   Number two?

Emile   I'm hungry.

Shanice   Yu fat bloater.

Emile   Shut up, I ain't fat.

Shanice   Hate to break it to yer, Emile, but yer gettin a little bit wide in the gut department. Anyhow, yu turn into one a dem big fat men who can hardly walk, I'll step.

Emile   Yu won't leave me.

Shanice   Yu wan bet?

Emile   Yu love me.

Shanice   I know I love yer, juss as long as yu don't turn fat on me. Oderwise, I juss have to go and check one a yer brers dem.

Emile   Yu ain't jokin.

Shanice   Course I'm jokin.

Emile   Yu really tink I'm gettin fat?

Shanice   Yu are so easy to tease.

Emile   Do yer?

Shanice   No.

Emile   Yu shouldn't say dat.

Shanice   It was a joke, I'm sorry.

Emile   Wat if one a dem had heard yer?

Shanice   I don't care.

Emile   They'd dive on yu like dat, if they had the chance.

Shanice   Let dem try.

Emile   Dwayne man, he wants yer.

Shanice   Well, I don't want him, I got wat I want.

Emile (*slaps her hand away*)   Move!

Shanice   Emile! Yer wrong anyway. I ain't Dwayne's type.

Emile   Oh shut up, yeah.

Shanice Yu shut up.

Emile Yer everybody's type. Yer so fit.

Shanice Awright.

Emile Yer are.

Shanice Yes! I'm fit. (*Beat.*) Wass botherin yu?

Emile Saw Kwame's mum yesterday. Stuck up, man, always was. Lookin down on me like I'm shit. Come like her bwoi, well, he find out, innit.

Shanice Don't.

Emile See her face in the paper, appealin fer help. Den deh got de blasted funeral tomorrow, why can't she juss let it go, man? She don't even live round here no more.

Shanice Her son's dead, she can't let it go.

Emile I thought yu were on my side.

Shanice I am.

Emile Well, show it den.

Shanice Wat do yu think I'm doin?

Emile I keep seein him.

Shanice Shush.

Emile His face, man.

Shanice He'll go soon. He'll go.

Beat.

Emile Put the oder top back on.

Shanice Yu hate it.

Emile (*smirks*) It look good.

Exit **Shanice** *and* **Emile**.

Enter **Matt** *and* **Joe**.

Joe   So what did they say?

Matt   They dumped the car about a mile away. They shat all over the back seats. I mean, there's no need for that.

Joe   They don't make teenagers like they used to. They ought to burn that fucker down.

Matt   I'm sorry?

Joe   The estate.

Matt   It's not the estate, it's the people.

Joe   Them as well. Young ones anyway.

Matt   Are you trying to provoke me, Joe?

Joe   Provoke?

Matt   How am I supposed to react to that?

Joe   We're all friends here, you act how you feel.

Matt   And then what?

Joe   You're losing me.

Matt   Am I supposed to agree with you?

Joe   Do you?

Matt   No.

Joe   That's exactly why they took your car. They can see right through you. Take it easy! Do you think it was them who attacked Kwame?

Matt   Well, they fit the description.

Joe   I'm surprised you can tell. You can't tell them apart in the day now, let alone night-time.

Matt   Excuse me?

Joe   Joke.

Matt   I don't find that funny.

Joe   Sorry.

Matt   Our witness named one of them.

Joe   Which one?

Matt   The leader. Dwayne Edwards.

Joe   I thought it might have been the one who goes out wid the girl. What's a nice-looking gal doing with a little bwoi like that?

Matt   I couldn't say.

Joe   I'm going to get a headache tonight, just thinking about it.

Matt   Shall we go?

Joe (*smiles*)   You're very polite.

Matt   Thank you.

Exit **Joe** *and* **Matt**.

Enter **Ronnie** *and* **Shanice**.

Shanice   Twenty grand!

Ronnie   Tellin yu.

Shanice   Fer Kwame?

Ronnie   Yes! Yu know wat I'll do if I had dat money?

Shanice   Tell me.

Ronnie   Buy car.

Shanice   Yu can't even drive.

Ronnie   I'd buy it fer yu. Get sum clothes. Yu can tell me wat to buy, dress me up.

Shanice   I don't think the world is ready fer yu in a dress.

Ronnie   We go ravin every night. Hunt fer sum bwois. But only if deh buff.

Shanice Of course. So wat about Dwayne?

Ronnie Mek him jealous, innit? Emile as well. Can't wait, man. If yu weren't goin out wid him, we could claim dat money right now.

Shanice Yu shouldn't say things like dat.

Ronnie True though.

Shanice I don't care if it's true, don't say it.

Ronnie Yeah, but it's true.

Shanice Shut up.

Ronnie Yu sound like Emile.

Shanice Sorry.

Ronnie Call me troll while yer at it.

Shanice Are yu deaf, wat did I juss say? I've never called yu dat, not even behind yer back. Ronnie, have yu told anyone wat yu saw?

Ronnie No.

Shanice Promise me.

Ronnie I haven't.

Shanice It's important.

Ronnie I know.

Shanice Ca we ain't at school no more, I can't aways be deh fer yu.

Ronnie I know.

Shanice Gotta think fer yerself.

Ronnie I said I know.

Shanice Be careful wid wat yu say.

Ronnie Wat yu gettin wound up fer? Yu didn't do it.

Shanice   I feel as though I have.

Ronnie   Behave, man.

Shanice   I had him cryin his eyes out to me.

Ronnie   Wat, again?

Shanice   Goin on about seein Kwame's face.

Ronnie   Ejut.

Shanice   He ain't the only one, dread. I'm seein Kwame too, every day. Him standin right here. Him leavin, wavin to me. I'm the lass person who saw him alive, Ronnie.

Ronnie   No yu ain't.

Shanice   Yu know wat I mean. He had his lass food in here, double cheeseburger, large fries and a Coke. Dat was the lass food he ever had, double cheeseburger.

Ronnie   I don't know why yu gettin stressed.

Shanice   It's runnin thru my head, every day. Shit won't go.

Ronnie   I know it won't, ca yu love to chat about it.

Shanice   Why did Emile have to do it?

Ronnie   Ask him.

Shanice   Juss ignore me, yeah.

Ronnie   I know wat yu need.

Shanice   Tell me.

Ronnie   Barbados.

Shanice (*laughs*)   Is it?

Ronnie   Definitely. Go stay wid yer gran. I'll come wid yu, yeah.

Shanice   We go chase, man?

Ronnie   Trust.

Shanice   Awright.

Ronnie   We go swimmin.

Shanice   Bacardi Breezer.

Ronnie   Tropical Lime.

Shanice   Ruby Grapefruit.

Ronnie   Lie on beach.

Shanice   Sun in my face.

Ronnie   Yu see?

Shanice   Oh Ronnie man! If only.

Ronnie   We can, yu know.

Shanice   No, we can't. Come on, enuff daydreamin.
Clean up.

Ronnie   Yer gonna love me, Shanice.

Shanice   I love yu awready.

Ronnie   Well, yer gonna love me even more.

Shanice   Wat yu tief now?

Ronnie   Nuttin. Guess who I saw? Guess?

Shanice   I don't want to guess, juss tell me.

Ronnie   Miss Douglas.

Shanice   Is it?

Ronnie   The slag herself.

Shanice   She see yu?

Ronnie   Yeah, she saw me.

Shanice   So wat she have to say fer herself?

Ronnie   Nuttin. She was comin outta Tesco's when I
clocked her. She couldn't get across dat road fast enuff. She
was clutchin her bag, like they do, well desperate to get

away from me. She nearly walk right into the side of dis car, nearly get run over. Man scream out from his window, cussin her, I goes, yes, blood, tell her. I kept followin her though.

Shanice   She didn't see yu?

Ronnie   No, I was careful. Yu wanna know ware she lives now? Ashwood Gardens.

Shanice   Ain't much help without a number.

Ronnie   Twenty-nine C. Yu gonna get her, Shanice? I'm comin wid yu, yeah, I have to come wid yu.

Shanice   Calm yerself.

Ronnie   I'm juss sayin, I'm comin wid yu. Let's get her back, man, let's do her good, fer kickin us out. Please, Shanice?

Shanice   Awright!

Ronnie   Yes!

Joe *enters.*

Ronnie   Wass my man doin here?

Shanice   Yu here again?

Joe   No, it's what can I get you? You won't get many customers talking like that.

Ronnie   Chat is dry.

Joe   Ginger beer please.

Ronnie   Buff dough.

Shanice   I don't think so.

Ronnie   Oi oi buff bwoi!

Shanice   Yu mad?

Ronnie   Yu tellin me yu wouldn't?

Shanice   He's Five 0.

Ronnie   So yu would, if he wasn't? How old are yu?

Shanice   Ronnie!

Ronnie   How old?

Joe   Old enough.

Ronnie   Thirty-five or summin. Has to be. Yu look good though, fer an old man.

Shanice   Thirty-five ain't dat old.

Ronnie   She thinks yer buff.

Shanice   Will yu stop shamin me?

Ronnie   So ware's the oder one?

Joe   My partner?

Ronnie   No! Guy's a minger. The oder one. Fit one who wears uniform. Looks like Duncan from Blue. Yu should see dis guy, Shanice.

Shanice   Yu told me.

Ronnie   Oh man!

Shanice   Yu mind? Don't go creamin yer knickers in here.

Ronnie   So ware is he?

Joe   You mean PC Adams?

Ronnie   Yeah, him, ware is he?

Joe   I have no idea. I don't know him.

Ronnie   Well, yu can find out fer me.

Shanice   Yu love to drool. Yu don't feel slack?

Ronnie   Yu should see him dough.

Shanice   Since when yu go fer white bwois? Yu muss be well moist.

Ronnie   Juss tell him I gonna come lookin fer him. It's gonna be me and him soon, tellin yu. 'Me so horny . . .

Shanice   '. . . me so sexy . . .

Ronnie/Shanice   '. . . me love yu long time!'

Laughter from the girls.

Ronnie   Wanna share him, Shanice?

Shanice   I don't do white men.

Ronnie   But if yu had to, who would yu go fer?

Shanice   None.

Ronnie   Shut up.

Shanice   None, right.

Ronnie   If I put a gun to yer face, yu still wouldn't choose?

Shanice   No.

Ronnie   Lie bad.

Shanice   White bwois too soff.

Ronnie   Blah, blah, bloody blah, who would yu choose?

Shanice   David Rees.

Ronnie   David Rees!

Shanice   Yu have to shout?

Ronnie   Oh shame.

Shanice   Only if I had to.

Ronnie   Oh yes?

Shanice   Yu open yer mout to anyone, and yu die.

Ronnie   I can see dat, yu and him.

Shanice   Ain't gonna happen.

Ronnie   Oh but he's nice, really sweet and dat.

Shanice   Oh don't chat like a white girl, please.

Ronnie   I reckon he looks like Will Young.

Shanice   No!

Ronnie   Only ca him gay.

Shanice   He don't look like Will Young!

Ronnie   Ask him out.

Shanice   Move.

Ronnie   I know his brudda.

Shanice   Don't involve me in yer stupidness.

Ronnie   Yu might be missin out.

Shanice   On wat?

Ronnie   He might have a PhD, yu get me?

Shanice   A white bwoi?

Ronnie   Why not? Ain't juss bruddas who have dem. I know sum bruddas who don't have dem. Yu have one?

Joe   What?

Ronnie   PhD?

Shanice (*laughing*)   Shut up, Ronnie man.

Ronnie   Bet he don't.

Shanice   Yu don't feel no shame.

Ronnie   Watch my man's face turn red now.

Shanice   Oi, go and get sum change fer me.

Ronnie   Oh I see.

Shanice   No yu don't see.

Ronnie Want sumtime alone wid yer man here. I'm tellin Emile. How yu know he ain't here to chirps me?

Shanice He ain't chirpsin neither of us.

Ronnie All the shops are shut.

Shanice Costcutter's ain't.

Ronnie Dass miles.

Shanice Pound coins and twenties.

Ronnie Awright, I'm gone. Comin back dough. She go eat yu alive, dread.

Exit **Ronnie**.

Shanice She's mad.

Joe No need to apologise.

Shanice I ain't, I'm juss sayin she's mad. So ware is he?

Joe Who, Adams? I don't know him.

Shanice Yer partner.

Joe Conducting interviews or something. I don't know. I gave him the slip.

Shanice Naughty.

Joe When you hear him ask the same questions 'bout twenty times, it gets a bit boring, you know.

Shanice Is it?

Joe You're a bit young to be running this place on your own.

Shanice Is it?

Joe Should be at school.

Shanice Is it?

Joe Oh, I see, you don't want chat to no policeman.

Shanice   Is –

Joe   – Is it? Beat you.

Shanice   Gimme summin worth chattin about.

Joe   Did you go to his funeral today?

Shanice   His parents wouldn't want me deh.

Joe   Why's that?

Shanice   They don't want none of the kids from round here deh.

Joe   Can't say I blame them. I wouldn't want a whole heap of kids comin to my boy's funeral when I know it's one of them that killed him, or know who did.

Shanice   I don't know who kill him.

Joe   I never said you did. Did yu know him?

Shanice   Course I knew him.

Joe   How well did you know him?

Shanice   I answered dis awready.

Joe   Yeah, but do it fer me. I'm new. Please.

Shanice   We were at school togeder.

Joe   He was attacked after leaving here.

Shanice   Yes!

Joe   How did he seem?

Shanice   Awright, he was fine.

Joe   He was here for ten minutes.

Shanice   He had to wait fer his food.

Joe   Wat did you talk about?

Shanice   Stuff, his college and that.

Joe   College?

Shanice   He had to leave home, he was scared about going away.

Joe   That's quite a conversation to have in ten minutes.

Shanice   Is it?

Joe   Was he a regular, Shanice?

Shanice   He aways used to pop in here after he went swimmin. He would sit down deh, read one of his books. Kept tellin him.

Joe   Telling him what?

Shanice   About his books. Guy loved to study, man.

Joe   And what is so wrong wid that?

Shanice   He was aways gettin teased.

Joe   By who?

Shanice   Bwois.

Joe   What boys? The same ones who were in here the other day?

Shanice   And others. Dass the way it was at school. Yu strut round wid books in yer hands, yer askin to get beat up.

Joe   Or killed.

Shanice   Ain't wat I said.

Joe   I know.

Shanice   He loved to carry on, like he was better.

Joe   What's wrong wid that?

Shanice   Sum people don't like dat.

Joe   What people?

Shanice   I'm juss sayin.

Joe   Like yer boyfriend?

Shanice   He couldn't tek a joke.

Joe   How so?

Shanice   One time we had dis new teacher in, yeah. So we all decided to play a joke on him. No one was gonna speak fer the whole lesson, not do any work, juss stare out, see wat happens, wat he does. Everyone was up fer it right, except Kwame. Deh he was, sittin deh, doin his work. He ruined the joke.

Joe   He wanted to work.

Shanice   It was juss a joke.

Joe   It was his choice, he didn't have to, if he didn't want to.

Shanice   Den he was a fool. I could tell yu oder tings 'bout him.

Joe   So tell me.

Shanice   Yu don't wanna know, yu juss want catch the guy who did it.

Joe   So, I'm lookin for a guy?

Shanice   No. I don't know.

Joe   Tell me.

Shanice   First day he come to our school, teacher put him next to me, so I had to look after him. I ask him, why me?

Joe   Because you have a nice face?

Shanice   Yeah.

Joe   You have.

Shanice   Yu come like my gran.

Joe   How so?

Shanice   Ca she aways sayin, sum people have it in their nature to be nice. No matter wat they do to hide it, it's aways deh. They can't help it. Well, I could help it, I didn't want no smelly-head African next to me, followin me. I told him to move, nuff times, but he wouldn't go. I felt sorry fer him after a while, especially when other kids would start on him.

Joe   You looked after him.

Joe   I bet Emile loved that.

Shanice   He weren't my boyfriend den.

Joe   And now?

Shanice   Kwame loved to show how smart he was, like deh is two kinds of black, and he come from the better one, he was havin a laugh. People weren't gonna tek dat.

Joe   Including Emile?

Shanice   Why yu love to chat about Emile, yu love him?

Joe   It's just a question.

Shanice   Yu ask too many questions.

Joe   It's my job.

Shanice   So's listenin.

Joe   Ain't I listening to you now?

Shanice   All dat shit in the paper, chattin like they knew him. He weren't special, he was juss anoder kid, he was nuttin.

Joe   So, he had it coming?

Shanice   I didn't say that.

Joe   So wat was he doing chatting to you about college?

Shanice   I dunno, he juss talked. I can't stop him from chattin.

Joe   But why you, Shanice?

Shanice   I dunno.

Joe   Maybe cos he thought the same way as your gran.

Shanice   Yer wastin yer time.

Joe   Why?

Shanice   Go back to ware yu come from.

Joe   This is where I come from.

Enter **Dwayne**, **Emile**, **Clinton** *and* **Perry**.

Dwayne   Tyson's soff.

Clinton   Awright, watch.

Dwayne   Wass he got, after my man Lennox give him a slappin?

Clinton   He's still a force.

Dwayne   He's a joke. He ain't never bin the same since he come outta prison after wat dat gal said about him. He grind her, and wat happen, get banged up. Dat ain't right.

Perry   My dad says, women are here to fuck up the black man.

Clinton   Yu don't even know yer dad.

Perry   Yer mama don't know yer dad.

Clinton   Dry!

Dwayne   Like her pussy.

Joe *laughs*.

Dwayne   Awright, awright, who call the Feds?

Emile   Was it yu, P?

Perry   Yeah, I want dem to catch the bastard dat cut up Clinton's hair?

Clinton   Ha, yer so funny.

Dwayne   So wass my man doin here?

Shanice   We're juss chattin, so leave him, yeah.

Dwayne   Yu sexin him?

Shanice   Oh man, juss step.

Dwayne   Emile, have a word, man.

Shanice   Excuse me, I'm right here.

Emile   So ware's yer massa?

Shanice   Emile?

Emile   Ware him deh?

Clinton   Cold.

Perry   Gwan.

Emile   Him let yu off the ball and chain fer the night? Him lose his tongue or wat?

Joe   Toothpaste.

Emile   Wass he say?

Clinton   He said toothpaste.

Emile   Yeah, I know wat he said.

Joe   Well, you might want invest, ca yer breath stink, bredren.

Laughter.

Perry   Oh shame!

Dwayne   It's awright, Emile.

Emile   Get off.

Dwayne   Wat, yu go cryin to yer mummy now, ca the brudda here lick yu down wid sum lyrics?

Emile   He didn't lick me down.

Dwayne   And it was a dry one too.

Clinton   Toothpaste.

Emile   He ain't no brudda.

Dwayne   Look like one to me.

Perry   Yu want invest in sum specs as well, Emile.

Clinton   As well as toothpaste.

Emile   Look at the fool.

Dwayne   Yeah?

Emile   Don't even know he's bin used.

Joe   Why don't you enlighten me?

Emile   We ain't tellin yu shit.

Joe   So, you do know something?

Emile   No.

Joe   But you just told me you ain't telling us shit.

Emile   See, awready I know wat yer doin.

Joe   I'm only repeating wat you said.

Emile   Yu go try twist my words, watch him now.

Joe   You're twisting your own words.

Shanice   Emile?

Emile   Is who ask yu fer anythin?

Joe   You said you ain't telling us shit.

Emile   Yes.

Joe   Which implies, that you know something, but you refuse to share it with us.

Emile   No.

Joe   No, you refuse to share, or no, it isn't true?

Emile   See wat I mean about him?

Joe   You better watch yourself, Emile, that's a bad habit you picked up there.

Emile   Why don't yu juss go?

Dwayne   Shut up, yu fool.

Joe   Thank yu, Dwayne, control yer bwoi.

Clinton   Comin out wid dry lyrics himself now.

Joe   You had better keep a leash on this one, Dwayne. He may fold under questioning.

Dwayne   Sit down.

Joe   Bwoi.

Shanice   Why yu stressin him fer?

Perry   Rah, woman tougher than yu, Emile.

Shanice   Why don't yu juss go home?

Joe   I am home.

Dwayne   Wass dis?

Shanice   He say he comes from here.

Dwayne   Is it? Ware?

Joe   Dickens.

Dwayne   Knew it! Dat estate is soff!

Joe   Let me guess, Cleveland?

Perry   Believe.

Joe   Yu ain't all dat.

Dwayne   Shut up, man.

Clinton   Wid yer dry chat.

Perry   Yu definitely ain't bin back from time.

Joe   You Cleveland bwois are wurtless and you know it.

Dwayne   Talk to the hand.

Joe   Yu know it.

Dwayne   Dat was back in the day. Tings change.

Clinton   Believe.

Perry   Yeah.

Dwayne   Wat matters is now.

Joe   Awright, I'm down with that.

Dwayne   No yer not. Yu ain't from round here no more, dread. So don't carry on like yu tink yu know.

Clinton   Chump.

Perry   If yer so bad, why yu leave fer?

Joe   I wanted a change. Cleaner air.

Emile   Well, gwan den, if dass how yu feel.

Joe   Yeah, but there's a little matter of a murder, Emile, remember?

Emile   Yu ain't gonna find him here.

Joe   Maybe, maybe not.

Emile   Dis guy drive me mad.

Dwayne   Chill.

Emile   Juss say wat yu feel, yeah.

Joe   Your boy is losing it again, Dwayne, have a word.

Emile   Yu tink it's one of us, innit?

Joe   You'll find out soon enough what I think.

Emile   Wass so special about dat bwoi anyhow? How many black bwois bin kill up round here?

Joe   That ain't my business.

Emile   Course it ain't. But Kwame was different, right. Ca he loved to act like a white man.

Clinton   Believe.

Joe   Whatever.

Emile   Go run back to yer slave masters.

Joe   Slave masters?

Emile   How yu know it weren't a white guy dat beat him?

Joe   I don't.

Emile   So wat yu doin here? A little bit of trouble.

Joe   A little bit?

Emile   And the first ting deh do is reach fer us. Always.

Joe   Oh look, don't gimme the 'police pick on us ca we're black' line. Ca I'd juss laugh in yer face. Why should people care about you, when you don't care about yourselves?

Emile   Ooh, man get vex.

Clinton   Oh yes.

Joe   Bwoi, you'll know when I get vex.

Emile   Is it?

Joe   You juss can't keep yer tail quiet, the lot of yer.

Dwayne   Awright, awright, let's juss chill now please, yeah. Peace. He don't speak fer the rest of us. Catch the rass dat did dis. Innit, bwois?

Chorus of agreement.

Joe   I see.

Dwayne   Good. Dass good.

Joe   Don't go mistaking me for some other fool, yeah. Cos I ain't leaving here till I catch somebody, and I will catch, trust. I'm gone. Shanice, always a pleasure.

Exit **Joe**.

Dwayne   Fool.

Clinton   He say he go catch sumone.

Dwayne   Catch wat? We supposed to be scared of dat?

Clinton   Nuh, man.

Perry   Safe.

Dwayne   And yu, lettin him get to yer.

Emile   I weren't.

Dwayne   He come like yer dad.

Emile   He don't look nuttin like my dad.

Dwayne   I didn't say he looked like yer dad, I said he come like yer dad, clean out yer ears. He's right, yu nuh, yer too touchy. No wonder my man's ridin yer arse. Hold it down, bwoi.

Emile   I was.

Dwayne   Yu want get catch?

Shanice   Leave him.

Dwayne   Gal, shut up, I'm juss tryin to stop my bwoi here from goin to prison, yeah.

Shanice   And yerself.

Dwayne   Yu want control yer woman please?

Shanice   Yu gonna let him speak to me like dat, Emile?

Dwayne   Emile!

Emile   Leave me!

Shanice   Oh man.

Emile   Every time yu two start, it's me in the middle. Yu want fight, gwan.

Exit **Emile**.

Dwayne   Bring dat fool back.

Shanice   Let him sulk.

Dwayne   Gwan.

Exit **Perry** *and* **Clinton**.

Shanice   Wat am I doin?

Dwayne   Yu gonna cook me sum food?

Shanice   No.

Dwayne   Rude!

Shanice   Wat yu want?

Dwayne   Number two.

Shanice   Wat yu starin at?

Dwayne   Nuttin.

Shanice   I'm up here, yu know. Perv man. 'Bout yu lookin down my top.

Dwayne   I weren't.

Shanice   I saw yu.

Dwayne   Yu look nicer in dat oder top. Put it on.

Shanice   I don't have it.

Dwayne   Get anoder one. I'll pay fer it.

Shanice   Dry.

Dwayne   I chat better than Emile. Wat yu doin wid him?

Shanice   Who, yer best friend? I love him.

Dwayne (*sucks his teeth*)   Yer juss lookin after him. Like yu look after troll.

Shanice   Don't call her dat.

Dwayne   Shut up.

Shanice   Yu know she fancies yer.

Dwayne   Who's lookin after yu? When yu go have sum fun?

Shanice   Yu think I want fun wid yu?

Dwayne   Don't yu get bored?

Shanice   I'm gettin bored right now.

Dwayne   Come on.

Shanice   Don't touch me.

Dwayne   Yer lucky dass all I'm doin. Nuff brers round here want ride yu, yu nuh.

Shanice   Yu on crack?

Dwayne   How yu gonna fight dem all off? Dass how bad it's gettin. Yu don't know wat yer doin, yu got no idea. The fact dat yer goin wid sum fool, mek dem want it even more. I keep tellin dem nuff times, no one touches yu, but I can't hold dem off for ever, Shanice.

Shanice   Yu couldn't hold yerself.

Dwayne   Yu wanted it dat night.

Shanice   I was drunk.

Dwayne   Yu were sexed up. Yu know if one a dem so much as looks at yu funny, I'd kill dem.

Shanice   How nice.

Dwayne   Yer so fit. Wat? Yu rather I chat rubbish to yu?

Shanice   Go on den, try.

Dwayne   Move.

Shanice   Deh's no one else here. Come on, I want to see dis. Try. Come on. Fer me.

Beat.

Dwayne   I love yer hands, yu got nice hands.

Shanice *laughs.*

Dwayne   Yu want die?

Shanice   Yu are so sad. Yu run Emile down day and night, den yu have nerve to steal his lines. Sad!

Dwayne   Move.

Shanice   But oder than dat, not bad, I'd have to think about it.

Dwayne   Yu know wat else I can't get over. Seein yu, yer first day at school, I thought, Rah! Dat can't be the same Shanice Roberts who I used to live next door to, went primary school wid. Wid yer pigtails, and her nappy head. Playin football wid me.

Shanice   I whopped yer arse at football. Remember dat five-a-side tournament?

Dwayne   Yu score a couple of goals and yu think yer it.

Shanice   Three.

Dwayne   Dat third one was not a goal.

Shanice   Deh yu go.

Dwayne   It weren't.

Shanice   Oh Dwayne man, it was seven years ago.

Dwayne   It weren't a goal.

Shanice   Give it up.

Dwayne   I can't stop thinkin about yu.

Shanice   Dwayne, please.

Dwayne   Yer hauntin me, yu know dat?

Shanice *laughs.*

Dwayne   Don't laugh at me.

Shanice   Yu want have yerself a cold shower, dread.

Dwayne   Yu carry on.

Shanice   I will.

Dwayne   Yer gonna get hurt, yer gonna get hurt bad! Wass dat fool Emile gonna do den?

Shanice   He wouldn't be if he stopped mixin wid yu.

Dwayne   Is it my fault he keeps reachin out to me?

Shanice   I'm the one dass holdin him when he has his nightmares.

Dwayne   Is it? Ware?

Shanice   Yer nasty.

Dwayne   Chill.

Shanice   'Kick him in the head, kick him.'

Dwayne   I didn't tell him.

Shanice   Yu made him.

Dwayne   No, Shanice, yu made him. Yu told him Kwame was sexin yu. Sorry, yeah.

Shanice   Don't touch me.

Dwayne   Shanice.

Shanice   Go brush yer teeth.

Dwayne   Yu go free it up soon, yu know it.

Shanice   Not fer yu.

Dwayne   I hope they rape yu up bad.

Enter **Ronnie**.

Ronnie   Got yer change. Yu know how far I had to go. Awright, Dwayne?

Dwayne   Troll.

Exit **Dwayne**.

Shanice   Gimme my change.

Ronnie *throws money to the ground*.

Shanice   Oh Ronnie.

Exit **Ronnie**.

Shanice   Yeah, gwan, run!

Exit **Shanice**.

Enter **Joe** *and* **Matt**.

Joe   See that basketball court.

Matt   You are changing the subject.

Joe   That is where the old huts used to be, for the dustbins.

Matt   Really?

Joe   I lost my virginity in there.

Matt   I beg your pardon?

Joe   I was fifteen. Mandy Cook, oh man, she was fine. Huts were the only place we could go to. Mandy Cook. First white girl I had, you know. Tellin you, she was –

Matt   Fit, thank you.

Joe   Just trying to lighten the mood.

Matt   Look, Joe, I know you haven't been with us for long.

Joe   Uh-huh?

Matt   So you might not be up to speed with how we do things here.

Joe   Probably not.

Matt I'd appreciate it if you did not go off on your own. We work together.

Joe Of course.

Matt We follow our lines of inquiry together.

Joe Absolutely.

Matt So we understand each other?

Joe Of course, Matt.

Matt Good.

Joe The thing is though.

Matt Yes?

Joe The girl knows something.

Matt Did you think you could charm it out of her?

Joe Well, we don't have much else.

Matt I'm aware of that.

Joe Haven't you noticed, everything's scaling down?

Matt I'm aware of that as well.

Joe It's not news any more. Soon, he'll just be another dead black kid. Kids round here aren't made to feel important. They never have. They know a token gesture when they see it.

Matt I was beginning to think you didn't care.

Joe I don't. (*Beat.*) I want to know what he was doing in there.

Matt Ordering food.

Joe So she said. But he never came out wid any.

Matt He was eating in.

Joe For ten minutes? Counting the five or six it takes to cook. I was thinking, maybe he was buying drugs there.

Matt   Joe, can I ask you something?

Joe   Just tell me, don't ask.

Matt   Why are you so eager to demean him?

Joe   Oh man.

Matt   He was a bright young lad. Four weeks away from starting university, he had a future, he didn't deserve to die like that.

Joe   You trying to impress me, Matt?

Matt   With what?

Joe   What a cool liberal you are.

Matt   Meaning?

Joe   Meaning that. I mean, come on, it's really got to get to you, all this PC shit.

Matt   Not particularly.

Joe   Not even a little?

Matt   The Met needs to change. We can't keep making mistakes.

Joe   It's the uniforms I feel sorry for. Now they're thinking of asking them to provide written records for every stop and search. I mean, what kind of stupidness is that?

Matt *sighs.*

Joe   What? What is it?

Matt   I don't understand you.

Joe   Good.

Matt   Joe, if you have a problem working with me on this case . . .

Joe   What case? We both know why I'm here. It's bring out the poster boy. Make the Met look good. McPherson report. Well, that's fine, but you had better step back, boy, and let me do my job.

Matt First off, I am not your boy. Second, I am the senior officer.

Joe Yes! Go, Matt! Stand yer ground, don't take shit from anybody.

Matt Please, don't patronise me.

Joe Ditto.

Matt I was not.

Joe It's always going to be in our job, prejudice.

Matt I am not prejudiced.

Joe Easy, Matt, it's only a word, you don't have to shit yourself.

Matt I'm not. Alright?

Joe If you're walking down the street at night, you see a bunch of black lads walking towards you

Matt Oh, come on.

Joe – you know you're gonna cross that road, as fast as your legs can tek you. You know! It's all preconceived. Maybe this Kwame was a good kid, I don't know.

Matt He was.

Joe But he's from that estate. We've got to find out if he's a bad boy. We have to ask those questions, and I don't care.

Matt That doesn't make it right.

Joe It's the way it is.

Exit **Joe** *and* **Matt**.

Enter **Shanice** *and* **Emile**.

Emile Rape yer!

Shanice   Dass wat the bastard said.

Emile   Wat yu mean rape?

Shanice   Wat yu think I mean? The bwoi nasty, dass wat I keep tellin yu.

Emile   Like he meant it?

Shanice   Whether he meant it or not, it was a nasty ting to say, don't yu think? Emile?

Emile   I don't blasted know.

Shanice   Yu don't know?

Emile   Wat yu stressin me fer?

Shanice   It's not a hard thing to work out, Emile. Was he right or wrong to say it?

Emile   He was wrong.

Shanice   Don't strain yerself.

Emile   I said he was wrong, wat yu want?

Shanice   Deal wid it.

Emile   I'm aways dealin wid it.

Shanice   Talk to him.

Emile   Yu mad?

Shanice   Tell him I'm yer gal, tell him he can't treat me like dis.

Emile   Awright!

Shanice   Why yu so soff?

Emile   Yu gonna dog me out now?

Shanice   No.

Emile   Lie.

Shanice   I want things the way they were.

Emile   Go college like Clinton?

Shanice   Yes.

Emile   Gal, dat ain't fer us, Miss Douglas took care of dat.

Shanice   Don't worry yerself about her.

Emile   Maybe yu should.

Shanice   Should wat?

Emile   Fuck him. Fuck him, Shanice. One time, yeah.

Shanice   No, yu did not say dat.

Emile   Dwayne's right, yeah, yu don't know wat yer doin, wat yer givin out. I can't tek it, man. Whenever my back's turned, wonderin all the time if Dwayne or anyone else is sexin yu. It's drivin me mad, not knowin, so juss fuck him, yeah. Least I'll know, I'll have sum peace, I'll forgive yu, we'll move on.

Shanice *screams. Attacks* **Emile**.

Emile   I'm sorry, I'm sorry!

Shanice   Yu love doin dis to me or wat?

Emile   I don't know wat I'm doin, yeah.

Shanice   It's aways about yu.

Emile   I keep seein his –

Shanice   – his face, yeah!

Emile   I'll talk to Dwayne.

Shanice   Don't worry yerself.

Emile   I said I'll talk to him. Don't leave me.

Exit **Emile**.

Enter **Ronnie**.

Shanice   Yu sure dis is the right road?

Ronnie   Yes.

Shanice   Ashwood Gardens?

Ronnie   Yes.

Shanice   Not Ashwood Square?

Ronnie   No.

Shanice   Twenty-nine C?

Ronnie   Yes.

Shanice   Are yu gonna say more than word to me tonight?

Ronnie   No.

Shanice   Bet yu do.

Ronnie   Bet I don't.

Shanice (*laughs*)   See!

Ronnie   Oh, juss leave me.

Shanice   Yer soff, Ronnie. Ronnie?

Ronnie   Get off me, don't do dat, Shanice. Move!

Shanice   Oh, so yu want fight me now?

Ronnie   Kick yer arse. It's big enuff.

Shanice *grabs her, holds her playfully in a headlock.*

Ronnie   Get off.

Shanice   Say it.

Ronnie   Get off me.

Shanice   Say it!

Ronnie   Yer arse ain't big.

Shanice   Better.

Ronnie   It's Jurassic!

Shanice *grabs her again.*

Ronnie   Awright!

Shanice (*backs off*)   Well, gimme a smile den.

Ronnie   I don't feel like smilin.

Shanice   Oh Ronnie.

Ronnie   Don't Ronnie me.

Shanice   Come here and gimme a hug. Come here.

Ronnie   I don't hug hos.

Shanice   Excuse me?

Ronnie   Yer a ho.

Shanice   Listen, I'm gonna say dis one lass time, yeah, deh is nuttin goin on between –

Ronnie   – between me and Dwayne!

Shanice   So yu think yer funny now?

Ronnie   Yer a liar.

Shanice   I ain't lyin to yu, Ronnie.

Ronnie   Yu lied to me before, den I had to find out from Clinton, yu were grindin Dwayne.

Shanice   Once, I grind him once.

Ronnie   Yu still lied dough.

Shanice   Only cos I know how yu go all menstrual when it comes to Dwayne.

Ronnie   Yu love to do dis to me.

Shanice   Yu know wat, yu can fuck off, yeah.

Ronnie   Wat?

Shanice   Fuck off. Move. Now.

Ronnie   Wass up wid yu?

Shanice Yu! Yer so jealous.

Ronnie Yu got everythin.

Shanice I got nuttin but grief.

Ronnie Yu got Dwayne droolin.

Shanice I don't know wat yu see in de fool, I really don't.

Ronnie He likes yu.

Shanice So?

Ronnie Why can't I be yu?

Shanice Yu not turnin lesbian on me?

Ronnie Move.

Shanice Dat I don't need.

Ronnie I said no.

Shanice Look at me. I said look. (*Beat.*) Don't chat fuck ries in my face again, yu understand?

Ronnie Yes.

Shanice Don't be me, Ronnie. It's overrated.

Ronnie I won't den.

Shanice We awright?

Ronnie Yeah.

Shanice Yu sure?

Ronnie Yeah.

Shanice Cool.

Ronnie She's comin.

Shanice Right.

Enter **Miss Douglas**.

Shanice Awright?

Miss Douglas   Yes, thank you.

Shanice   Yu got a light?

Miss Douglas   I don't smoke.

Ronnie   She don't recognise us.

Miss Douglas   That's not true.

Shanice   See, yu get Ronnie all upset now.

Miss Douglas   Then I apologise.

Shanice   Ain't yu gonna say hello?

Miss Douglas   Hello, Shanice.

Shanice   Hello, Miss.

Ronnie   I love yer house, Miss. Nice.

Miss Douglas   Thank you.

Shanice   Ware yu goin?

Miss Douglas   I'd like to go home.

Shanice   Stay and chat.

Ronnie   Yeah, stay and chat.

Shanice   Yu bin shoppin, Miss?

Miss Douglas   Yes.

Shanice   Let me see.

Miss Douglas (*pleads*)   Please.

Shanice   Please wat?

Ronnie   Ain't even touched her yet, and she's sweatin awready.

Miss Douglas   What do you want?

Shanice   To chat.

Ronnie   Yu deaf?

Shanice   So how's it goin, Miss?

Miss Douglas   Fine.

Shanice   How's school?

Miss Douglas   Fine.

Shanice   Yu miss us?

Ronnie   Do yu miss us?

Shanice   Course she does, Ronnie, check her face.

Ronnie   She's sorry.

Shanice   Is dat true, Miss, yu sorry?

Miss Douglas   Yes, I am sorry.

Shanice   Yu lie bad.

Ronnie   She'd say yes to anythin, to get away.

Shanice   Believe.

Ronnie   Yu a prostitute, Miss? Say yes.

Miss Douglas   I don't know what it is you want.

Shanice   To chat.

Ronnie   Still deaf.

Miss Douglas   Please don't do this.

Shanice   Don't do wat, Miss?

Miss Douglas   You are only making things worse for yourself.

Shanice   Is it?

Miss Douglas   Let me pass.

Ronnie   Yu don't tell us wat to do no more.

Shanice   Nice watch. Take it off.

Miss Douglas (*removes watch*)   May I go now?

Ronnie   Yu know, I'd shut up if I were yu.

Miss Douglas   You haven't changed at all.

Shanice   Don't chat to her like dat. We're out here now.

Ronnie   Believe.

Shanice   Dis is our school.

Miss Douglas   Look, I will not be intimidated like this.

Shanice   Is it?

Ronnie   Can hear her heart pumpin from here.

Miss Douglas   I won't allow it.

Shanice   Yu won't allow it?

Ronnie   Gonna put us in detention? Miss tink she bad now.

Miss Douglas   You cannot keep doing this, blaming everyone else for your mistakes.

Shanice   Wat have I said about talkin like dat? 'Bout yu darkin us?

Miss Douglas   You stole Mr Ferns's wallet, girl.

Shanice   I was puttin it back.

Miss Douglas   Oh come on.

Shanice   I was.

Ronnie   Yu were puttin it back?

Shanice   Quiet.

Miss Douglas   We have been through this.

Shanice   We go thru it again.

Miss Douglas   I caught you red-handed.

Shanice   Yu caught me puttin it back.

Ronnie   Yu soff.

Shanice Shut up.

Miss Douglas You had his money in your pocket, explain that to me.

Shanice I don't have to explain shit.

Miss Douglas Oh Shanice.

Shanice Step!

Ronnie Wat yu tryin to touch her fer? Yu a dyke, Miss?

Miss Douglas Listen to me.

Shanice Couldn't wait, man, yu wanted me outta deh.

Miss Douglas You know that isn't true.

Shanice And den yu had to start on Emile.

Miss Douglas He threw a chair at me.

Ronnie Did yu like wat I did, Miss?

Miss Douglas Oh yes, Veronica, you trashing my car was a nice touch.

Ronnie Cool. Gimme yer money.

Miss Douglas Shanice, please listen to me.

Ronnie Gimme it.

Miss Douglas Why are you still letting yourself get led around by her?

Ronnie She is dead.

Shanice Hold it down.

Ronnie Nuh, man.

Shanice Hold it down, Ronnie.

Ronnie Shanice!

Shanice Go stand over deh. Go. Yu betrayed me.

Miss Douglas What is it you think you did to me?

Shanice   It's all yer fault.

Miss Douglas   All I ever did was try and help you. I had no choice.

Shanice   It was juss a wallet, man.

Miss Douglas   It was wrong.

Shanice   I was puttin it back, yu deaf?

Miss Douglas   It was too late. You came so far, you were doing so well.

Shanice   So why open yer mout den?

Miss Douglas   Why did you take it?

Shanice   I dunno, I juss did.

Miss Douglas   Was it her?

Shanice   Leave her.

Miss Douglas   Did she put you up to it?

Ronnie   Wass she say?

Miss Douglas   When are you going to learn, Shanice, people like her don't want to be helped? They don't want to listen.

Shanice   I am people like her.

Miss Douglas   No, you are not. You're just scared.

Shanice   Don't play me. I wasted nuff times listenin to yu, and I still got fling out.

Ronnie   I'm bored now, man, do her, den let's go.

Shanice   Hand over yer money.

Miss Douglas   No.

Shanice   Miss!

Miss Douglas   I will not. You won't hurt me.

Shanice   I will.

Miss Douglas   No, you won't.

Shanice   I will.

Ronnie   Juss do it.

Miss Douglas   Stay out of this, Veronica.

Ronnie   Stop callin me dat.

Miss Douglas   Still thinking a foul mouth is going to get you everything you want.

Ronnie   Let's juss tek her money and go, Shanice man.

Shanice   I want her to gimme it.

Miss Douglas   You are going to have to take it.

Shanice   Gimme it.

Miss Douglas   No.

Ronnie   Shanice!

Shanice   Leave me!

Miss Douglas   Why couldn't you leave her alone?

Ronnie   She renk!

Miss Douglas   You are nothing, Veronica Davis, you always were.

Ronnie   Yu gonna let her chat like dat?

Miss Douglas   Please, Shanice.

Ronnie   Yu think yu be sellin burgers if yu didn't get fling out?

Miss Douglas   Listen to me.

Ronnie   Wid yer shit money every month, hair smellin of onion.

Miss Douglas   Shanice?

Ronnie   Every night, dread.

Miss Douglas (*pleads*)   Please.

Ronnie   Do her!

Shanice *strikes her.*

Ronnie   Oh! Shame! I felt dat from here. Tek her money and let's go.

Shanice   Yu happy now?

Ronnie   Shanice!

Shanice   Yu happy?

Ronnie   Wat yu goin on wid?

Shanice   Are yu?

Ronnie   Come on!

Exit **Shanice**.

Ronnie   Ware yu goin? (*To* **Miss Douglas**.) Ware yu goin? Money.

Miss Douglas   I knew you'd end up like this.

Ronnie   Is my name Shanice? I don't business wat yu think of me, yeah. I know yer scared. Believe.

Exit **Ronnie** *and* **Miss Douglas**.

Enter **Dwayne**.

Dwayne   I'm here. Come on!

Enter **Emile**.

Dwayne (*laughs*)   Wat?

Emile   Bastard, man.

Dwayne   Shut yer noise.

Emile   Yer a bastard, Dwayne. Leavin me like dat.

Dwayne   Is it my fault yu can't run?

Emile   I know how to run, I can run faster than yu.

Dwayne   So wat happened? Yu go cry?

Emile   Shoulda told me yu weren't payin him.

Dwayne   We done it before.

Emile   Still shoulda said. Coulda bin prepared.

Dwayne   Bwoi love to moan.

Emile   Guy nearly caught me.

Dwayne   I bet he's still lookin.

Emile   I bet he calls the police.

Dwayne   Hey, it's me who should be callin. 'Bout he charge us ten squid from town. Tief! Hear how the controller said it would be seven or summin. But my man deh try and shake us fer ten. Hear how he spoke. 'Ware yu goin, boss, ten pound, boss.' Stupid Arab. Should tell him about him claart! Go back to Iraq! See how long his beard was? Bin Laden's brudda. Yu know how many bruddas dat man's got? Untold! His mama's hole muss be dat big.

Emile   Ain't his mum. His dad have a whole heap of women.

Dwayne   Must be a bro. Gimme a draw. Bloody cheer up, man, wass up wid yu?

Emile   Juss don't leave me like dat again.

Dwayne   Yeah, wass yer wurtless rass gonna do?

Emile   I ain't no rass.

Dwayne   Rass.

Emile   Don't call me dat.

Dwayne   Rass! Yu still comin out wid nish, Emile, wat yu gonna do?

Emile   Yu'll find out.

Dwayne   Chill. Before I slap yu.

Emile   Juss tell me wat yer doin.

Dwayne   I'm tellin yu to chill. Hey, don't step up, unless yu gonna jump.

Emile   Yer mad.

Dwayne   Is it?

Emile   Outta control, dread.

Dwayne   Me?

Emile   Yu didn't have to hit the guy.

Dwayne   He ask fer it.

Emile   Six times? Have a heart, blood.

Dwayne   Like yu had fer Kwame?

Emile   He deserved it.

Dwayne   So yu tink yer bad now?

Emile   I want respect.

Dwayne   Wat yu goin on wid?

Emile   Shanice said –

Dwayne   Shanice? Don't come to me wid shit from yer gal, 'bout Shanice!

Emile   Yu still don't respect me, do yer?

Dwayne   Yer chattin like a spas.

Emile   I did wat yu all wanted.

Dwayne   Yu don't want to start dis wid me.

Emile   I want respect, I want it now, bredren.

Dwayne   Well, yu ain't gonna get it.

Emile   Yu love to put me down.

Dwayne   Yer too soff.

Emile   I've had enuff.

Dwayne   Is it?

Emile   Wat more I have to do?

Dwayne   Yer soff!

Emile   And stop tryin to sex Shanice, she's my woman.

Dwayne   I'll sex who I like, bwoi!

Emile   Yu ain't.

Dwayne   Yu really are stupid, innit? Dat policeman know it too.

Emile   Leave her alone, Dwayne.

Dwayne   Watch me stroke her leg, every time yer deh. Watch me run my train up her arse, watch me. Yu might learn summin. I'm gonna run it good, man, gonna run it. And yu ain't gonna do nuttin, ca yer soff.

Emile *pulls out his blade, aims it at* **Dwayne**'*s face.*

Dwayne   Yeah? Wat? Wat?

Emile   Yu see it?

Dwayne   Yu tink I'm blind?

Emile   I buy dis fer yu.

Dwayne   Yu pull it, yu best use it.

Emile   I will.

Dwayne   Wat she see in yu?

Emile   She my woman. And I want respect!

Dwayne (*laughs*)   Yu.

Emile   Idiot? Fool? Arsehole? Who's soff now? Who's soff now?

Dwayne   Me?

Emile   Who have the blade?

Dwayne   Yu.

Emile   Yu know who yu look like, Dwayne? Like one a dem white cunts who clutch their bags warever we see dem.

Sound of police sirens.

Dwayne   Yu hear dat?

Emile   Yu a white cunt, Dwayne?

Dwayne   Dass the cab driver tellin dem about us, we gotta go.

Emile   Are yu a white cunt?

Dwayne   Yeah.

Emile   Believe.

Exit **Dwayne**.

Enter **Joe**.

Joe   Bwoi, Emile! You know how to run fast, man! Look at me, I have no breath left. You alright? Take deep breaths, my man.

Emile   Move.

Joe   Alright.

Emile   Yer lucky I trip up.

Joe   Yeah.

Emile   No way could yu catch me.

Joe   I almost had you.

Emile   Yu want go again?

Joe   You mad?

Emile   Yer soff.

Joe   I bet you used to run for your school. Am I right?

Emile   Yeah.

Joe   Medals and shit?

Emile   Untold.

Joe   Me too.

Emile   Yu?

Joe   What, you don't believe?

Emile   Yer outta shape, blood.

Joe   That was then, this is now.

Emile   Believe.

Joe   So what happened to you, Emile? Didn't you want to be an athlete? Why aren't you running now?

Emile   Dunno.

Joe   Don't chat like you're an idiot.

Emile   Move.

Joe   What happened?

Emile   I dunno. Shit, shit 'appens.

Joe   Like what? What shit? Tell me what happened to you.

Emile   Yu tink I want tell yu?

Joe   Fine. Stay stupid.

Emile   So wat about yu?

Joe   Me?

Emile   Dickens, bwoi. Wat 'appen to yu? Didn't yu want to be a policeman?

Joe   Are you cussing me?

Emile   Yeah, I'm cussin yu.

Joe   Lose the tone, Emile. Have some respect.

Emile   Yer not my dad.

Joe (*laughs*)   Look, just tell me what you were running from just then?

Emile   Heard the sirens.

Joe   Yeah, so what you running for? What's your naughty little black arse been up to now, Emile? What you do?

Emile   Nuttin.

Joe   You're a bad liar.

Emile   Is it?

Joe   People who run have something to hide.

Emile   Is it?

Joe   Yes, it is.

Emile   People also run ca they don't like gettin stressed by all yer friends, innit? I ain't got time fer dat.

Joe   You? Where the hell you going, work? (*Laughs.*) I was lookin for yu, I want to chat to you.

Emile   I don't wanna chat to yu.

Joe   Now you're hurtin my feelins.

Emile   Is it?

Joe   I was hoping we could spend some quality time together.

Emile   Wat yu tink I am?

Joe   Come, stand up.

Emile   Ware we goin?

Joe   Take a guess.

Enter **Matt**.

Joe So, Emile, the guy on your left is your boy Clinton, and over there, we have Perry, and that has got to be Dwayne, right here, see that boy there, you see him?

Emile I ain't blind.

Joe That's Kwame.

Emile I know.

Matt You know?

Emile Yeah. I know. I went school wid him.

Joe Well, that's good, because you're going to recognise this young fella right here. That's you.

Emile That ain't me.

Joe Hold up a second, I've got a better picture here. It really gets your face. You wouldn't believe the trouble we went through to get these pictures.

Emile Is it?

Joe Trust. Here we are. See it there?

Emile Yeah. Ain't me.

Joe That's not you?

Emile Ain't me.

Joe Well, that's a big relief.

Emile Yeah?

Joe Yes, cos then, if that was you, and your friends, at this particular place, at this particular time, with Kwame, approximately five minutes before he died, then you and your friends would have some serious explaining to do, me and my friend here wouldn't have to reach for a search warrant, knock on your mother's door, you still live at home, course you do, go through all her things, same thing with your friends, bring them all in here, one by one, see what they say, find out if they are a bigger jackass than you. But like you said, dat ain't you.

Emile Can I go now?

Joe Sit down.

Emile Yu can bring in who yu like. Deh won't say nuttin.

Joe Say what? What aren't they going to say?

Emile Nuttin.

Joe So, they do know something?

Emile Don't play me, yeah.

Joe Play you with what?

Emile Wid dem words.

Joe Are you stupid?

Matt Joe?

Emile Yeah, tell yer bwoi to chill.

Matt Why don't you stop wasting our time.

Emile I'm juss messin wid yu.

Matt Tell us about these.

Joe You're all laughing in this one, what's that about?

Emile Nuttin to say. We're juss laughin about, havin a laugh.

Joe Did you kill Kwame for a laugh?

Emile No.

Joe So why did you kill him?

Emile I didn't.

Joe You know who did?

Emile No.

Joe   This picture was taken five minutes before he was beaten up, Emile.

Emile   And yer point is?

Joe   You are probably the last ones to see him.

Emile   Yer point?

Joe   And you don't know anything?

Emile   Is wat I said.

Joe   Alright. So tell me something you do know. What was the conversation about. (*Holds up photo.*) Tell me. What were you laughing about?

Emile   Can't remember.

Joe   Try.

Emile   I was tellin a joke.

Joe   A joke?

Emile   Yeah.

Joe   Must have been a good joke.

Emile   It was.

Joe   Well, let's hear it then. The joke.

Emile   Yer soff.

Joe   And you're a liar.

Emile   Wat do yu call a lesbian dinosaur?

Joe   I give up.

Emile   A lickalottapus.

Joe   That's it?

Emile   Yes.

Joe   Weren't that funny.

Emile   Yeah, well, dass yu.

Joe   That was the same joke you told Kwame?

Emile   It's wat I said.

Joe   But it isn't funny. Ignorant, yeah, but not funny.

Emile   We laughed.

Joe   I don't see Kwame laughing.

Emile   Well, he was.

Joe   It looks he's crying.

Emile   He weren't cryin.

Joe   Like he's scared. What has he got to be scared about?

Emile   Yu tell me.

Joe   You threaten him?

Emile   No.

Joe   What did you do to him?

Emile   Nuttin. We pass him by the street, told the joke, and we left him.

Joe   You left him there to die.

Emile   No.

Joe   Yes.

Emile   We juss left him.

Joe   Did you like him?

Emile   He was awright.

Joe   Why?

Emile   Wass dis fool sayin now?

Joe   Why did you like him? He was nothing but a bookworm, a nerd, a little fool. What was he going do with his life? Go to university, get a nice job, forty grand a year, you think? He was heading out of the estate for good. Then, there's you. Dashed out of school at fifteen. What have you got in common with him? How could you be friends with him?

Emile   Did I say we were friends?

Joe   Alright, now we're heading somewhere.

Emile   I said I liked him.

Joe   Are you a battyman, Emile?

Matt   Joe!

Emile   Yer the battyman.

Joe   You liked him? That Zulu warrior, who's as black as coal? Who thought he was smarter than the lot of you?

Emile   Yer words, dread.

Joe   You liked him?

Emile   Yeah.

Joe   Does Dwayne know you're this soft?

Emile   I ain't soff.

Joe   He was a nice-looking boy though.

Emile   Yu are a battyman.

Joe   He must have had a lot of girls reaching for him.

Emile   Yeah?

Joe   Him and Shanice would've made a nice couple, don't you think, if she wasn't going out with you, that is.

Emile   She is goin out wid me.

Joe   I know. But if she weren't. Did he step to your woman, Emile, is that how it was? You ain't having that, some bwoi tryin to grind your woman. I wouldn't have that. Is that what occurred, Emile? Is that what occurred?

Emile   No.

Joe You can talk to me.

Emile I am talkin.

Joe See, what I can't figure out, what I can't get my head round, is this. This picture. You and your friends, other end of the high street, laughing your heads off, look at the time, five minutes after Kwame was found in the street, with his head cracked open. You lot, laughing like it didn't mean a thing.

Emile Ca we didn't know.

Joe Tell me.

Emile I am.

Joe Tell me what happened. We all get a little upset.

Emile I ain't upset.

Joe Especially over a woman. I know how it goes, come on, Emile, bend my ear, bro to bro.

Emile I ain't yer bro. I ain't yer nuttin. Yu love to tink yer down wid us.

Matt Alright.

Emile Yer nuttin to me.

Matt Sit down, Emile.

Emile So don't come it, yeah, don't play the big man.

Matt Sit down please.

Emile Well, tell yer bitch to chill den. Ca dass all yu are now, dis fool's bitch! And I ain't growin up to be no white man's bitch, yu get me?

Joe You don't like bitches, do you, Emile?

Emile No.

Joe Was Kwame a bitch?

Emile Yes.

Joe Is that why you killed him?

Emile No.

Joe So why did you kill him?

Emile I didn't.

Joe You couldn't stand it.

Emile I don't talk to yu.

Joe He was a reminder.

Emile I'd rather chat to him.

Joe Of what a wurtless, useless rass you are.

Matt Let's take a break.

Joe Innit, Emile?

Matt Interview suspended at 16.10 p.m.

Exit **Emile**.

Matt I'm releasing him.

Joe Are you mad?

Matt We're going round in circles in there. We've got nothing to charge him with. You need to calm down.

Joe For fuck's sake.

Matt Will you please calm down?

Joe Facety little nigger.

Matt Joe?

Joe You want to see yourself, eyes as big as saucers. Yes, Matt, I said nigger. Do you want say it, go on, give it a try, let it out. Cos if I'm thinking it, so are you. Nigger!

Matt Stop it.

Joe Little shit.

Matt Are you done?

Joe Boy wanna learn respect.

Matt Calm down, please.

Joe Oh, will you stop saying please, it drive me mad! He did it. I know he did it. You know he did it. Bwoi thinks he's bad, him and his crew. I'll show dem who's bad. Ain't nuttin but a low-life useless cold-blooded black bastard. He thinks he's summin, he ain't nuttin. I'm havin him.

Matt With what exactly? You've got nothing.

Joe Don't butt in like that again.

Matt I'm sorry?

Joe Mek me look bad.

Matt You were losing it.

Joe It was working.

Matt He wanted to talk to me more than you.

Joe Love to hold his hand.

Matt Your way wasn't working.

Joe (*laughs*) Fool don't even know he's bin insulted.

Matt Don't push your luck.

Joe You do nish for one black kid, too much for the other one.

Matt Oh that's right, go there.

Joe You all think you're doing them a favour by patronising them.

Matt I wasn't patronising him. Look, I do not wish to fight you, Joe.

Joe Why? What you so bloody 'fraid to say, man?

Matt Hold it down.

Joe   I don't want to hold it down. I want to talk. I want us to talk. I want us to have the conversation. Yeah? So let's have it.

Matt   I'm releasing him.

Exit **Joe** *and* **Matt**.

Enter **Shanice, Ronnie, Perry, Emile, Clinton** *and* **Dwayne**.

Shanice   Perry, dat had better not be spliff yer smokin.

Perry   Nuh, man.

Shanice   Wat have I told yu? Not in here.

Perry   Shut up and gimme my fries.

Shanice   Who yu tellin to shut up? Yu mad?

Perry   Emile?

Emile   Chill.

Shanice   Dat had better be him yer sayin dat to.

Perry   Emile?

Shanice   Emile!

Emile   Yer shamin me, Shanice.

Perry   Thank yu.

Ronnie   Yu shame yerself.

Perry   Yu gonna take dat?

Emile   Shut yer mout.

Perry   Oh right, so bwoi tink he man now.

Emile   I don't think, I know.

Perry   Dwayne, put dis fool under manners again fer me please.

Emile   Why don't yu?

Perry   Awright den, come.

Dwayne   Sit down.

Perry   Yu fight like a gal anyhow.

Emile   Is it?

Perry   Believe.

Dwayne   Put out the spliff.

Perry   Dwayne man.

Dwayne   Yer fuckin up my sinuses wid dat, put it out.

Clinton   Are we all done now? Can we divvy up now please?

Clinton *produces a handbag, the boys rifle through it.*

Perry   See dat woman's face? See how scared? Feel my heart.

Clinton   Move.

Perry   Feel it, dread.

Clinton   Like a drum.

Perry   Better than weed.

Emile   Better than speed.

Clinton   Better than a line.

Perry   Yu tek line?

Clinton   Yes.

Perry   Since when?

Clinton   A boy at college had sum.

Perry   I thought I tell yu to stay away from dat?

Clinton   Step off, P.

Perry   I'm telling yer mum, yu get dis! (*Raises his hand.*)

Emile   Yu got the rest of the money in yer pocket deh, Dwayne?

Dwayne   Wat?

Emile   Rest of the money, dread.

Dwayne   Rest of the money here.

Emile   Nuh, man. I saw yu open the purse, deh was more deh.

Dwayne   Is it?

Emile   Yer holdin out on us, bro. Come on, man, cough up the rest, ain't got all night.

Dwayne   Deh is no more.

Emile   Right now, on the table, if yu please.

Perry   Emile, yu mad or wat?

Dwayne   I'm tellin yu now, Emile, dis was all the money dat was in dat bag.

Emile   Well, yu mus be high from Perry's weed den, ca I definitely saw more dough in dat purse. Now I know yu don't wanna skank us, so wa gwan? Yer dad still fleecin yu or wat?

Dwayne   Don't do dis. Awright? Yu understand?

Emile   Awright, blood, ease up.

Dwayne   Yu ease up.

Emile   I'm cool. Keep the money.

Dwayne   Deh's no more money.

Emile   Awright, man, watever, I made a mistake den.

Dwayne   Yer damn right.

Exit **Dwayne**.

Emile   Oh come on, Dwayne!

Clinton   Yu are well and truly mad, yu nuh.

Perry   Believe.

Emile   I thought he was skankin us.

Clinton   Sounded like yu knew, a minute ago.

Perry   Bwoi sweatin now.

Clinton   Must be.

Emile   About wat?

Perry   I know my man Dwayne longer than yu, Emile.

Emile   Yer point is?

Clinton   Leave him, cous, his time comin.

Perry   Yu know.

Emile   Speak English, yu fools.

Perry   Dwayne comin fer yu now, rude bwoi, when yu least expect it. Him comin fer yu. Yu challenged him.

Exit **Perry** *and* **Clinton.**

Ronnie   Oh man, yu fucked up!

Shanice   Shut up, Ronnie.

Ronnie   Tell me now, if dat ain't wat he did.

Emile   I don't business.

Shanice   Emile.

Emile   Let him come, I had him before.

Shanice   Listen to me.

Emile   I'll tek him again, let him come.

Ronnie   Yu sweatin big time, Emile.

Shanice   Clean up.

Ronnie   Yu know he's got a gun now.

Emile   Move.

Ronnie   I've seen it. Watch him put a hole in yer head.

Shanice   Enuff.

Emile   Dis is a test.

Shanice   Emile man.

Emile   I'm ready fer him. I ain't tekin any more of dis, I ain't tekin it from nobody.

Shanice   Yu best listen to me now.

Emile   Yu want me, Dwayne! Well, I'm ready now. Come fer me now!

Shanice   Yu gotta go.

Emile   Don't start.

Shanice   No. Leave.

Emile   Wat do I have to go fer? It's Dwayne dass gotta go. He's goin. And if Perry and Clinton don't like it, they can go too. He's the one who's soff, I tell him who's soff. Me. Emile. Say summin. I defended yu. Tell him yu my woman. No one sexes yu.

Shanice   Did you think he'd listen?

Emile   I did wat you wanted, man.

Shanice   He only backed off cos yu had a knife, wat happens if Ronnie's right, wat if he's got a gun now?

Ronnie   He has!

Emile   It'll be awright.

Shanice   No, it won't.

Emile   Why yu love to piss on everythin I do?

Shanice   Ca yu don't think.

Emile   I dealt wid him. Like I said.

Shanice   I meant talk.

Emile   Deh yu go again, wid dis talk business.

Shanice   Prove yer better dan him.

Emile   Yu mad or wat?

Shanice   Dan all a dem.

Ronnie   He's gonna kill him.

Shanice   Ronnie!

Ronnie   It's true and yu know it, man. Run and hide, Emile, cos Dwayne is gonna fuck yu up.

Shanice   I'll come wid yu.

Ronnie   Shanice man.

Shanice   Quiet! (*To* **Emile**.) We'll go anyware. We'll leave now, yeah. Right now, come. Emile?

Emile   Dis was supposed to be my time. It was me who had Kwame, not dem. Deh jealous.

Ronnie   Fool.

Shanice   Yu don't have time fer dis.

Emile   They love to put me down, love to mek joke. Do they wake up every night, seein his face?

Ronnie   I thought yu said the nightmares were gone. Ain't so big now.

Shanice   Do yu wanna die, Ronnie?

Ronnie   Oh bloody hell, Shanice.

Shanice   Do yu wanna die? Shut yer hole! Emile, ware yu goin?

Emile   It's my time.

Shanice   No.

Emile   I don't business no more!

Exit **Emile**.

Ronnie   Yu were gonna go?

Shanice   Ronnie man!

Ronnie   Without me?

Shanice   We ain't even blood, wass up wid yu?

Ronnie   Yu go, they'll know it was him.

Shanice   And if we stay, he's dead.

Ronnie   Juss don't leave without me, yeah? Shanice?

Shanice   Beg yu, girl, get a life.

Ronnie   I hate it when yu come like dis. Look yer nose down.

Shanice   Calm down.

Ronnie   Plannin on goin without tellin me.

Shanice   I was gonna tell yer.

Ronnie   Yu lie bad. Yu love to lie.

Shanice   Fine, if dass wat yu tink.

Ronnie   And yer still a ho.

Shanice   I dunno wat I am.

Ronnie   Yer a ho, Shanice. Love to have man fuss over yu. Yu get all moist cos of it.

Shanice   Ronnie?

Ronnie   Don't Ronnie me. Go run off wid dat fool, run! I tek care of myself, I don't need yu.

Shanice   Are yu done? Come here.

Ronnie   Fer wat?

Shanice   Come here.

Ronnie   Yu go slap me?

Shanice   I'll slap yu if yu don't come here.

Ronnie *approaches.* **Shanice** *kisses her on the forehead.*

Shanice   Don't ever chat fuck ries in my –

Ronnie   – in my face again, yeah, watever.

Shanice   I'd never set out to hurt yu.

Ronnie   Yu ain't goin.

Shanice   I have to.

Ronnie   Not without me.

Shanice   Deh's gonna come a day, when yu have to look after yerself, Ronnie.

Ronnie   I don't care.

Shanice   I don't have time fer dis.

Ronnie   I'll do it.

Shanice   Wat?

Ronnie   I'll tell dem wat I saw. I'll get the money, den we can both go.

Shanice   Ronnie!

Ronnie   If Emile's in prison, Dwayne can't hurt him. Right? Am I right? Well, deh yu go den, problem solved. I'll tell the police, Dwayne can't hurt Emile, den we can go. Yer up fer it? Shanice? Are yu up fer it?

Shanice   He wanted to be a designer.

Ronnie   Buildings and that. He was a smart-arse.

Shanice   So he had it comin, he deserved to get beat up?

Ronnie   Don't yell at me.

Shanice   It's not right. Wat 'appened to him weren't right, he didn't deserve to have us comin into his life, man, endin it fer him. It's not right, and no one's sayin it.

Ronnie   I'm sayin it.

Shanice   Yu want the money.

Ronnie   Was it yu who saw him gettin kicked in the head? Lyin on the ground bleedin, cryin fer his mum? I don't think so. Let me tell the police. Yu want Emile alive and in prison, or dead? It's a good plan, Shanice, it'll work. Please! Let me. Yeah? Yeah?

Shanice   Awright.

Ronnie   Awright wat?

Shanice   Yes, go on, do it.

Exit **Shanice** *and* **Ronnie**.

Enter **Dwayne**, **Perry** *and* **Clinton**.

Perry   Yu shoulda had his claart deh and den.

Clinton   Juss tell me ware and when yer gonna do it, Dwayne. Please. Ca I wanna see dat fool on his hands and knees, cryin like a gal in front of my laughin face, before yu kill him. Please, Dwayne, tell me, a favour to me, man.

Perry   He heard yu, Clinton.

Clinton   Well, tell him to speak up den, can't hear him.

Perry   Dwayne?

Dwayne   Yeah, man, watever.

Clinton   Thank yu. I dunno why yu let it get dis far.

Dwayne   Yu my mum?

Clinton   He pulled a knife on yu, dread, shoulda taken care of business deh and den.

Dwayne   He proved his worth, I thought he was due.

Clinton   Now he's tekin the piss.

Dwayne   Who yu barkin at?

Clinton Awright, man, ease up.

Dwayne Yu wanna come it as well, Clinton?

Clinton All I said was –

Dwayne Don't say anytin.

Perry Clinton, leave us alone fer a minute, yeah.

Clinton I didn't say nuttin –

Perry Juss go stand over deh. (*To* **Dwayne**.) So, wat?

Dwayne Guy gives me a headache wid his voice, man.

Perry Try livin wid it. Yu go tek care of Emile, everytin sweet, yeah?

Dwayne Yeah.

Perry Cool. Crack a smile fer me nuh, man. I tell yu wat though. When dat fool's gone, Shanice.

Dwayne Shanice?

Perry It's me and her, man. Trust.

Dwayne No.

Perry Wat yu mean, no?

Dwayne I mean, no. She's off limits, before and after, yu understand?

Perry Don't tell me yer still sweet fer her? It is, innit?

Dwayne None of yer business.

Clinton Oh man.

Perry Wat yu want?

Clinton Yer dad, Dwayne.

Dwayne Oh man.

Enter **Manny**.

Manny Good evenin, gentlemen. Wat say yu?

Clinton Bwoi! (*Waves the air.*)

Perry Bredren!

Manny Yu don't have a hug fer yer Uncle Manny?

Perry I'm awright, Manny, juss stand over deh please.

Manny Who loves yu more than me?

Clinton Don't touch me, yeah.

Manny Bwoi, yu can't say hello?

Dwayne Hello.

Manny My bwoi, yu nuh, my bwoi.

Dwayne Yeah, they know.

Manny Yu have a pound fer me? Juss a pound, bwoi, please.

Dwayne Wat yu want it fer?

Manny I have to go see my mudda, yer granmudda, I need bus fare.

Dwayne Yeah.

Manny Gimme a pound please.

Perry Dwayne, we're not here now, catch yu later, yeah. Let's go up west, catch a bus.

Clinton Yu get it, I'll walk.

Perry Yu want walk all the way up west?

Clinton I don't mind, it keep me fit. Seriously.

Manny Son?

Perry Why can't yu jus say it?

Clinton Say wat?

Perry We have to go through dis every time.

Clinton Say wat?

Perry Yer skint.

Clinton I ain't skint.

Manny Listen.

Perry Yu want me to pay fer yer bus fare.

Clinton If yu want to pay fer me, dass up to yu, innit.

Perry Clinton! Juss say it.

Clinton Awright. I'll come wid yu, if yu don't want to come on the bus by yerself.

Perry Shut up, will yu, please, can yu do dat? Shut up. Hold up. Yu got money, from the purse.

Clinton Yeah, I got money, but I ain't got change fer the bus.

Perry Yu woulda walked all the way up west, even though yu have money?

Clinton I don't have change.

Perry Yu are gone, Clinton man, yu are so far gone.

Exit **Perry** *and* **Clinton**.

Manny Hey, yu my bwoi, yu nuh.

Dwayne Don't touch me.

Manny Juss gimme two pound.

Dwayne Yu said one pound.

Manny Two pound fer me, please.

Dwayne Do yu even know wat yer sayin, half the time?

Manny Yu my bwoi.

Dwayne Go brush yer teet, man.

Manny Juss gimme sum change. Yes, yes. Hey, let me have sum more of dem silver ones yeah, please.

Dwayne   Take it all. Juss take it.

Manny   My bwoi.

Dwayne   Two words fer yu yeah, please. Soap and water.

Manny   Yu my bwoi.

Dwayne   Yeah, yeah.

Manny   Yu my bwoi. Good bwoi, Junior.

Dwayne   Wat?

Manny   Wat?

Dwayne   Wat did yu juss call me?

Manny   Yu my bwoi.

Dwayne   Yu juss called me Junior.

Manny   Nuh, man.

Dwayne   I ain't deaf, yu called me Junior.

Manny   Junior? Who dat?

Dwayne   Who is Junior? Did I hear yu right? Who is Junior?

Manny   Bwoi?

Dwayne   Junior is yer son, who live up by Shepherd's Bush, my half-brudda, dass who Junior is. Junior live wid his two little sistas, Tasha and Caroline, yer daughters, my half-sistas! Remember dem? Nuh, it muss be Anton yu remember, yer son who live up by Dagenham way. Or is it Stuart, my little brudda, who live two minutes away from my yard, who I never see. Nuh, nuh, it muss be the latest one, Kenisha. Wass my name?

Manny   Bwoi?

Dwayne   Move yer hand away from me. Wass my name? Yer so drunk, yu don't even know which yout of yours yer chattin to. Wass my name? Say my name before I buss yer claart all over dis street. Say it.

Manny   Dwayne. It's Dwayne, yer name Dwayne.

Dwayne   Yu musta bin beggin to God, to tell yu.

Manny   Yu Dwayne.

Dwayne   Get off me.

Manny   The one in trouble.

Dwayne   Who tell yu I was in trouble?

Manny   It was yu who beat up dat bwoi, weren't it? Weren't it?

Dwayne   It weren't me dat beat him, right.

Manny   One a yer friends den.

Dwayne   Who tell yu?

Manny   Everyone know, 'bout who tell me? See, I do know yu. I know my own children right, I know! Don't tell me I don't know.

Dwayne   So, wat yu gonna do?

Manny   Why yu do it, son?

Dwayne   Answer my question first. I didn't do it, I told yu. So, wat yu gonna do? Wat yu gonna do?

Manny   Yu shame me.

Dwayne   Yu want chat 'bout shame? Shame is seein yu, in the off-licence tryin to buy a can of beer wid only twenty pence in yer hand. Beggin dat Indian man to let yu have it.

Manny   So wat, yu gonna mess up yer life?

Dwayne   Wat are yu gonna do?

Manny   Yu mad?

Dwayne   Wat are yu gonna do?

Manny Dwayne?

Dwayne Wat are yu gonna do? Wat are yu gonna do? Wat are yu gonna do?

Exit **Dwayne** *and* **Manny**.

Enter **Joe**, **Matt** *and* **Ronnie**.

Ronnie Is dat it?

Joe Not quite.

Ronnie So, when I get my money?

Joe Hey.

Ronnie Wat?

Matt Why do they call you troll? Can't be nice.

Ronnie Wat yu think?

Matt Do they call you it? The boys?

Ronnie Not just dem.

Matt Is that why you're here?

Ronnie Wat?

Matt To get back at them.

Ronnie No.

Matt Get them into trouble.

Ronnie No.

Matt You had better tell us the truth now.

Ronnie (*to* **Joe**) Him deaf?

Joe Answer his question.

Ronnie I just did.

Matt This is a serious allegation you're making.

Ronnie I know.

Matt   I want you to be sure now.

Ronnie   I am, I saw dem kill him. I thought they were jackin him at first. They were standin around him, in a circle, scarin him. They were shoutin and laughin, darin Emile to beat him, so he did.

Matt   Did what?

Ronnie   Kicked him. He was kickin him in the head.

Matt   Anything else?

Ronnie   One a dem, I think it was Perry, knocked off his glasses.

Matt   What else?

Ronnie   I saw dem run off. I ran too, in the opposite direction.

Matt   What else?

Ronnie   What else wat? I saw him beat him, Emile beat him up, they run off. Wat? Wat!

Joe   Tell me about the trainers.

Ronnie   Whose trainers? My trainers?

Joe   Kwame's trainers.

Ronnie   His?

Joe   Yes!

Ronnie   Oh, right!

Joe   Well?

Matt   Ronnie?

Ronnie   Wat?

Matt   We're waiting.

Ronnie   Cool. (*Nervous laughter.*)

Joe   Listen to me, Ronnie, yeah. You told us all about what you saw, Kwame gettin attacked, that's good, that's all good. But we still need you to help us clear up a few things. Such as the trainers, Kwame's trainers. You saw them take them off him, right, right?

Matt   Joe?

Ronnie   Right, yeah, I saw dat. They took the trainers off him.

Joe   Before or after he was attacked, Ronnie?

Ronnie   Before. It was before.

Joe   Good. That was all I wanted to know. When I turn on the tape, yeah –

Matt   I need to speak with you.

Joe   – that's what yer going to tell me. Right?

Ronnie   Cool.

Matt   Joe!

Exit **Ronnie**.

Matt   Tell me you didn't just do that.

Joe   Believe.

Matt   She had no idea what you were talking about.

Joe   That's not how I read it.

Matt   We held back that info about the trainers, for a reason.

Joe   Yeah yeah yeah.

Matt   She didn't see a thing.

Joe   She must have done.

Matt   Her story was all over the place.

Joe   So she couldn't string two sentences together, so what? It's the way those kids talk. You're treating them like they don't belong. That's how they feel, they're not stupid.

Matt   Do you have any idea what will happen if we screw this? Do you?

Joe   She knew about the BMW.

Matt   That was in the local paper.

Joe   She saw it happen. We got him, what did I say? You don't like it, you should have spoken up, Sarge!

Matt   You had no right leading a witness like that, without consulting me.

Joe   I didn't think you'd be comfortable with it.

Matt   Do not patronise me!

Joe   You telling me you haven't bent a few rules in yer time?

Matt   Of course I have. What kind of a wanker have you got me down as?

Joe   So you'd fit up some white kid? Oh, but this is different though, innit?

Matt   You know it is.

Joe   A black kid. You have to watch yourself. Got be Mr Politically Correct Man of the Year.

Matt   You just won't give that up. You have done nothing but push me and push me.

Joe   So push me back.

Matt   I have had enough.

Joe   It should only matter if it's true.

Matt   I won't have it.

Joe   You know he did it.

Matt Course I know.

Joe So, what?

Matt So I need to think, is that alright with you?

Joe There are two kinds of people.

Matt Are you going to let me think?

Joe Ones that break the law, ones that don't. I'm just dealing with the ones that do.

Matt What do you think I'm trying to do?

Joe Prove it.

Matt Why do you hate them so much?

Joe Prove it.

Matt It's really got to hurt that you're not black enough for them.

Joe Wass this fool going on with?

Matt Joe, I'm warning you.

Joe I'm gone.

Matt Answer my question.

Joe You think you can get to me like this?

Matt I'm not trying to get to you, I want you to answer my question. They're your people, why do you hate them?

Joe Listen, yeah, those boys are not my people. You think I care what they think?

Matt Yes, I do think you care. You were Kwame. Weren't you? Look, I'm sorry, Joe.

Joe Hey, don't you dare apologise to me. Don't turn soff now. Just keep your *Guardian*-reading shit to one side, yeah, or whatever it is you read . . .

Matt I'm not like that!

Joe You fucking people!

Matt That is enough, Constable!

Joe Wid your wishy-washy liberal crap. Are you so afraid to say what you really feel?

Matt No.

Joe Give me back the old school of police. Give them boys something to really cry about.

Matt Not another word.

Joe At least they'd know where they stand.

Matt Don't push me.

Joe To do what? To say what?

Matt Leave it.

Joe Come on, Matt, let them know where they stand. That's all they want.

Matt Is that what you want, Joe?

Joe This isn't about me.

Matt You don't know where you stand?

Joe All yer doin is cloudin the issue.

Matt And you're running away. You're hiding. Alright, you want to hear about the time when I was in uniform, when I had to stop my first black person?

Joe Yes.

Matt He had a defective headlamp, I waved him down in the middle of the night, he comes out of his car screaming, I'm only picking on him cos he's black. He was doing forty. How the hell did I know what colour he was? All I saw was a defective headlamp.

Joe Dumb nigger. Worst kind.

Matt   He was a prat. A stupid ignorant prat. That's what I thought, it's what I said. I got a reprimand.

Joe *claps slowly.*

Matt   There's no clouding of the issue for me, Joe. You'll never get me to say it. I don't want to say it. I'm not going to feel bad for what I believe in, and I do believe in it. The job, wishy-washy views, everything.

Joe   He's going to walk then.

Matt   You don't know that, that's not up to you.

Joe   Are you going to man up or what?

Matt   It's not our call. We'll let the DI decide if we have enough to charge him with, alright? And you're lucky, I'm not going to mention what you just did.

Joe   Well, thanks.

Matt   You can fuck off, I'm not doing it for you. Because, you see, Joe, I know where I stand. Now I'm going to tell you where you stand. Right here, beside me with your mouth shut.

Joe *goes to leave.*

Matt   You move one more inch, and you're finished. You speak when I say, you do as I say. Is that clear enough for you, Constable? This is what you wanted, to be like everyone else. Well, come on then, crack a smile, Joe. That's an order.

Exit **Joe** *and* **Matt**.

Shanice   Yu ain't gonna do nuttin.

Dwayne   Is who yu darin me?

Shanice   Yer soff.

Dwayne   Is who are yu?

Shanice   Can't yu see wat he's doin?

Dwayne   Playin big man.

Shanice   Like yu.

Dwayne   I'm better.

Shanice   Let me have him.

Dwayne   Ware yu gonna go?

Shanice   Sumware.

Dwayne   Yu ain't gonna go. Yu ain't.

Shanice   Gonna miss me, Dwayne?

Dwayne   See yu. Love to flirt.

Shanice   Yu can't say it.

Dwayne   I ain't backin down, Shanice, he dissed me.

Shanice   Yes yu can.

Dwayne   Don't chat rubbish to me. Why him? Wat is special 'bout him?

Shanice   He's the first one to ask me out.

Dwayne   I've asked yu out.

Shanice   He didn't juss yank my arm, and say, come!

Dwayne   I bet he can't even kiss.

Shanice   Him kiss better than yu. When we first went out, I knew he wanted to put his arm round me, I look at him, and goes, get on wid it. He was so shy.

Dwayne   Soff.

Shanice   He asked if he could kiss me.

Dwayne   Him a bwoi!

Shanice   He asked me, Dwayne.

Dwayne   Yu don't ask to kiss, yu juss kiss.

Shanice   I couldn't believe it.

Dwayne   Ca yer a slapper.

Shanice   Dass why I went wid yu. Ca I didn't want to believe it. Whenever anyone says I'm good, or nice, I don't wanna believe it.

Dwayne   I wanna kiss yu.

Shanice   Wat?

Dwayne   Is that awright?

Shanice   Yu mad?

Dwayne *kisses her.*

Shanice   Wanna grind me as well now, Dwayne?

Dwayne   No. (*Strokes her face.*)

Enter **Emile**.

Emile   So now wat, yu want me to beat him up now?

Dwayne   Come.

Shanice   Emile, no.

Emile   Why?

Shanice   Cos he'll kill yu.

Dwayne   No, let him come.

Emile   He was sexin yu, like Kwame, I have to.

Dwayne   So, come. (*Pulls out gun.*) My friend here waitin fer yu, come.

Shanice   Dwayne, back off, man, please.

Dwayne   Tell yer bwoi first.

Shanice   Put the gun down, wass wrong wid yu?

Emile   I can get a gun too, Dwayne.

Dwayne   Is it?

Emile   Believe.

Shanice   STOP! Dwayne man?

Dwayne   Yu love to think I won't do it.

Shanice   I know yu can do it, I know yu will do it. But I'm askin yu, I'm beggin yu, yeah, please don't do it. (*Beat.*) Emile, come on, man, yu don't want to do dis.

Emile   Well, stop makin me. It's yu dass makin me, it's yu dass makin me do dis.

Dwayne   Yer soff.

Emile   I might as well fling yu at him.

Dwayne   Yer givin me yer gal, Emile, cheers.

Emile   Yu love to have man chase yu.

Shanice   Awright, do it, fight him, go fight him, kill each oder ca I don't business no more, bloody fight him.

Dwayne   Come.

Shanice   He's waitin.

Dwayne   Yu comin or wat, Emile? I tell yu wat, I let yu mek a move first, yeah?

Shanice   Emile?

Dwayne   Come!

Shanice   He ain't.

Dwayne   Ca him soff.

Shanice   Dwayne, juss leave us, yeah.

Dwayne   Yu best start runnin.

Exit **Dwayne**.

Emile   Well, go on den.

Shanice   Wat?

Emile   Go follow him.

Shanice   Go follow him ware, Emile? I told yu not to hang round wid him. I told yu wat he was like.

Emile   First Kwame, now him.

Shanice   No. Kwame weren't tryin to sex me.

Emile   Shut up.

Shanice   He was juss bin nice. He didn't do anythin, he weren't after anythin.

Emile   Yu told me.

Shanice   I know wat I told yu.

Emile   So, why?

Shanice   Yu made me feel special, I weren't juss sum yattie to yu. Dwayne comes along, and yu stop noticin me. Yu were too busy impressin him. Yu made me lose faith, not juss in yu, but in me, man. So I goes, fuck yu, Emile, fuck yu. I thought Kwame fancied me, so I thought yes! I'll rush dat.

Emile   He did try and sex yu.

Shanice   Hello! I tried to sex him, he blew me off, Emile. Ca he was nice! Juss nice.

Emile   Yu?

Shanice   Ronnie's gone to the police. I told her to. Don't look at me like dat. Yu were supposed to juss give him a slap or summin. Why yu have to kill him?

Emile *grabs her.*

Shanice   It's dis place! Let's go, right now, come. I'll look after yu. Ronnie, she's so stupid, man, she thinks we're gonna run off togeder wid the reward money. Yer the one I want to run off wid. Yu were right all the time. I can't keep lookin after her, I don't want to. Yu ain't got a choice no more. Emile!

Exit **Shanice** *and* **Emile**.

Enter **Ronnie**, **Matt** *and* **Joe**.

Ronnie   And I want a room wid cable.

Matt   Don't start.

Ronnie   It best have a telly wid cable.

Matt   You might have a video.

Ronnie   I want DVD.

Matt   What's the difference?

Ronnie   Obvious yu don't have one.

Matt   You will go where we put you.

Ronnie   Yu joke.

Matt   So be quiet.

Ronnie (*to* **Joe**)   Yu gonna let dis geezer chat to me like dat?

Matt   Take it or leave it.

Ronnie   I'll leave it den.

Matt   Where do you think you're going?

Ronnie   Home.

Matt   That is the last place you want to be, Veronica.

Ronnie   It's Ronnie, how hard is it to say dat, Ronnie!

Matt   Alright, Ronnie. I don't think you realise how serious this is.

Ronnie   I do.

Matt   You are, potentially, an important witness in a murder investigation.

Ronnie   Yeah, yeah. Love to go on.

Matt   What do you think your friends would do if you went home?

Ronnie   I don't know, go mad fer me, innit? (*Laughs.*) Call me troll, I don't care. Used to it. Don't care wat they think. Except Shanice, but she knows why I'm doing it, she knows.

Matt   This is as serious as it gets. Right, Constable?

Joe *nods his head.*

Matt   Right, Ronnie?

Ronnie   Yes! Awright. Bloody hell.

Matt   So we'll have no more talk about cable TV, MTV base, DV bloody Ds, PlayStation.

Ronnie   PlayStation 2, actually. Get it right. Joke!

Matt   Constable?

Joe   Hold it down, yeah.

Ronnie   Why don't yu kiss his arse while yer at it.

Joe   Just ease up, OK.

Ronnie   Yu white man's bitch.

Joe   This is it for you. Focus. Behave.

Ronnie   So I'm supposed to stay in sum room and do nish?

Matt   We can take you out.

Ronnie   When do I get my money?

Matt   You know when.

Ronnie   You can't even dash me a few dollars till den?

Matt   That is not up to me.

Ronnie   Can I use a phone?

Matt   Who do you want to call?

Ronnie   Shanice.

Joe   Why Shanice?

Ronnie   Tell her I'm awright.

Matt   I think your mind should be on other things.

Ronnie   I want call Shanice. I want a McDonald's Happy Meal.

Matt   Later.

Ronnie   I'm hungry, dread.

Matt   I said later. We're expecting company. Our inspector would like to speak with you.

Ronnie   Why yu lot love to ask borin questions?

Matt   Hey!

Ronnie   Awright.

Joe   Ronnie?

Ronnie   Wat?

Joe   Come on, just behave yourself, please.

Ronnie   I said awright.

Joe   This is important.

Ronnie   I know.

Joe   Right!

Ronnie   Yes, man!

Matt   This is hopeless.

Ronnie   Yu want calm down, dread. Can I have my McDonald's now?

Enter the **Inspector**.

Inspector   How far away were you?

Ronnie   A bit.

Inspector   A bit what? Give it to me in yards.

Ronnie   I dunno, juss a bit. I can't remember exactly.

Inspector   Well, you will have to remember.

Ronnie   Wat fer? I don't know.

Inspector   How could you forget that?

Ronnie   I didn't forget, I said I don't know.

Inspector   The point I am trying to make, Veronica –

Ronnie   Ronnie.

Inspector   – if you were there –

Ronnie   I was.

Inspector   – I do not think it is something you could forget.

Ronnie   Love to chat.

Inspector   Listen to me, you may find this amusing, Veronica –

Ronnie   Ronnie! Yu deaf?

Inspector   – I can assure you, those people in the courtroom will not.

Ronnie   Watever.

Inspector   You thought there was a robbery going on over the street, that they were 'jackin' somebody?

Ronnie   Yeah.

Inspector   You were standing behind the bus-stop shelter, across the road?

Ronnie   Yeah. Bloody hell.

Inspector   And you were hiding behind the bus-stop shelter because you did not want the boys to see you.

Ronnie   Dwayne don't like it when I'm followin him.

Inspector   Yes or no?

Ronnie   Yeah.

Inspector   Now, at that point in the evening –

Ronnie   Yer talkin too fast again.

Inspector   – At, that, point, in the evening, a silver BMW pulls up, by the bus stop, the window of the front-passenger side rolls down, a young white woman leans out, and you have a conversation with this woman.

Ronnie   Yeah.

Inspector   She asked if you lived in the area.

Ronnie   Yeah.

Inspector   She asked you for directions.

Ronnie   Yeah, yeah, yeah!

Inspector   Whilst Emile and his friends were attacking Kwame?

Ronnie   Yes. (*Aside.*) Slag.

Inspector   I beg your pardon?

Joe   Ronnie!

Ronnie   Nuttin.

Inspector   Furthermore, the music playing from the car radio is rather loud.

Ronnie   At first, but her man turned it down.

Inspector   But you could still hear the music?

Ronnie   Yeah, it was Jay Z.

Inspector   I'm sorry?

Ronnie   Jay Z the rapper. Dass who was playin on the radio. Are we done now?

Inspector   Not yet. Now help me out here. Despite the conversation, despite the 'Jay Z' music playing from the car radio, you were not distracted at all, from witnessing the attack?

Ronnie No.

Inspector And the boys do not notice that you are watching them?

Ronnie No.

Inspector You didn't hear about the BMW from the newspaper, did you?

Ronnie No.

Inspector But you knew we were looking for it, so did you decide to use it, to make your story more credible?

Ronnie No.

Inspector Did you really speak to that woman?

Ronnie Why she carryin on?

Inspector Did you see those boys?

Ronnie Callin me a liar?

Inspector I need you to be absolutely sure about this.

Ronnie I thought yu wanted me to help?

Inspector So you weren't following the events in the newspaper quite closely then?

Ronnie No.

Inspector You weren't desperate to grab the opportunity, to be the centre of attention?

Ronnie Look, I might have glanced at summin in the paper, yeah.

Inspector So, you do admit to lying?

Ronnie Everyone was readin it. It had a picture of our estate and dat, it was cool.

Inspector   You didn't do more than read?

Ronnie   Why, why would I, wass so special about him?

Inspector   Twenty thousand pounds?

Ronnie   Oh man, I've had enough of dis. I'm done.

Joe   Come on, Ronnie!

Inspector (*to* **Joe**)   Yes, thank you, Constable. Sit down, Veronica.

Ronnie   Call me dat one more time.

Inspector   Sit down please. Just tell us the truth.

Ronnie   I am tellin yu the truth.

Inspector   I don't think you are.

Ronnie   I don't care.

Inspector   You were lying when you said you were on the street.

Ronnie   No.

Inspector   You were lying about seeing what happened, you know everyone is going to be watching you.

Ronnie   Yer point?

Inspector   You love it.

Ronnie   No I don't.

Inspector   You will love anything that will stop you from being reminded of what you really are, a sad, lonely little girl, with no friends.

Ronnie   I've got loads of friends. Shanice is my friend.

Inspector   What is your nickname? What do your friends call you?

Ronnie   I'm tellin the bloody truth, is dis wat happens when yu tell the truth? Well, fuck dat!

Inspector   Calm down please.

Ronnie   Try and help the police, say wat they want me to say, dis is the thanks I get.

Inspector   What was that? What was it that we told you to say? Ronnie?

Joe   Alright, look, I made a mistake, yeah.

Inspector   Quiet.

Joe   It's my fault.

Inspector   Sergeant?

Joe   But she saw him kill him.

Matt   Joe?

Joe   She saw the boy do it.

Matt   Don't.

Ronnie   Him goin mad or wat?

Joe   Tell her, Ronnie, tell her what it felt like seeing Kwame lying there on the ground, how it made you feel. That it made you care. Tell her.

Ronnie   Is who yu screamin at?

Inspector   Look at me, Ronnie. I said look at me.

Ronnie   This is fuck ries.

Inspector   What did they tell you to say?

Ronnie   Dat I saw dem tek the trainers.

Inspector   You said before you saw them do that.

Ronnie   I know. Musta happened when I was talkin to dat woman, innit?

Inspector   So, you were distracted.

Ronnie   No. Fer a second, yeah.

Joe   Shit.

Inspector   You have just lied to me. If we had put you in a courtroom, you would have committed perjury.

Ronnie   I'm not lyin. I saw dem do it, man. I saw dem kill him. Yu know wat they'll do to me if I go back home? How can I be lyin?

Inspector   I see.

Ronnie   Yu don't bloody see. Yu don't see us. None of yer. 'Bout yu see! I ain't lyin.

Inspector (*to* **Joe** *and* **Matt**)   What the hell are you two playing at?

Joe   Ma'am?

Inspector   Not another word. You've got nothing.

Ronnie   So we done now? Are we done?

Inspector   Get her out of here.

Ronnie (*pleads*)   Shanice!

Exit **Inspector**, **Ronnie** *and* **Matt**.

Enter **Emile**.

Joe   See, Emile, dis is gettin vex! I wanna tell you something, yeah? Cos, that's all I got time for now, thanks to that little friend of yours, that troll. One time, when I was in uniform, yeah, early in the afternoon, it was 'bout four or summin, got a call, two pissheads fighting outside a pub, one black, one white. One a dem spilled the other one's drink, I can't remember who, whatever. Anyhow, they were having a right go at each other. Pushing, and sum shoving. Both a them are as bad as each other, effing and blinding, tellin you! I didn't want to get involved. Shitting myself, if truth be told. But I stepped in, arrested them both, boom boom! (*Slaps* **Emile**.) The white guy, calmed himself down, straight off, he stood there, knew he was in the wrong, didn't even try to run off. Black guy, different story. He couldn't stop mouthing off to me. What do you think he said? Guess.

Emile Dunno.

Joe Cocksucker. Pig. Bastard. Traitor to my own, white man's bitch. The lot. Goin on about, how I was only nickin him cos he was black and I want to be white. By the time we got him back to the station, he was still carrying on. Still shoutin, mekin up all kinds of noise. It took five of us to throw him in a cell. (*Slaps* **Emile**.) You know what the white guy was doing during all this? Nothing, nish. From the time I showed up on the street, to when we got back to the station, he didn't say a word. And he was the one throwing out the most licks, when they were havin the fight. You see wat I mean, Emile? (*Slaps him.*) You see where I'm goin wid this? White man get caution, get sent home the very same day, black man spend the rest of the day and night in the cell, cos he couldn't keep his stupid wurtless mout shut, couldn't play the game! White man played the game, played it beautifully, I wanted to shake his hand and go, 'Yeah, nuff respect.' I tell you, Emile, when it comes to that, them white bwois are poles apart. Niggers, Emile, can't play the game. You can't play the game, Kwame played the game, Kwame had a life. He was a decent kid. But you, you! (*Slaps him repeatedly.*) You want a life, bwoi, get yer own. Why you have to tek his? You know what, it's fuckers like you, like that pisshead, is why I had to leave. Now it's fuckers like you that bring me back to where I started. You had to drag me down, innit? You had to drag Kwame down. You feel good about that? You love that? Is it? Do you? Do you? (*Slaps him.*) Do you?

Enter **Shanice**.

Joe Yer wurtless!!

Shanice (*stands between* **Joe** *and* **Emile**)   Leave him.

Joe Shanice, move.

Shanice Are yu mad?

Joe Move.

Shanice Leave him.

Joe I'm letting him know where he stands.

Shanice   Yu think dis is gonna change him?

Joe Bwoi drowning, girl.

Shanice Wat else yu expect him to be?

Joe You want drown too?

Shanice Wat yu know about him? Wat yu know about me?

Emile Get off.

Shanice Emile?

Emile Leave me!

Exit **Emile**.

Joe Where you goin?

Shanice Yu best step back.

Joe Don't go after him, Shanice, remember your gran. He ain't even sorry for wat he did.

Shanice Yu don't know him.

Joe I know him.

Shanice Yu don't know him.

Joe Fine, go drown with the idiot.

Shanice Wat about yu? Yu sorry? Yu sorry fer wat yu did, Joe? Say yer sorry, say it.

Joe Sorry for what? You know what him and that friend of yours have done to me? You want drown yerself, go.

Shanice Yu go. Carryin on like we should tek after yu, why should we be like yu?

Exit **Joe**.

Shanice (*aside*)   Yer fool.

Enter **Manny**.

Manny   Hey, pretty gal.

Shanice   Oh please.

Manny   Yu know yu love me.

Shanice   Is it?

Manny   Yu have a pound fer me? Beg yu fer a pound, please.

Shanice   Do yu even know how to wash yerself?

Manny   Beg yu.

Shanice   Yu stink.

Manny   Juss a pound.

Shanice   Step.

Enter **Dwayne**, *carrying a football*.

Manny   My bwoi, yu awright? Yu have a pound fer me? Beg yu fer a pound. Son? Bwoi?

Exit **Manny**.

Shanice   Yu see how black his teet is?

Dwayne   Yu hear from Emile?

Shanice   No.

Dwayne   Yu don't know ware he's gone?

Shanice   Stay wid his sista.

Dwayne   Wat about troll?

Shanice   Gone sumware wid her mum.

Dwayne   I dunno wat she's gonna do without yu.

Shanice   She's gonna have to learn, innit? They both are. I told her to do it.

Dwayne   I ain't here fer dat. Yu don't have to be scared, yeah.

Shanice   I ain't.

Dwayne   Yu are. Don't.

Shanice   Fine, I won't.

Dwayne   Did I tell ya? Clinton pass his BTEC.

Shanice *laughs.*

Dwayne (*feeling self-conscious*)   Wat?

Shanice   Nuttin. Dass good. Wat yu doin wid dat?

Dwayne   Wanna show yu summin.

Shanice   Wat?

Dwayne (*places football on ground*)   Gonna prove to yu dat third one was no a goal.

Shanice   Oh man, yu are sad.

Dwayne   Scared I'm right, Shanice?

Shanice   No.

Dwayne   So come.

Shanice   It was seven years ago, how am I supposed to remember ware I was, please?

Dwayne   I'm Neil, remember him?

Shanice   Yes.

Dwayne   I'm here.

Shanice   Yeah, and?

Dwayne   Yer outside the box, Perry's in goal, he's clocked yu makin yer move.

Shanice I knew exactly ware I was gonna shoot.

Dwayne Bottom right-hand corner.

Shanice Right.

Dwayne I'm givin yu chase, tryin to stop yer.

Shanice But yu can't.

Dwayne I nearly had yu.

Shanice Right, den I scored.

Dwayne No.

Shanice Rest yer lip 'bout no.

Dwayne Yu did strike, I'd give yu dat, but it bounced right off Clinton's knee.

Shanice Deflection. Case rested.

Dwayne If it hadn't, it woulda gone wide.

Shanice No.

Dwayne Tellin yu.

Shanice Shut up.

Dwayne Ask Clinton.

Shanice Dwayne, put the ball down. Put the ball down. Wat are we doin?

Dwayne Yu really think I woulda shot Emile?

Shanice Yeah.

Dwayne Believe. Yu know wat stopped me?

Shanice Wat?

Dwayne Yu, Shanice.

Shanice So, wat now?

Dwayne Go out and dat.

Shanice (*laughs*)   Go out and dat.

Dwayne   Yeah.

Shanice   Awright.

Dwayne   Wat?

Shanice   Yu deaf? I said awright.

Dwayne   Cool.

Shanice   But Dwayne?

Dwayne   Wat?

Shanice   Yu ain't grindin me.

Exit.

Simon Stephens

Motortown

This play is for Oscar and for Stan and also for Mark

'For something to begin something has to end
The first sign of hope is despair
The first sign of the new is terror'

Heiner Müller, *Mauser*
(translated by Marc von Henning)

Simon Stephens began his theatrical career in the literary department of the Royal Court Theatre where he ran its Young Writers' Programme. His plays for theatre include *Bluebird* (Royal Court Theatre, London, 1998); *Herons* (Royal Court Theatre, London, 2001); *Port* (Royal Exchange Theatre, Manchester, 2002); *One Minute* (Crucible Theatre, Sheffield, 2003, Bush Theatre, London, 2004); *Christmas* (Bush Theatre, London, 2004); *Country Music* (Royal Court Theatre Upstairs, London, 2004); *On the Shore of the Wide World* (Royal Exchange, Manchester, and Royal National Theatre, 2005); *Motortown* (Royal Court Theatre Downstairs, London, 2006); *Pornography* (Deutsches Schauspielhaus, Hanover, 2007, Edinburgh Festival/Birmingham Rep, 2008, and Tricycle Theatre, London, 2009); *Harper Regan* (Royal National Theatre, 2008); *Sea Wall* (Bush Theatre, 2008, Traverse Theatre, 2009); *Heaven* (Traverse Theatre, 2009); *Punk Rock* (Lyric Theatre Hammersmith and Royal Exchange, Manchester, 2009); and *A Thousand Stars Explode in the Sky* (with David Eldridge and Robert Holman; Lyric Hammersmith, 2010). His radio plays include *Five Letters Home To Elizabeth* (BBC Radio 4, 2001) and *Digging* (BBC Radio 4, 2003). Awards include the Pearson Award for Best Play, 2001, for *Port*; Olivier Award for Best New Play for *On the Shore of the Wide World*, 2005; and for *Motortown* German Critics in Theater Heute's annual poll voted him Best Foreign Playwright, 2007. His screenwriting includes an adaptation of *Motortown* for Film Four; a two-part serial *Dive* (with Dominic Savage) for Granada/BBC (2009) and a short film adaptation of *Pornography* for Channel 4's Coming Up series (2009).

I am indebted to Ian Rickson for all his support over the past seven years, and in particular for his inspiration in the writing of this play. I am indebted too to Ramin Gray and Marianne Elliott and Graham Whybrow and Ola Animashawun and Nina Lyndon and all the rest of the staff and writers of the Royal Court Young Writers' programme. And to Mel Kenyon. I am grateful to the British Council and to Mark Amery and Playmarket, New Zealand, for all of their support in the beginning of 2006 and all of the writers and actors I worked with there. Thanks to Chris Mead for the quote.

This play owes a massive amount to the spirit of B. R. Wallers and The Country Teasers.

Happy Anniversary Princess Sarah.

SWS,
Gothenberg, March 2006

Motortown was first performed at the Royal Court Jerwood Theatre Downstairs, Sloane Square, London, on 21 April 2006. The cast, in order of appearance, was as follows:

Lee	Tom Fisher
Danny	Daniel Mays
Marley	Daniela Denby-Ashe
Tom	Steve Hansell
Paul	Richard Graham
Jade	Ony Uhiara
Justin	Nick Sidi
Helen	Fenella Woolgar

Director and Designer Ramin Gray
Lighting Designer Jean Kalman
Sound Designer Ian Dickinson
Choreography Hofesh Shechter

Characters

Lee
Danny
Marley
Tom
Paul
Jade
Justin
Helen

The play should be performed as far as possible without décor.

Scene One

Danny *and* **Lee**.

Lee She doesn't want to see you. She told me to tell you.

A brief pause.

She told me to tell you that you were frightening her. Your letters were frightening, she said.

A brief pause.

I'm really, really, really, really sorry.

A very, very long pause. The two brothers look at each other. Then **Danny** *looks away. He moves away from* **Lee**.

Lee You sleep all right?

Danny I did. Thank you.

Lee That's good.

Danny I had some extraordinary dreams.

Lee Did yer?

Danny I did, yes.

Lee What about?

Danny I can't remember, to be honest. I say that. I'm not entirely sure if it's true. I'm not sure if it's that I can't remember or I can't quite believe them, yer with me? My dreams! I'm telling yer! What time is it?

Lee It's nine o'clock. I've been up for a while. I was waiting for yer.

Danny Were yer?

Lee I get up at five-thirty.

Danny Do yer?

Lee Most days.

Danny   Right. That's quite early, Lee.

Lee   Yes.

Danny   You should join the fucking army, mate.

Lee   Don't swear.

Danny   You what?

Lee   It's ignorant.

Beat.

Danny   That I was 'frightening' her? Are you sure that's what she said?

Lee   With your letters.

Danny   That's a bit of a surprise to me, I have to say.

A pause.

Lee   You sleep with a frown on your face. Did anybody ever tell you that?

Danny   No.

Lee   Well, it's true. I went in to check on you. You were frowning.

Danny   What have you been doing since half-five?

Lee   I was cleaning the flat.

Danny   Good idea.

Lee   Can I get you some breakfast?

Danny   That'd be lovely, Lee. Thank you.

Lee   I've got some Coco Pops. Would you like some Coco Pops or would you prefer Sugar Puffs?

Danny   Coco Pops is fine.

Lee   And a cup of tea?

Danny   Lovely.

Lee With milk and two sugars and the tea bag in first before the hot water?

Danny That's right.

Lee Would you like some toast as well?

Danny I would, please.

Lee I've got butter, margarine, Marmite, jam, marmalade, peanut butter, honey, Nutella and lemon curd.

Danny Butter would be nice. And a little bit of marmalade please.

Lee Right. Coming right up!

He doesn't move.

Danny How've you been, Lee?

Lee I've been all right. I've been very good. I've been healthy. I had to clean up quite quietly while you were sleeping. But that isn't a problem.

Danny Good.

Lee And how are you?

Danny I'm fine, mate. I'm fine. It's nice to be back.

Lee I should have asked if you wanted to sleep in my bed.

Danny No, you shouldn't have done.

Lee I should have done. I just chose not to.

I passed my driving test.

Danny Nice one. Well done. When was that?

Lee In January. It was easy. Passed first time.

Danny I should think so. I did too.

Lee Did you?

Danny At Pirbright.

Lee You didn't tell me.

Danny   We should get a car. Shouldn't we?

Lee   Yeah.

Danny   Put it in the driveway. Give it a clean. Show it off. You could wear a suit. Get a cup of tea in the morning. Go to work. With yer tie on. You'd love that, wouldn't you?

Lee   Ha!

Danny   How *are* Mum and Dad?

Lee   They're very well, thank you. I think they're pleased you're home.

Danny   Great.

Lee   They talk about you incessantly. It's like a kind of water torture for visitors.

Danny   I can imagine.

Lee   You gonna go and see them, you think?

Danny   I don't think so, no.

Lee   Right. Why?

Danny   I don't think I really want to, Lee, that's all.

Lee   I ironed your shirts for you. While you were sleeping. And after I tidied up.

Danny   Right. Thank you.

Lee   That's all right. I like ironing. I'm really good at it.

He exits.

Danny *stands alone. Long pause.*

Lee *returns with a cup of tea for both of them.*

Lee   We saw you on telly. On the news. On *Newsnight*. I went round to Mum and Dad's. They videotaped it. (*He drinks his tea.*) It didn't look anything like you.

Danny   I've not seen it.

Lee Well, go round then. Ask Mum and Dad. They'd definitely let you watch it. You'll be astonished. It's like you're a completely different person.

He leaves again. Comes back almost immediately.

I go round. They seem increasingly old to me. They're getting smaller. Their backs are arched. Their skin is getting wrinkly.

He leaves again. He comes back in with some toast, no plate. He passes the toast to **Danny**.

Danny Thanks, Lee. This is smashing.

He eats, then looks at **Lee**, *who is watching him.*

Danny London?

Lee (*immediately*)   7,465,209.

Danny Paris?

Lee (*immediately*)   2,144,703.

Danny Mexico City?

Lee (*immediately*)   8,605,239.

Danny *gives him a big smile.* **Lee** *smiles back, proud and shy.*

Lee Were you all right out there then, Danny?

Danny I was, it was fine.

Lee You spent most of your time giving out chocolates from what I could tell. They seemed quite friendly.

Danny They were. See their little faces light up. All big grins. A mouthful of fucking Mars bar and they're putty in yer hand, Lee, I'm telling yer.

Lee You're gonna be on *Trisha* soon, you. Knowing you. I think.

Danny Fuck off.

Lee 'My addiction to swearing and being a swear monkey!'

Danny   When did she come round?

Lee   Last week.

Danny   Where's she staying?

Lee   Up Goresbrook, behind the field.

Danny   In her old house?

Lee   I think so, Danny, yes. But she told me not to tell you that.

Danny   Right.

Lee   She seemed very sure about it.

Danny   Yeah.

Lee   See Denise Van Outen?

Danny   Yeah. What about her?

Lee   I'd like to *be* her.

Danny   You what?

Lee   Just thinking out loud. How's your breakfast?

Danny   It's fine thank you, Lee. It's lovely.

Lee   What are you going to do today?

Danny   I don't know.

Lee   We should do the washing up together. Bring back memories. For old times' sake.

Danny   We could do. What you reading?

Lee   You what?

Danny   At the moment.

Lee   I'm reading a true-life book about ghosts and haunted houses.

Danny   You're a big inspiration to me, Lee.

Lee *walks off. He comes back with a ghost book in his hands. Shows* **Danny** *a picture in it.*

Lee   Have you seen this one? Back of the car. The car is a hearse. On the way to a funeral. And that woman, it's her funeral. Fake or real? Do you think?

Danny   I don't know.

Lee   Your hand's shaking.

Danny   Yeah.

Lee   It's always done that. What's that about, do you think?

Danny   I don't know.

Lee   West Ham got promoted.

Danny   I heard.

Lee   You missed it. And you missed my thirtieth birthday party.

Danny   I was at the camp.

Lee   It was a weekend. You stayed put. Watching *Grandstand*.

And you never, ever ring me, ever.

Did Degsie go out with you?

Danny   Degsie?

Lee   From the passing out.

Danny   I don't think I knew anybody called Degsie.

Lee   I talked to him at your passing out.

Danny   I don't remember.

Lee   He was from Goole, in Yorkshire. His father was a mechanic.

Danny   I don't remember anybody called Degsie.

Lee   Or Francis Stifford. Or Charlie Sturt? Did they go out with you?

Danny How many people did you talk to at my passing out?

Lee I –

Danny You had a good day, that day, didn't you?

Lee I did. It was great. I'm sorry about the Coco Pops. I feel like I've led you down the garden path. I've got no food in at all. I should have got some and I just didn't.

Danny You still get your lunches?

Lee Yeah.

Danny They still bring them round?

Lee Yeah. They do. Yeah.

Danny Will they bring one round for me?

Lee No. They won't.

Are you going to go out today, do you think?

Danny I might do, Lee, yes.

Lee I might go out today, too. After my lunch gets here.

Danny We could fucking go out together.

Lee I'm gonna start a swear box. I'll be able to buy a dishwasher by the end of it.

Danny How much deodorant have you got on?

Lee A bit.

Danny Don't go fucking swimming, will yer?

Lee Why?

Danny You smell like a tart's boudoir!

Lee Like a what?

Danny Seriously. Show us yer teeth.

Lee   My teeth?

Danny   You wanna get them sorted Lee, they're fucking disgusting. Here. Have a Polo. Have two. Have another, save it for later.

Lee   I told her she should tell you herself.

Danny   Did yer?

Lee   At first I did, but then I promised.

Danny   Thanks.

Lee   I didn't know what to do really.

Danny   Don't worry about it.

Lee   I never liked her anyway.

Danny   No.

Lee   The way she spoke to me. She was really rude.

Pause. **Danny** *smiles at him.*

Danny   We should go for a day trip. Us two, I think.

Lee   A day trip?

Danny   Go up Southend. Go to the seaside. Get a few drinks at The Northview. Look out to sea. Go and ride on the fairground. I'd look after you. See you all right. Be good that, I think. Don't you think, Lee, wouldn't you like that?

Lee   Maybe. After lunch.

Danny   I don't know if I can wait until lunch-time.

Lee   I have to, they're coming round.

Pause.

Are you incredibly angry with me, about Marley?

Danny   No, Lee, I'm not.

Lee   It's not my fault, is it?

Danny   No.

Lee   Don't shoot the messenger they say, don't they?

Danny   They do, yeah.

Lee   I'm glad you're a soldier.

Danny   Thanks.

Lee   I'm glad you're brave.

Danny   Thanks.

Lee   But you're incredibly messy.

Danny (*with a chuckle*)   Sorry.

Lee   Why are you laughing at me?

Danny   I just enjoy you. And I've not seen you.

Lee   I hate the summer. I get a bit sweaty.

Danny   You know the thing about you, Lee?

Lee   What?

Danny   You can kind of hold stuff in a bit. I quite admire that, as it goes.

Lee   That's not true.

Danny   It is, you know.

Lee   I can't hold anything in, me. I can't even hold my farts in.

Danny   That wasn't what I was talking about.

Lee   No.

Danny   I'm not going to wait until after lunch.

Lee   Right.

Danny   I think I'm going to go out on my own. Have a wander.

Lee   Will you be home for your tea?

Danny   I think so.

Lee   Give me a ring. On the phone. If you won't.

Danny   Right.

Lee   Are you going to go and see Marley?

Danny   No. Not if she doesn't want me to.

Lee   It's just what she says.

Danny   Yeah.

Lee   We've not got the same hair. Or the same bone structure. Or the same eyes. Or anything. We did once. But now we don't.

Danny *looks at* **Lee** *for a long time.*

Danny   Will you be here when I get back?

Scene Two

Danny *and* **Marley**.

Danny   Lee told me that you went to see him. He told me that you didn't want to see me any more. That you told him I was frightening you. Is that true, Marley?

No response.

Was I frightening you?

No response.

Was I frightening you, Marley? Were my letters frightening you?

Marley   Calm down.

Danny   I was writing you letters. They were letters, that's all.

Marley   Calm down, Danny, people are starting to stare at you.

Danny   Who is? Who's starting to stare at me?

Marley   There's no need to shout. I'm sitting right here.

Danny   If I was frightening you, then you could have told me yourself. You could have written to me. You could have come to see me. You didn't need to leave me a poxy message. I'm not sixteen anymore.

Marley   –

Danny   I never wanted to frighten you. It was never my intention to frighten you.

Marley   All right.

Danny   I had nobody else I knew I could write to.

Marley   Fine.

Danny   Don't say that.

Marley   What?

Danny   Don't just sit there with your face screwed up like that. It's like you're passing a note through a classroom.

Marley   Danny, look, I'm glad you're back. I'm glad you're safe. I'm glad you didn't get your head blown off. I hope you're going to be okay.

Danny   I am.

Marley   But I don't owe you anything. And if I ask you to leave me alone, through your brother, or through a letter, or through a text message or a note via our teacher, then I expect you to leave me alone.

Danny   I'm gonna be more than all right. I'm gonna be great.

Marley   'Cause if you don't –

Danny   What?

Marley   I'll call the cops. I'll go to court. I'll get an order out on you, no danger.

Danny   You what?

Marley   I mean it, Danny.

A long pause. He stares at her. She has to break his stare.

Where you staying?

Danny   Where am I . . . ?

Marley   You heard me, where are you staying, Danny?

Danny   What do you wanna know that for?

Marley   You staying with your Mum and Dad?

Danny   No. I'm not. I'm staying at Lee's. What do you wanna know that for?

Marley   So I can tell the cops if you ever contact me again.

Danny   You're lying.

Marley   Try me.

Danny   You must be.

A pause. **Marley** *smiles.*

Marley   I saw your Lee a while back, as it goes. Having his driving lesson. Driving down the Heathway. He was driving at about twelve miles an hour. There was a big queue building up behind him.

Danny   Don't.

Marley   Why did you come and see me when I asked you not to?

Danny   Why do you think?

Marley   I have no idea.

A very long pause.

I'm gonna finish my tea.

Danny   Right.

Marley   And then I'm gonna go home.

A very long pause. She drinks her tea.

Danny   How is it?

Marley   What?

Danny   Your tea?

Marley   It's lovely.

Danny   That's good. Mine's a bit tepid. Should have tasted the tea we had out there. It was horrible.

Marley   I bet it was.

Danny   It was powdered.

Marley   Great!

Danny   It tasted like concrete.

Marley   Lovely.

Danny   I really missed you.

Marley   You said.

Danny   Is this going to be the last time I ever see you? 'Cause if it is I don't quite understand why.

Marley   Some of the things you said . . .

Danny   I don't remember.

Marley   I was only your girlfriend for about three months.

Danny   It was more than that.

Marley   And then you write that.

Danny   You have a way of talking to boys, did you know? It makes me want to smash their faces in.

Pause. He grins.

You got a boyfriend now?

Marley   Stop it.

Danny   Have you, Marley? Are you seeing somebody?

Marley   I don't believe this.

Danny   That means you have, doesn't it? Who is it, Marley? Who is he?

Marley   I'm going.

Danny   Marley, who is he? Do I know him?

Marley   See you, Danny.

Danny   Did he go to our sixth form?

Marley   Fuck off.

Danny   Don't. Don't, Marley. Please don't.

He goes to her. Grabs her arm.

Marley   Get off my arm.

He lets go of her.

Danny   Please don't go.

Marley   Fuck off.

Danny   Please, Marley, don't. I'm sorry. I just missed you, is all. If that's out of order then I take it all back.

Marley   I stopped being your girlfriend years ago.

Danny   It wasn't years.

Marley   I thought you were my friend.

Danny   Yeah.

Marley   There's nothing wrong with that. I was going to university. You were down in Pirbright. I thought we were mates.

Danny   Yeah. I know.

Marley   Your letters were really weird and they were really frightening. You really hurt my arm.

Danny   I'm sorry.

A very long pause.

I wish you'd come. To Pirbright. To see me. It was an amazing place. Better than anywhere round here by miles. I wish you'd come to the passing out. Lee came. He was an embarrassment. With his big old glasses on. Looking like a freak.

Marley   How long you gonna stay with him?

Danny   Not long.

Marley   Where are you gonna move to?

Danny   I have no idea.

Marley   Don't they sort you out with somewhere?

Danny   No. I paid myself out.

Marley   So they just leave you?

Danny   They do, yeah.

Marley   To fend for yourself?

Danny   Yeah.

Marley   Well, you should be good at that, shouldn't you? You're trained for that, aren't you, Danny? You could go to the Marshes. Dig a hole.

Danny   I could, yeah.

Marley   You'd love that, you, I bet.

Danny   I can lie awake at night and imagine what it's like to kiss your face.

Marley   Don't.

Danny   You can too, I bet.

Marley   This is ridiculous. You couldn't even get it up half the time. Could you, though? When you think about it. Came in about two seconds when you did.

Scene Three

Danny *and* **Tom.**

Tom I think people are more like flowers than we ever give them credit for.

Danny You what?

Tom See me, Danny. I'm a little flower. Bit of sunshine like this and I bloom, mate. Get outside. Put yer shorts on. You wanna do a bit of that.

Danny You reckon?

Tom I didn't think they'd let you out yet, Danny.

Danny Didn't yer?

Tom I thought you'd still be out there.

Danny I came home early.

Tom You had enough, had you?

Danny I had, a bit.

Tom How was it?

Danny It was easy.

Tom Pushing on an open door.

Danny Mostly it involved waiting around all fucking day. Do a couple of patrols.

Tom Give out a few Spangles.

Danny We stayed in the airport. They turned the Basra international airport into our base. Had these big old statues and fountains and marble floors and everything.

Tom Lovely.

Danny Had a PlayStation. Watch a few DVDs. Get yer one ginger beer a day.

I just got bored.

Came home.

Beat.

They smile at each other.

Tom   I'm glad you did.

Danny   Me too.

Tom   It's good to see yer.

Danny   Yeah. It's good to see you, too.

Tom   You want a crisp, Danny? They're sea salt and malt vinegar.

Danny   Lovely. Thank you.

Tom *looks at* **Danny** *for a long time.*

Tom   You staying with your Lee?

Danny   I am, yeah.

Tom   How is he, Lee?

Danny   He's fucking completely puddled. But he's not so bad. I quite like him. I'm on his couch.

Tom   Nice. You not going see your folks?

Danny   I don't think so, Tom, no.

Tom   They still up in Becontree, are they?

Danny   They are mate, yeah.

Tom   How come you're not gonna go and see them?

Danny   'Cause they do my fucking head in, Tom.

Tom   Do they?

Danny   They do, yeah.

Tom   Right. Right. Right. Right. Good. And have you seen Marley?

Danny   I haven't, Tom, no.

Tom Best off out of that one, I reckon.

Danny Yeah, me too.

Tom I think she was completely insane.

Danny I think you're right.

Tom I saw you on the telly. With Paxo. I thought you looked all right. I thought you came off fairly well, as it goes.

Danny Thanks, Tom.

Tom Other people said they thought you looked a bit odd.

Danny Did they?

Tom Said it looked nothing like you. Are you as hard as fuck now?

Danny You what?

Tom Are you?

Danny I don't know. I don't think so.

Tom You look it, you know?

Danny Thanks, Tom.

Tom You look quite handsome, as it goes.

Danny That's very kind of you.

Tom In a kind of James Cagney kind of way.

Danny James Cagney?

Tom Definitely more James Cagney than Leonardo DiCaprio. What are you gonna do for money?

Danny I'm all right for a bit.

Tom You could come and work here, if you wanted.

Danny Thanks, Tom. I'll be fine.

Tom Work on the till. Count the cash. Place the orders. Any of that.

Danny That's kind of you, mate.

Tom And have you got long-term plans?

Danny Not completely, no.

Tom I think you should look into a career in film special effects.

Danny Do yer?

Tom You'd be good at that, I think.

Danny You reckon?

Tom I do, yeah.

Danny How much is this, Tom?

Tom Thirty-five pounds. I could give it you for twenty-seven.

Danny Thank you.

Tom That's not a problem. You're a friend of mine. I'm happy to help you out.

It's a Walther P99 replica. Semi-automatic. There's no hammer, see? The trigger's beautiful, I think. Although it is odd at first. It has a very long, double-action first shot. But then it's very clean, for the rest of the magazine. You don't need to exert any pressure at all. It has a six-millimetre calibre. It takes 0.2 gram pellets. I can *give* you a hundred of those as part of the deal. It's a very authentic model, this one. Probably the most authentic I've got in just now.

Danny Right.

Tom I've got a good deal on the Smith and Wesson at the moment. Which is a simple six-shot. At twenty pounds. I've got a Taurus PT92 in chrome, which I think is actually rather elegant. That's thirty pounds to you. I've got a KWC Beretta for you at fifteen quid, Danny. 0.12 gram pellets, nearly hundred metres a second. If you fancy it we could take them out.

Danny   Nice one.

Tom   Go up home. Go up the Chase. Shoot some ducks.

Danny   We could do.

Tom   Mind you, you could probably get us on Foulness, couldn't you? Get on the Island.

Danny   I could try.

Tom   You ever been up there?

Danny   I haven't, Tom, no.

Tom   I'd fucking love to go there, me.

Danny   Yeah. I'll take this, Tom.

Tom   Good choice.

Danny   It's a good weight, eh?

Tom   It's a cop gun. Special forces. Undercover. James Bond type of thing.

Danny   Great.

Tom   You got cash?

Danny   I do, yeah.

Tom   Lovely.

Danny   I've not been up the Chase since I've got back.

Tom   I've not been for fucking years, mate.

Danny   It's changed, hasn't it? The whole town.

Tom   I can never tell any more.

Danny   It has, it's got worse, I think.

Tom   The factory's almost completely closed up now.

Danny   I heard. I went down. To get the train up here.

Tom   The whole of Chequers is all completely burnt out. All of it. The whole fucking street.

Danny   Yeah.

Tom   There's a whole new array of drugs you can get down there. Drugs I've never even heard of before. It's like a supermarket for drugs.

Danny   I'm half tempted to go up Eastbrook.

Tom   Are you?

Danny   Take this with me. 'All right, sir?' Bang!

Tom   Ha! Don't.

Danny   No. Don't worry, I won't.

Tom   I know what we should do!

Danny   What's that?

Tom   We should go up Shoeburyness. Take my car up. Do some doughnuts. I've not done that since you left. Or go Southend. Go cockle picking.

Danny   Yeah.

Tom   Have you got the new 50 Cent album?

Danny   I haven't Tom, no.

Tom   It's fucking great.

Danny   Is it?

Tom   What about the new Outcast?

Danny   No.

Tom   Snoop Dog?

Danny   I've not.

Tom   Black Eyed Peas?

Danny   No.

Tom   I've got all of them. Jay-Z, featuring Beyoncé?

Danny   No.

Tom   He's a lucky cunt, isn't he?

Danny   He is, yeah.

Tom   I'll burn 'em for you! Have you got an iPod?

Danny   No.

Tom   You should get one, I think.

Danny   Yeah, I will.

Tom   I've got 6,324 songs on mine. Mostly hip hop. I got some Rod Stewart, for me mum.

Danny   If I wanted it converted, would you know where I could go?

Tom   Sorry, Danny?

Danny   The P99, if I wanted it engineered, to fire live ammo, do you know anybody who could do that for me?

Scene Four

Danny, **Paul** *and* **Jade**.

Paul   To ask about the meaning of life is about as philosophically interesting as asking about the meaning of wood or the meaning of grass. There is no meaning. Life is, as science has proven in the last two years, a genetic system. An arrangement of molecular structure. There is no solidity. Only a perception of solidity. There is no substance. Only the perception of substance. There is no space. Only the perception of space. This is a freeing thing, in many ways, Danny. It means I can be anywhere. At any time. I can do anything. I just need to really try. This is Jade. Say hello, Jade.

Jade   Hello.

Danny   Hello.

Paul   How's Tom doing?

Danny   He's all right, I think.

Paul   Good man. Good man. Good man. He's a bit of a weird old cunt though, don't you think?

Danny   I do, sometimes.

Paul   He is. He speaks very highly of you, but he is a bit of a weird old cunt.

Danny (*to* **Jade**, *lying*)   Jade was my wife's name.

Paul   Are you married, Danny?

Danny   I was.

Paul   How old are you?

Danny   Twenty-seven.

Paul   What happened to your wife, Danny?

Danny   She got killed.

Paul   No.

Danny   We got robbed. She got shot in the chest.

Paul   Good God, Danny, that's awful.

Danny   Yeah.

Paul   When was this?

Danny   A couple of years ago.

Paul   Did they catch the fucker?

Danny   Yeah. He was a soldier. Some squaddie.

Paul   For God's sake. I'm really sorry to hear that. Aren't you, Jade? Aren't you sorry to hear that?

Jade   Yeah. I am.

Paul   We're both of us really sorry to hear that, Danny.

A long pause.

Yes.

Is it Danny or Daniel?

Danny Danny.

Paul Good. How boyish! What do you do, Danny?

Danny What do I do?

Paul Your job, what is it?

Danny I'm in film. I do special effects for films.

Paul Do you really? That's rather remarkable to me! What a remarkable job. What films have you done?

Danny None that you know.

Paul Go on. Try me. I go to the cinema all the time, don't I, Jade?

Jade Yeah. He does.

Danny I worked on a few of the Bond movies. I worked on the gun scenes on some of the Bond films.

Paul Which ones?

Danny *Die Another Day*. Mainly.

Paul I never saw that. Did I?

Jade No.

Paul I hate James Bond. I think his films are fucking dreadful. Did you come in on the train?

Danny I did, yeah.

Paul I like the train ride. Out of Dagenham.

Danny Yeah.

Paul I like Dagenham.

Danny Do yer?

Paul It's full of fat kids in football shirts, isn't it? Lovely that. I like it round here more, though. I like the views, you understand?

Danny   I do.

Paul   Canning Town. London, E16. Do you like London, Danny?

Danny   I'm not sure.

Paul   You're not sure?!

Danny   It's a bit big for me.

Paul   A bit big. (*He smiles.*) You see, that's the problem with the Essex native, though, Danny, isn't it? They never fucking leave.

Danny   That's not completely true.

Paul   What's the furthest you've ever been to?

Danny   You what?

Paul   In the world?

Danny   France.

Paul   Is it?

Danny   Yeah.

Paul   Ha!

Jade *smirks too.*

Danny   Don't laugh.

Paul   No. You're right. I'm being rude. I'm sorry. It's just I'm quite the traveller. I travel almost constantly. I'm more familiar with aeroplanes than I am with buses. That's actually the truth. Do you want to know something about aeroplanes?

Danny   Go on.

Paul   You know the real reason why people tell you to adopt the brace position in the event of an emergency on an aeroplane? It's so the impact of the crash on the neck forces the spinal column into the skull and into the brain and kills you immediately. Rather than allowing you to suffer a prolonged and horrible death. That's the reason why, really.

Danny   This is my gun.

He pulls his gun out of his pocket and shows it to him.

Paul   Yes. Put it away. We'll sort that out in a bit. Can I get you a cup of tea, Danny?

Danny   No thank you.

Paul   Or a coffee? Or a beer? A whisky? Anything like that?

Danny   A water.

Paul   A water? You want a glass of water? Tap or mineral?

Danny   Tap.

Paul   Tap water. Very good. Ice? Lemon?

Danny   No thank you.

Paul   As it comes, as it were. Terrific. Jade, sweetheart, get Danny a glass of water, will you? There's a good girl.

Jade *leaves. They watch her go.*

Paul   She's fourteen. You wouldn't think it to look at her, would yer?

Danny   I don't know.

Paul   You wouldn't. Immoral really, but . . .

A long pause. **Paul** *stares at* **Danny**.

Paul   Can I ask you this? Do you ever get that feeling? When you're in, you're in, you're in say a, a, a, a bar or a restaurant or walking down a street, and you see a girl. A teenage girl. You see the nape of her neck. In her school uniform. With her friends. All pigtailed. And you just want to reach out and touch. You ever get that?

Danny   I'm not sure.

Paul   You see, when you can't tell the difference any more between what is real and what is a fantasy. That's frightening, I think.

They don't let you take anything onto planes anymore, Danny. Did you know that? Since 9/11. Fucking nothing. Apart from pens, oddly. They should take pens off you. That's what I think. The pen can be a lethal instrument. You can stab somebody in the eye. Push it all the way in. Cripple them at least. Cut into the brain. Leave them brain-damaged. It'd be easy, that. I'd leave the end sticking out, wouldn't you?

Danny   I don't know.

Paul   You would. I would. It would look hilarious.

I need a shave.

You know what I think about 9/11, Danny?

Danny   No, I'm actually in a bit of a –

Paul   Wait for your fucking drink!

Danny   –

Paul *glares at him.*

Paul   The best heist film Hollywood never made. That's what I think. The level of planning, the level of daring, the downright fucking scientific sexiness and brass-balled braveness that went into that operation! Christ! You should tell your friends. They could cast it up! Cast Bruce Willis. Black him up a bit. That'd be a fucking blockbuster all right.

Danny   Yeah.

Paul   They should make films out of everything, I think. Films and musicals. They should make musicals out of everything as well. Imagine it! *Bulger! The Musical!* I'd pay forty quid to see that.

Jade *returns. She gives* **Danny** *a glass of water.*

Danny   Thank you very much.

Jade   That's all right.

Paul *waits for* **Danny** *to drink. Watches him.*

Paul   How is it? Your water?

Danny   It's fine, thanks.

Paul   Look out there. Have you the slightest idea how many tube lines run under the square mile area you can see from out of that window, Danny, have you? It's completely fucking hollow down there. Beneath the surface of the ground. It's full of vermin and metal. Rats. Mice. Squirrels. Foxes. Soon there'll be dogs fucking everywhere. Stray dogs. Little pit bulls. Wandering around. They'll come in down the river. And then, in the future, in London, people will find foxes in their living rooms. You'll have to batter them with your broom sticks. Or shoot them in the head. Either method works just as well. Scabby fucking things. They'll eat your cat as soon as look at you. I'm gonna bring hunting for foxes with hounds back. But not in fucking Surrey. Not in Wiltshire. Down Oxford Street. A huge fucking pack of us.

He makes the noise of a hunting trumpet.

Show me.

Danny *shows him his gun.*

Paul   P99. Nice. Let me have a look.

He opens a small toolkit, takes out a tiny screwdriver and a tape measure and opens the gun. Goes to work adjusting it. He wears half-moon spectacles as he does so.

The notion of a War on Terror is completely ingenious. It is now possible to declare war on an abstraction. On an emotional state.

He continues to work.

God. Law. Money. The left. The right. The church. The state. All of them lie in tatters. Wouldn't you be frightened?

He continues to work.

The only thing we can do is feast ourselves on comfort foods
and gobble up television images. Sport has never been more
important. The family unit seems like an act of belligerence.
All long-term relationships are doomed or ironic. Therefore
sexuality must be detached. But, because of fucking AIDS,
detached sexuality is suicidal. So everybody goes online.

Hardcore black fucking MPEG porn . . . junky lesbian breast
torture . . . bondage fantasies, hardcore pics . . . free bestiality
stories, low-fat diet, free horse-sex, torture victims zoo . . .

Marvellous stuff!

You can get all the free trailers. And that's enough for me.
I wouldn't spend any fucking money on it. That's just a waste,
I think. I think that's when you're addicted to it.

He continues to work.

I saw a fifty-year-old man sit a sixteen-year-old Brummie girl
on his lap. He held her breast in his hand and got her to smile
at the webcam. Asked her what she thought all of the people
watching did while she masturbated. She said she thought
they masturbated. It was a truthful image. It sits in my
consciousness.

He looks up at **Danny** *and points with his tiny screwdriver.*

Paul You want to know the truth about the poor in this
country? They're not cool. They're not soulful. They're not
honest. They're not the salt of the fucking earth. They're
thick. They're myopic. They're violent. They're drunk most of
the time. They like shit music. They wear shit clothes. They
tell shit jokes. They're racist, most of them, and homophobic
the lot of them. They have tiny parameters of possibility and a
minuscule spirit of enquiry or investigation. They would be
better off staying in their little holes and fucking each other.
And killing each other.

They're on the way there already, of course. There's a guy
who lives downstairs. He got himself involved in all that.
Couple of fellahs come along. Cut his biceps in half with a pair
of garden shears. Absolutely extraordinary.

Every week entire towns are torn apart by the puking boozers and the French-cropped cunts of England. Whacked off their heads on customised national health prescription anti-depressants. And testosterone injections. And Turkey Twizzlers. They puke up in the lobbies of banks. They use their bank cards to go and puke in a bit of peace and quiet. Leave it there. Welcome to Barclays!

And the girls are so vapid. You know the type? All brown skin and puppy fat and distressed denim on their arses and ponchos.

He continues to work.

When Jade's gone I think I'm going to start spending my time in the bars of Borough Market. Or Sloane Street. Or Bloomsbury. Get myself a rich girl, a business girl. You see them. And below their suits and their handbags and their fresh, fresh skin and clean hair, you know, you just fucking know.

Royalty are the worst, of course. Mind you, if I was the king of this country I'd start every morning with a blowjob too. From my butler. With my coffee and my yoghurt and my fruit. It's the most civilised thing I can imagine. It's absolutely legendary.

Wait here.

He leaves. **Danny** *drinks his water.* **Jade** *shifts her position. He looks at her.*

Danny Will he be long?

Jade I don't know.

Pause.

Danny Doesn't he do your head in after a while?

Jade What do you mean?

Danny He goes on a bit, doesn't he?

Jade I like him.

Danny Is he your boyfriend?

Jade   Ha!

Danny   What's funny?

Jade   'Is he your boyfriend?'

Danny   What's funny about that?

Jade   Nothing. It doesn't matter.

Danny   You shouldn't laugh at people. Shouldn't laugh at me, definitely. Shouldn't you be at school?

Jade   I don't go to school any more.

Danny   Why not?

Jade   It's boring. I don't need to, anyway. Paul teaches me all kinds of stuff.

Danny   I can imagine.

I used to go Eastbrook. In Dagenham. You ever heard of it?

Jade   No.

Danny   It's a fucking remarkable place. For a thousand reasons. But I never really felt completely comfortable there, you with me?

Jade   –

Danny   I always wanted to go out. See, you'd get a day like this. Go down the docks. Fuck that lot. Go and watch the river. Go over the Chase. Don't you think, Jade?

Jade   –

Danny   Have a day trip. We should have a day trip. Us two. Me and you, Jade. What do you think?

Jade   I don't think Paul would like it.

Danny   He wouldn't mind. Would he?

Paul *comes back in with the gun complete.*

Danny   Would you Paul? Would you mind if I took Jade for a day trip? Hop in the car. Go to the seaside.

Paul *looks at him for a long time. Hands him back his gun.*

Paul Do you need ammunition?

Danny I do, yeah.

Paul Here. 125 gram, nine-millimetre standard pressure hollow-point. Fifty rounds, ten pounds. Sixty pounds total. That's a very good price.

Danny Thank you.

Paul *hands him a small, plain, red box.* **Danny** *hands him sixty pounds. He examines his gun with a confidence and proficiency that belies the notion that he is anything other than a soldier.*

Paul This weather.

Danny Yeah.

Paul This whole planet is in a terrible state, Danny, you know? The ecological fallout of the decisions that you have made – you, Danny, personally, today, you, not anybody else, you – the ecological fallout of those decisions is catastrophic. And it's the same for all of us. Times sixty million. Times six billion. And nobody says anything about it. There are too many people. There is not enough water. There is not enough oxygen. And nobody admits it. And so now we're gonna consume China. And then we're gonna consume India and then we're gonna consume Africa and we'll carry on consuming. We'll continue to eat it all up and eat it all up and eat it all up until the only thing we've got left to fucking eat, Danny, the only thing we've got left to eat is each other.

Scene Five

Danny *and* **Marley**.

Danny We could get a car. Get a nice one. CD player. Seat belts. Airbags. All that. A really silent one. Get a couple of kids. Drive them to school. Nip off to work in yer suit. See you later, Danny. See you later, Lee! Have a good day, boys. Do all that.

Marley Danny.

Danny Are you cold?

Marley What are you doing here?

Danny I got something for yer.

Marley You can't come round here any more.

Danny You could make us all a cup of tea in the morning. We could buy a fucking Teasmade! You'd be in for Danny and Lee when they got home from school. I'd be at work but get home later and watch the news!

Marley This is stupid.

Danny Do you remember my flat?

Marley –

Danny It was good there, wasn't it? I wish I never sold it. I've nowhere to go now.

Marley Danny, you're shaking. I'm gonna call your brother.

Danny I'll tell you something. The amount of fucking snatch I'm gonna get now, Marley, you wouldn't believe.

Marley The amount of what?

Danny I already met somebody. We're going on a date. Jade, she's called. Black girl. A fucking coon. How d'yer like that?

Marley Don't, Danny.

Danny Don't what?

Marley It's boring.

Danny You know how old she is?

Marley –

Danny   Have a guess.

Marley   No.

Danny   She's forty-three.

Marley   Great.

Danny   That's the level I'm pitching it at nowadays.

Marley   Lovely.

Danny   Did you see me on the telly, by the way?

Marley   I didn't, no.

Danny   I was fucking brilliant. Made fucking Paxo look like . . .

Marley   That's not what I heard.

Danny   You what?

Marley   I heard you could barely speak. Didn't look anything like you. You look terrible, Danny. What have you been doing?

Danny   I've been at my folks, all day, really.

Marley   How they doing?

Danny   They're doing all right. They're well. I mean, I hate them so it's difficult for me to tell.

Marley   You hate them?

Danny   I do a bit. My dad mainly. Drunken fucking contradictory wanker. I find him completely ridiculous. I hope I get to bury him.

She looks at him for a long time.

What are you thinking?

Marley   Are you gonna go up London soon? And look at things?

Danny   What do you mean?

Marley All the tourist attractions. You used to go, do you remember? Stand outside them. Looking in.

Pause. He glares at her. Then grins.

Danny When I've finished with you I'm going to go and find every boyfriend you ever had and every friend you ever had and get them and shoot them in the face.

Marley You what?

Danny And all your family.

Marley That's nice, Danny.

Danny Do you think I won't, Marley, do you think I wouldn't? This is what I'm trained to do.

Marley I think you need to go to the hospital.

Danny I've got something for you. I went out, into town, up London, this afternoon and got a present for you. I've not decided whether you're gonna get it yet.

Marley A present?

Danny I don't know if you'll like it or not. You probably won't.

Marley What are you like, Danny? Jesus!

Danny You look quite sexy when you get angry.

Marley I'm going now.

Danny What about your present?

Marley I don't want your poxy present. What is it? Box of chocolates, is it? Box of Black Magic?

You should know. I wanted to tell you. I do have a boyfriend. I've been seeing him for years. We're gonna get married, I think. We're gonna have kids. I'm gonna be a mum to his kids.

He can't look at her.

All you ever do is talk and talk and talk.

I can't do this any more. It does me no good.

Danny

Marley You're shivering.

Danny I'm sorry.

Marley What are you sorry for?

Danny It's not me. It isn't me.

Marley What isn't you? Fucking hell!

Danny I'm really sorry.

Marley I wanted to be your mate. I wanted to come round for tea and fags and biscuits.

Danny I don't think so. Not now. No.

Marley.

Marley What?

Danny Marley.

Marley Are you crying?

Danny Marley.

Marley What, Danny? Jesus!

Danny Go back in. You should go back inside. I don't think I should see you any more.

Scene Six

Danny *and* **Jade**.

Danny It's lovely here, isn't it?

Jade –

Danny Most people don't even know this place exists. Some maps don't even show the road onto it.

See his face, on the checkpoint, when I showed him my pass.
That was a bit of a surprise for him, I think. What do you
think?

Jade I don't know.

Danny Sorry?

Jade I said I don't know.

Danny It was, I think. I think it was a big surprise. Uptight
cunt. Officer class. Failed.

Jade What are you gonna do?

Danny See miles from here and all, can't you? See France,
I reckon, on a good day.

Jade Are you gonna hurt me?

Danny Or Holland. What do you think, Jade? Do you
reckon you could see Holland from here?

Jade I don't know.

Danny Do you think he'll notice you've gone – Paul?

Jade Yeah.

Danny Do you?

Jade Yes, I do.

Danny Do you think you were very important to him?

Jade Yes.

Danny Do you think he was a bit in love with you, Jade?

Jade I don't know.

Danny You looked very funny when I turned up. Did you
get the fright of your life?

Jade I did a bit.

Danny Did you?

Jade Yeah.

Danny (*as though to a cute puppy*)   Aaahhh.

A pause. He moves away from her. Looks out to sea.

Were you good at school?

Jade   What?

Danny   When you went to school, Jade, were you quite good at it?

Jade   Yeah.

Danny   I bet you were. You look as though you were. You're quite confident, aren't you? Did you *ever* like it?

Jade   Yeah.

Danny   When did you enjoy it?

Jade   In primary school. Year seven was all right.

Danny   And then it all went a bit wrong for you?

Jade   –

Danny   Would you ever go back, do you think? Go sixth form?

Jade   I think so, yeah.

Danny   'Cause you're quite brainy, aren't you? For your age?

Jade   I don't know.

Danny   What would you do if you did?

Jade   I'm not sure.

Danny   What A levels would you take?

Jade   I –

She starts crying a bit.

Danny   Well, that's clever. You're gonna stay on at sixth form but you don't know what you're going to study there.

Jade   I haven't decided.

Danny   See, that's the fucking thing, isn't it? Nowadays. Young people today! They have no idea what they're going to fucking *do* with their lives. They have no clarity. No vision. No perspective. I find it very dispiriting I have to say.

Stop crying.

I hate students.

Jade   Do you?

Danny   I *fucking* hate sixth-formers. All fucking iPods and crappy T-shirts with band names on.

Do you like the sea, Jade, do yer?

Jade   Yeah.

Danny   Have you ever been out past Southend before?

Jade   No.

Danny   Foulness Island. What a funny name! How old are you Jade?

Jade   I'm sixteen.

Danny   That's not what Paul told me. He told me you were fourteen. Are you fourteen or sixteen?

Jade   Sixteen

Danny   Are you lying to try to impress me?

Jade   No.

Danny   Have you ever actually had sex before?

Jade   What?

Danny   You could look all right, you, you know? If you sorted yourself out a bit, I think you could. Sort your hair out. Your hair looks shit. There could be something of the Britney Spears about you. Do you like her? Britney? Do you, Jade? Stop crying. Jade, do you like Britney Spears?

Will you sing one of her songs for me? Jade? Have you got a good singing voice? Come on, Jade. Sing that, do you know that, that one with the school uniform on, that one 'Baby One More Time'?

Do you know that one, Jade?

Come on. You know it. Britney Spears, Jade.

He sings the first line of the song, encouraging her to sing along with him. He does a little dance while he's singing.

He forgets the words, hums them. Can't stop himself laughing while he's singing.

He remembers the chorus. Sings it. At his manic encouragement she begins to join in.

He stops singing before the final line of the chorus. Waits for her to finish the line. Leans right in on her. Big grin on his face. She sings the final line of the chorus alone.

He nearly hits her. Hard. On the side of her head. Stops his fist just in time. Bursts out laughing.

Danny   Do you want to travel, Jade, do you think?

Jade   What are you going to do to me, please?

Danny   Where do you want to go? Tell me somewhere. Tell me where you wanna go. Tell me some places.

Jade   –

Danny   Do you want to do a geography quiz?

Jade   –

Danny   Capital cities! Ask me a capital cities question, Jade. Go on. Ask me, 'What's the capital of . . . ?', Jade. You ask me. 'What's the capital of . . . ?' Go on, Jade.

Jade   I don't know.

Danny   You say, 'What's the capital of . . . ?' Say that, Jade! Say it! Please!

Jade   What's the capital of . . . ?

Danny   And then you think of a country. Say it again, Jade, and think of a country.

Jade   What's the capital of . . . ?

Danny   Go on, Jade.

Jade   Bulgaria?

Danny   Sofia! See! Sofia! How fucking brilliant is that?! How many men could do that, Jade?! Not fucking many, that's how many! Not. Fucking. Many!

Do you know how many words I can spell? Do you? Jade? Thousands of words. I can spell thousands of words, Jade. More than anybody I know.

Do you know how many press-ups I can do? Jade, look at me. I can do a hundred press-ups.

Here. Feel my muscles, Jade. Feel them.

He flexes his bicep. She refuses to move her arm to touch it.

FEEL MY MUSCLES, JADE!

She does.

They're hard, aren't they? Aren't my muscles hard, Jade?

Jade   Yes.

Danny   I know. Here. Watch this!

He falls to the floor and does ten one-armed press-ups. Counts them all as he does them.

Isn't that great?! Not many people can do that, Jade. Not many people can.

She barely dares look at him.

I like your jacket.

Jade   Thank you.

Danny   Is it new?

Jade   No.

Danny   It looks it.

Jade   It isn't.

Danny   It looks all shiny. Clothes are funny when they feel all new, aren't they? When they smell new. It's a good feeling, that, I think.

Take it off.

Jade   What?

Danny   I wanna take a photograph of you. On my phone.

Would you mind if I took a photograph of you, Jade? Here. Take your, your, take your jacket off, will ya? That's better. There. That's lovely. Gissa smile. Lovely.

He pulls a mobile phone out of his pocket and takes a photograph of her.

Do you want a Coca Cola? Do you? You want some Coke? I've got some Coca Cola in the car. Or how about a smoothie? Do you want a yoghurt and honey smoothie? I love yoghurt and honey smoothies, me.

Put your hand down. On the ground.

Jade   –

Danny   Put it there.

Jade   Don't.

Danny   Jade. Now.

She puts one hand on the ground. He takes another photograph.

Now keep it there.

Jade   –

Danny   I'm going to go and get some Coca Cola and a yoghurt and honey smoothie from the car. I'm not going to tell you when I'm coming back. But when I come back I want your hand to be there.

Jade   Please don't.

He smiles at her briefly, then leaves. She keeps her hand on the ground.

He comes back in with a bottle of Coca Cola, a small honey and yoghurt smoothie, a canister of petrol, a body-bag folded up, a cushion and a cigarette in his mouth.

He lights the cigarette. He smokes it for a while, watching her. He puts the cigarette out on her hand. She screams. Starts crying.

Danny   Did I say that you could move your hand?

Jade   No.

Danny   No, I didn't. I didn't tell you you could move your hand. So why – Jade, Jade, look at me – why did you move your hand, Jade?

Jade   Because you burnt me.

Danny *bursts into a giggle. Then stops. Gathers himself. Takes another photograph with his phone. Looks at her for a while.*

Danny   Sometimes there are days when my heart fills up.

Here. Take your shoes off. Take your socks off.

We had. There was. Our sergeant-major. He was a funny man. I quite liked him, as it goes. You hear all these stories, don't you? Attention! But, no, he was all right. He'd get drunk. Do this to you.

He hits the soles of her feet with the butt of his gun.

With a hammer. Never did it to me. Hurts, doesn't it? And when he shouts at you. SIT FUCKING STILL, JADE! The feeling of spittle on yer face. Here. I'll wipe it off.

He wipes her face.

And you can't tell anybody. You can't pull rank. You can't do that. Get a bucket of shit and piss from the slops of the drains there. Get some little geek cunt. Pour it over their head. It was quite funny. And out there. Everybody says about the British.

How fucking noble we are. I used to like the Yanks. At least they were honest about it. At least they had a sense of humour. Yer get me?

He imitates the famous Lynndie England 'Thumbs up!' sign right in her face. And takes an American accent.

Thumbs up, Mac!

Some of the things we did, down in Basra. It was a laugh. I'll tell yer that for nothing. Here, Ali Baba. Get that down yer throat, yer raghead cunt.

You never know. Fucking fourteen-year-old girl? Don't matter. Could've strapped herself. Underneath her fucking burka. Take it off!

Jade   What?

Danny   Take it off! Take you're burka off, this is a body search. I've seen boys with their faces blown off. Skin all pussed up and melted. Eyeballs hanging out on the cartilage.

Yer helmet holds it all together. Bits of yer skull held in.

Will you pretend you're my sister? Jade?

Jade   –

Danny   Will you, Jade?

Jade   If you want.

Danny   Thanks.

Takes another photograph with his phone.

Jade   It's muscle.

Danny   What?

Jade   It's muscle, not cartilage – that holds the eyeball into the skull.

He looks at her for a bit.

Danny   Yeah.

Looks at her for a bit more.

Course you come back. Go up London. Fucking burkas all over the place.

He picks up the petrol canister.

Now here's a question for you. Is this really petrol or is it water?

He opens the canister. Holds it open, under her nose, for her to sniff.

What do you think? Jade? What do you think? Answer me.

Jade   I don't know.

Danny   No, I know. But have a guess. What do you reckon?

Jade   I think it's petrol.

Danny   Do yer?

Jade   It smells like petrol.

Danny   Are you sure that's not just your imagination?

Jade   No. I don't know.

Danny   Your imagination plays terrible fucking tricks on you in situations like this.

He pours some over her head.

You look quite funny. Your hair's all wet.

Takes another photograph with his phone.

You want a cigarette?

He pulls a cigarette out of his packet. Offers it to her. She doesn't take it. He pops it in his mouth. Crouches down. Pulls out a box of matches.

Jade   No.

Danny   Should we?

Jade   No, please, no, don't, don't, don't, don't. Please.

Danny   Chicken. Coward.

He pulls out his gun and presses it into the cushion against her chest. He shoots her in the chest four times. There is no scream. Not much blood is apparent at first. Just four dull thuds. She slumps over a bit. He takes another photograph with his phone.

He drags her body towards the body-bag, leaving a massive trail of blood behind her. The shots have blown her back off. Puts her into the body-bag. Zips it up. He talks to her while he's working.

Yer see them, don't yer?

Fucking leave university and get a fucking house together and spend all day in their shitehawk little jobs hoping that one day they're gonna make it as a fucking big shot. But they're not. They never will. They're shrivelled up home counties kids and they march against the war and think they're being radical. They're lying. They're monkeys. They're French exchange students. They're Australians in London wrecked on cheap wine and shite beer. They're Hasidic Jews in swimming pools. They're lesbian cripples with bus passes. They're niggers, with their faces all full of their mama's jerk chicken, shooting each other in the back down Brixton high street until the lot of them have disappeared. They're little dickless Paki boys training to be doctors or to run corner shops and smuggling explosives in rucksacks onto the top decks of buses. It's not funny, Jade. I'm not joking. I fought a war for this lot.

I want to get it right. That isn't the right word. What's the right word? I want to get the right word. Don't tell me. Don't tell me. Don't tell me. I want to get it right.

I need a massage.

I can't even see straight.

Have I got a stammer? Have you noticed that?

Scene Seven

Danny *and* **Justin** *and* **Helen**.

Danny   Do you know any good dentists?

Justin   I'm sorry?

Danny   I was just wondering if you knew any good dentists. I've got the most fucking horrible toothache.

Justin   Not round here.

Helen   We're not actually from round here.

Justin   I've a good dentist in Chalk Farm, but that's no use.

Danny   No.

Justin   I'm sorry.

Danny   That's okay.

Helen   Toothache's dreadful.

Danny   Yeah. I fucking hate the dentist and all. It's terrifying. The sound of the drill and that.

Is that where you live? Chalk Farm?

Helen   It is, yes.

Danny   Whereabouts?

Helen   Do you know Chalk Farm?

Danny   A little, yeah.

Helen   Fitzjohn's Avenue. Just west of Rosslyn Hill. Do you know that bit?

Danny   No. I don't. I've no idea.

Helen   It's lovely.

Danny   Is it very expensive?

Helen   It is, yes.

Danny   Great!

Helen   I'm Helen.

Danny   Hi, Helen. I'm Danny.

Helen   Hello, Danny. How lovely to meet you.

Danny   And you, yeah.

Justin   I'm Justin.

Danny   Nice one. Arright, Justin?

Justin   Hello mate.

Danny   What brings you down here then?

Justin   We often come to The Northview.

Danny   Oh yeah?

Justin   It's our favourite hotel.

Danny   Right.

Helen   For a day out. A night off. A night out.

Danny   Great.

Helen   We just get in the car. Book a room. Spend the night.

Danny   Lovely.

Helen   I love the sea.

Danny   Yeah, me too.

Helen   The pier. And the funfair.

Danny   Do yer?

Helen   It's marvellous.

Danny   That's funny to me, that.

Helen   Why?

Danny   You just don't strike me as the funfair type.

Helen   Don't I?

Danny   No.

Justin   Doesn't she?

Danny   No.

Helen   Well, I am.

Justin   She is.

Helen   What kind of type do I strike you as, Danny?

Danny   I have no fucking idea.

Justin   Whereabouts are you from Danny?

Danny   I'm from Dagenham.

Justin   Marvellous.

Danny   In Essex.

Justin   Yes. I know it. Up the A13.

Danny   That's right.

Justin   The Ford Factory.

Danny   Uh-huh.

Justin   The World of Leather!

Danny   I'm sorry?

Justin   There's a massive World of Leather in Dagenham. You can get leather sofas there.

Danny   I never knew that.

Justin   It's a marvellous place. Would you like a drink?

Danny   I'm – I don't know.

Justin   We're having a drink.

Helen   Join us.

Justin   Come on, mate, join us for a drink.

Danny   I don't know if I should. I'm driving. I've got a delivery in the boot. I've not eaten – it'd go right to my head.

Justin   We're just about to eat ourselves.

Helen   Yes. Would you like something to eat?

Danny   I don't have –

Helen   Maybe we could buy you a meal or something?

Danny   Thank you. I'll – I'll have a beer with you.

Helen   We'll see about the meal.

Danny   Yeah.

Justin   Yes.

Helen   Good. Lovely.

Justin   What are you delivering?

Danny   I'm sorry?

Justin   In your boot, what is it that you're delivering?

Danny   Fireworks.

Justin   Fireworks?!

Helen   How exciting!

Danny   Is it?

Justin   Why on earth have you got a delivery of fireworks in the boot of your car?

Danny   I arrange firework displays.

Justin   Do you?

Danny   You know, for football matches. Things like that.

Helen   Terrific.

Danny   When West Ham got promoted. I did that.

Helen   Isn't that marvellous?

Justin   Trevor Brooking!

Danny   Yeah.

Justin   What beer would you like?

Danny   Er . . .

Justin   They have a fantastic selection of multinational lagers.

Danny   A lager's fine. A pint of lager would be smashing. Thanks, Justin.

Justin *leaves.* **Helen** *crosses her legs. Stares at* **Danny**. **Danny** *feels his tooth. A time.*

Helen   You're rather gorgeous, aren't you?

Danny   I'm sorry?

Helen   Don't apologise. (*Beat.*) Do you work out?

Danny   Do I? No. No. No, I don't.

Helen   You've got very broad shoulders.

Danny   I used to be a soldier.

Helen   Did you?

Danny   Until a year or so ago.

Helen   I see.

Danny   I was out in Basra, as it goes. When that all kicked off.

Helen   Good God.

Danny   Yeah.

Helen   That must have been awful.

Danny   No. No. No. No. It was all right. It was fine.

Helen   Are you married, Danny?

Danny   I am, yeah.

Helen   What's your wife called?

Danny   Marley.

Helen   What a lovely name! How long have you been married to Marley, Danny?

Danny   Ten years. We were at school together. We got married just after we left sixth form.

Helen   How lovely.

Danny   Yeah.

Helen   Where's Marley now?

Danny   She's at home.

Helen   Is she expecting you back?

Danny   She is, yeah.

Helen   I see.

Justin *returns with a pint of lager.*

Danny   Thanks, Justin.

Justin   That's my pleasure.

Danny   You not having one?

Justin   No, no. We're all right.

Helen   We're fine.

A pause. **Danny** *drinks a big gulp of lager.*

Helen   A hard day?

Danny   Yeah. It was a bit, as it goes.

That tastes lovely.

What do you do, Justin?

Justin   I'm a schoolteacher.

Danny   Are you?

Justin   I am, yes. Well. I'm the head of year. At a grammar school. In Tottenham.

Danny   I always hated schoolteachers.

Justin   Is that right?

Danny   Well. I say that. It's actually a lie. They always used to hate me. I would often hanker after their affections. Never got it. It was a big disappointment to me.

Justin   I can imagine.

Danny   Do you work?

Helen   I do, yes.

Danny   What do you do?

Helen   I manage a television production company.

Danny   That sounds pretty, er, exhausting.

Helen   It is.

Danny   Does it affect you at all?

Helen   How do you mean?

Danny   My dad was in management. It gave him a certain demeanour. I think it affected his posture a bit. He used to stand up incredibly straight.

Helen   I'm not sure. I've never thought about it. You have a look. Let me know.

She stands to leave. Speaks to **Justin** *first.*

Helen   I think so, don't you?

Justin *smiles. The two men watch her leave.* **Danny** *drinks.*

Some time passes.

Danny   Thank you for the beer. It's lovely. Really hits the spot.

Justin   That's my pleasure. Honestly.

Pause.

Danny   Yeah.

Some time.

Justin   So. Fireworks.

Danny   That's right.

Some time passses. **Justin** *looks right at him.*

Justin   Helen's my wife.

Danny   I guessed that.

Justin   We've actually got two children.

Danny   Oh, right.

Justin   David is four and Phillipa's two.

Danny   Lovely.

Justin   They're staying with her mother tonight.

Danny   Right.

Justin   Have you been to this hotel before?

Danny   I haven't, no.

Justin   I didn't think you had.

Danny   It's all right, isn't it? The views and that.

Justin   It is. Yes. We're staying in Room 21.

Danny   I'm sorry?

Justin   Room 21.

Some time passes.

Danny *breaks into a big grin.* **Justin** *smiles with him.*

Danny   Fucking hell.

Justin   Don't say anything now.

Some time.

Helen *comes back. They sit together for a bit.* **Justin** *and* **Helen**
exchange glances, slight smiles, while **Danny** *drinks more of his beer.*

Danny   Justin was just telling me about your children.

Helen   What did he say about them?

Danny   He told me how old they were.

Helen   Did he? Did you?

Justin   I did.

Danny   Four and two, wasn't it? David and Phillipa?

Helen   That's right.

Justin   Pip, I call her.

Helen   He's completely devoted to her. Aren't you?

Justin   I am a bit, I'm afraid.

Helen   He's absolutely under her thumb. She's got him twisted round her little finger.

Danny   He invited me up to your room.

Helen   Did he?

Danny   I'm a bit fucking freaked out, as it goes.

Helen   I thought you would be. There's no need to be.

Danny was telling me, Justin, while you were at the bar. He used to be in the army.

Justin   You can tell that.

Helen   That's what I thought. He was in Basra, apparently.

Justin   Were you really?

Danny *chuckles a bit.*

Justin   Would you like another beer?

Danny   No, thank you. I'm all right.

Justin   It's not a big deal, you know? It's just an invitation. I think Helen finds you quite attractive. But you mustn't do anything that you don't want to do.

Danny   No. No. No. It's not that. It's just a surprise.

Helen   It's just sex.

Danny   Yeah. I think it's good. My mum never bothered asking my dad. I think it's very open-minded. Does that come with working in the media, do you think?

Helen   I'm not entirely sure.

Danny   And do you like to watch, do you?

Justin   Only if it's not a problem.

Danny   Or do you join in?

Justin   I think that's . . .

Helen   That can be up to you.

Danny   Right.

Helen *stands up.*

Helen   I think you two should decide that. I'll be back.

She leaves.

Danny   I guess it's one of those things, isn't it? That you read about.

Justin   I don't know, is it?

Danny   It goes on all the time, I bet.

Justin *nods.*

Danny   Do you like it? Watching?

Justin   I do, yes.

Danny   Why?

Justin   I think it's lovely. I like to watch her happy.

Danny   Right. That's quite sweet, as it goes.

Justin *smiles.*

Danny   It's not like it's the first time I've ever come across this kind of thing, you know.

Justin   No?

Danny   In our platoon. You could go, sometimes, into downtown Basra.

Justin   Really?

Danny   Or not even bother. You could just stay in the barracks. Fuck each other. That would happen. You can't blame people, can you?

Justin   I never would.

Danny   You do get a little bored after a while.

Justin   I can imagine.

Danny   Smell of a nice bit of aftershave. Nice but of stubble on a chin. All the same with your eyes closed, isn't it? There is a certain attraction, I think.

Justin   I think so, too.

Danny   I thought you would. I was lying. Yer gay cunt.

Justin   I don't believe you.

Danny   You what?

Justin   I don't believe you were lying.

Helen *comes back. There is a time. She stares at him. Grins.*

Helen   You're still here. I'm glad. (*To* **Justin**.) Thank you.

Justin *smiles at* **Danny**.

Danny   Did you go on the march?

Justin   On the –

Danny   On the anti-war march, up Hyde Park, did you two go on that?

Justin   Yes. We did.

Danny *laughs.*

Danny   Did yer?!

Helen   Why's that funny?

Danny   I wish I'd been there.

Justin   Do you?

Danny   With my SA80. Sprayed the lot of yer. Stick that up yer arse and smoke it, Damon Albarn, yer fucking pikey cunt.

Helen and **Justin** *smile at one another.*

Helen   Yes.

Danny   I come back home. It's a completely foreign country.

He reaches over to **Helen***. Strokes her cheek.*

'Do you work out?' What the fuck are you talking about? Two hours drill and forty lengths. Twenty-five minutes max. Alternate strokes. Breaststroke, front crawl, back-stroke, butterfly.

He puts his thumb in her mouth. She sucks on it.

Here, you'll like this. I saw, one time, a group of guys, at Pirbright, get another lad, a younger lad – no listen to this, this is right up your street. They get him. Hold him down. Get a broom handle. Fucking push it, right up his rectum. Right up there. (*He removes his thumb.*) And we all watched that. Joined in. That was funny, to be fair. It did feel funny. I imagine it's the same kind of feeling, is it?

Helen   Are you trying to unnerve us?

Danny   Mind you, you play that game out there and it's even funnier. 'Cause they don't like anything with the slightest sexual connotation. You two, out there! Fucking hell!

Justin (*smiling*)   I think he is.

Helen   Do you?

Danny   I'd put it on my phone. You wanna see what I've got on my phone? You wanna see Ken Bigley? I've got Ken Bigley on here. Nick Berg. All them! You wanna watch?

Justin   I think you are.

Danny   You wanna watch, Justin?

Justin   No, I don't.

Danny *stares at him.*

Danny   Do you know what I want to do?

Helen   What's that?

Danny   I want an arm-wrestle. Right now. I fucking love arm-wrestles, me. Do you want one, Justin?

Helen   You're rather funny, aren't you?

Justin (*chuckling*)   He's like a little boy.

Danny   Justin. Come here. Let's have an arm-wrestle.

He positions his arm. Glares at him.

Come on, mate.

Justin *braces* **Danny**'s *arm in an arm-wrestle.* **Danny** *holds his arm exactly where he wants it.*

Danny   I've put children into the backs of ambulances and they've not *got* any arms, actually.

It could happen here, all that. I reckon it will. There are too many people. Wait until the water runs out. And the oxygen runs out.

Justin   Are you trying your hardest?

Danny   I'm gonna convert to Islam. Save me from scumballs like you two.

I'm not apologising for anything. See me. I'm as innocent as a baby. I'm a fucking hero! I'm a fucking action hero! I'm John fucking Wayne! I'm Sylvester Stallone! I'm fucking James Bond, me!

He wins the arm-wrestle.

That was fucking easy.

Scene Eight

Danny *and* **Lee**.

Lee   I spoke to Mum.

Danny   Right.

Lee   I told them to tell anybody who asks that you were with them all day.

Danny   Right.

Lee   She said she would. She said that Dad would too. She said it's not a problem. They've not been out. They've not spoken to anybody.

Danny   Which is lucky.

Lee   Yes. Yes. Yes. Yes. It is. Yes. They won't ask.

Danny   What?

Lee   Mum and Dad. They won't ask why they've got to lie for you.

Danny   No.

Lee   They'll just do it. They'll do whatever I ask them to.

Danny   Right. Yeah. Course they will. What'll you say?

Lee   I, I, I, I, I, I, I, I –

They look at each other for a long time.

Danny   I've had one hell of a day.

They look at each other for a long time.

It's horrible round here. They should set it on fire.

They look at each other for a long time.

Don't tell anybody, Lee. Don't you dare. Do you understand me?

Lee   Of course I do.

Danny   You fucking better.

Lee   What are you going to do?

Danny   When?

Lee   If the police find you?

Danny   I'll shoot them in the face and then shoot myself in the face and all.

Lee   I'm being serious.

Danny   So am I, Lee.

Pause.

Lee   Can I see it?

Danny   See what?

Lee   Your gun.

Danny *gets his gun out of his pocket and shows it to* **Lee**. **Lee** *holds it with a mix of complete horror and absolute fascination.*

Danny   It's hot, isn't it? We should go out. Take our shoes off. Get the grass between our toes.

So.

Blackburn next week, Lee.

Lee (*completely transfixed by the gun*)   That's right. Mark Hughes was a good player. Sparky, they called him.

Danny   Are you going to go, do you think?

Lee   I don't think so, no.

Danny   Have you ever actually been? To a game?

Lee   No. I haven't, no.

Danny   Why not?

Lee   I don't know. I haven't.

Danny   I wish I had a sister. It would have been miles better.

Lee   How much money have you got, exactly?

Danny   Three thousand, two hundred pounds.

Lee   Right. That's one good thing. (*Beat.*) Where is she, Danny?

Danny   She's in the boot of the car.

Lee   What are you gonna do with her?

Danny   I have no idea.

Lee *gives the gun back.*

Lee   Have my fingerprints all over that now. They'll think I did it.

Danny   Nobody'll notice that she's gone, you know?

Lee   They will. She was fourteen.

Danny   You didn't know her. She wasn't like most fourteen-year-olds.

Lee   This is stupid. You're stupid. You're a stupid stupid stupid stupid stupid –

Danny   What?

I wish it hadn't happened, Lee.

Lee   Do you?

Danny   If that's any consolation.

Lee   It isn't.

Danny   She was like a doll. She was a cute little black thing.

How was your lunch?

Lee   It was very nice, thank you.

Danny   What did you have?

Lee   I had roast pork and apple sauce and roast potatoes and gravy and carrots and peas and cauliflower.

Danny You wouldn't get that free if you were living with Mum and Dad, would you? Doctors wouldn't come round then, would they?

Lee I don't think so.

Danny Is that the main reason you left, Lee, for yer dinners? Do you really think you deserve this place?

Lee I don't know.

Danny Is that why you keep it so fucking clean?

Lee Danny.

Danny Do you think it's Mum and Dad's fault, what's happening to you? Is it genetic, do you think?

Lee Don't you start swearing your head off again!

Danny Did you have a hundred fucking mercury fillings or what?

Lee Danny.

Danny You don't have the slightest idea what I'm going through.

Lee I spend my nights watching reruns of *The Simpsons* on the television. I have videos of *Mork and Mindy* that I watch sometimes. And I spend my days trawling sex-contact pages on the internet. Don't you tell me that I don't know what you're going through. I *live* what you're going through. And I never did anything like that!

Danny Ha!

Lee Did you go and see Marley?

Pause.

Danny I did, yeah.

Lee I told you not to go.

Danny I know.

Lee You liked her, didn't you?

Danny I did, yeah.

Lee You liked her a bit too much, I think. You would've married her, I bet.

Danny Lee.

Lee She would never have married you, would she though, Danny? You were completely deluding yourself.

I'm so much cleverer than you, in real life, it's embarrassing.

When you were on television. I was incredulous. You couldn't even finish your sentences.

'It's important to think that we're making a difference. People have no idea what life was like here under Saddam's regime.'

Thing is. Mum and Dad were extremely proud of you. They had arguments. Over which one of them you took after and which one I took after.

He's ashamed of me, Dad. Which is ironic. People used to say I was a paedophile. Largely because of my glasses. I think he used to believe them. And if it weren't for you, I would have had a much more horrible time than I actually did. People were frightened you would have battered them. On account of you being a psychopath. I know that. But I can't do this, I don't think.

Danny Do what?

Lee Your eyes.

Danny What can't you do, Lee?

Lee I'm not surprised that girls like you. You've got nice eyes. They look for nice eyes in a man, I heard.

Danny Lee, I asked you a question.

Lee I don't think I can not tell. I think I'm going to tell the police.

Danny Lee.

Lee I don't think I can keep it to myself.

Danny   You can, you can, you can, you can, Lee.

Lee   Are you gonna batter my head in now?

Danny   You so can. You so can.

Lee   Why should I?

Danny   You're my brother.

They look at each other for a long time. The longest that they can manage. And then **Danny** *moves away.*

Ah, fuck it! Eh? Eh, Lee? Fuck it! You know?

It doesn't matter.

What does it matter?

Here. Bruv. Come here. I'm sorry I was mean to you! I think you're the best. I think you're fucking gorgeous. Come here.

Lee *approaches him.*

Danny   Touch my chest.

Lee *rests his hand on his chest.*

Danny   There. How hard is that? You like that? Here. Come here.

He beckons **Lee** *towards his face.*

Danny   Come on. Just a kiss. There.

He kisses **Lee**, *on the lips.*

Danny   There. You don't need to tell anybody. Do you?

Have you got a hard on? You have, haven't you? It's all right. It's all right, Lee. Straight up. It's all right. It doesn't matter.

All our years. All of them.

My brother!

He knows what I'm talking about.

When we were kids. Tell yer.

And everybody looks at him like he's some kind of fucked-up fucking weird old cunt. But he's not, yer know.

He's not.

He isn't.

He's all right

He's not gonna tell anybody.

And the way you smell! It's exactly the way I smell too. It reminds me of me. It makes me feel sick.

He kisses **Lee** *hard on the cheek. And breaks away. Lights a cigarette. His hands trembling.*

Lee You smoke the same brand as Dad's secret cigarettes.

Danny Right.

Lee It must be genetic.

Pause.

Danny Will you cut my hair?

Lee What?

Danny I need a haircut.

Lee All right.

Danny I've got clippers.

Lee I don't need your clippers. I've got my own clippers. I'll do it with my clippers. I'll do it great.

He pulls up a chair. **Danny** *sits in it.* **Lee** *wraps a towel round* **Danny**'s *neck. Leaves to go and get his clippers.*

Danny *stares out.*

Lee *comes back after a bit.*

Danny Shanghai.

Lee 12,762,953.

Danny   Moscow.

Lee   10,381,288.

He stands behind **Danny***, looks at the back of his head. He has the clippers poised in his hand.*

Danny   In Basra, when it all kicked off with the prisoners, I didn't do any of it. I never touched nobody. I had the rules, pinned above my head. My idiot's guide to the Geneva Convention pinned to the head of my bed. They used to call me a pussy cunt. It never used to bother me. I wish I'd told somebody. I might, still. I wish I'd joined in. I would've liked that.

I don't blame the war.

The war was all right. I miss it.

It's just you come back to this.

Lee   I never touched *any*body.

Danny   You what?

Lee   It's I never touched *any*body. Not I never touched *no*body. That's just careless.

Lee *turns his clippers on. He waits for a while before he starts cutting.*

The lights fall.

Mike Bartlett

My Child

To my family

Mike Bartlett's plays include *My Child* (Royal Court Theatre, 2007); *Contractions* (Royal Court Theatre, 2008); *Artefacts* (Bush Theatre/Nabokov/59E59, 2008, which won the Old Vic New Voices Award); *Cock* (Royal Court Theatre, 2009); and *Earthquakes in London* (National Theatre, 2010). Work for the radio includes *Love Contract*; *The Family Man* (both BBC Radio 4, 2007); *Not Talking* (BBC Radio 3, 2007, which won the Writers' Guild Tinniswood and Imison Prizes); *The Steps*; and *Liam* (both BBC Radio 4, 2009). He was Pearson Playwright in Residence at the Royal Court Theatre in 2007.

My Child was first performed at the Royal Court Jerwoood Theatre Downstairs, Sloane Square, London, on 3 May 2007. The cast was as follows:

Father	Richard Albrecht
Child	Adam Arnold
Mother	Jan Chappell
Karl	Adam James
Older Woman	Sara Kestelman
Another Man	James Livingstone
Man	Ben Miles
Another Woman	Antoinette Tagoe
Young Woman	Jodie Taibi
Other Woman	Romy Tennant
Woman	Lia Williams

Director Sacha Wares
Designer Miriam Buether
Lighting Designer Johanna Town
Sound Designer Ian Dickinson
Choreographer Juha Marsalo
Assistant Director Amy Hodge

Characters

Man
Mother
Older Woman
Woman
Child
Other Woman
Young Woman
Another Woman
Another Man
Father
Karl

The audience and actors come into the space together.
It is not clear who the actors are at first.

Actors can go anywhere in the space.

No actors should enter or leave the theatre during the
performance.

Note

/ means the next speech begins at that point.

– means the next line interrupts.

. . . at the end of a speech means it trails off. On its own,
it indicates a pressure, expectation or desire to speak.

A speech with no written dialogue indicates a character
deliberately remaining silent.

Blank space between speeches in the dialogue indicates time
drifting on with slightly less happening for a moment.

Darkness.

Man Mum?

Mother Shh.

Older Woman Love?

Woman Shh.

Man What do I do?

Mother Darling.

Child Mum.

Man Shhh.

Child Mummy.

Man Shush.

Excuse me.

Sorry.

Lights up.

Child My arm hurts.

Man Shut up.

Child My arm hurts bad.

Man Look, I'm really trying here. I'm trying to do my best.

Woman He looks ill to me.

Man We had a nice time.

Woman Did you?

Man Yes.

Woman He says / his arm hurts.

Man I know what he says. He just wants attention, I think. It's –

Woman He didn't fall or anything then?

Man   He's just tired.

Woman   Did he fall over?

Man   I would tell you –

Woman   So he didn't?

Man   I would tell you if he fell or anything. He didn't. Go to bed.

Child   But –

Man   Go to bed.

Child   You're rubbish. Simon's dad takes him to Hamleys when they go out. Says he can have anything he wants. Says he can choose anything. He's got a PS3.

Man   What's that?

Child   You don't know?

Man   Sorry. No.

Child   God.

Man   . . .

Woman   Go upstairs now.

Child   My arm hurts. Mum.

Man   You spoil him.

Woman   Would you just . . . just fucking go upstairs. Now. Please.

Child   You don't love me, Mum.

Woman   NOW.

I do not spoil him. He enjoys himself with me. What did you do? Take him to the job centre? He looks bored. He hates it with you.

Man   You shouldn't swear in front of him.

Woman   What have you done to his arm?

Man   What have *I* done?

Woman   Well, something's happened.

Man   I broke it.

Woman   What?

Man   He was mucking about, so I took his little arm, and snapped it across my knee.

Woman   What? What?

Man   Like a dry twig.

Woman   . . .

Man   I DON'T KNOW WHAT'S WRONG WITH HIS ARM. Perhaps he trapped it in something. He's just moaning again. He's spoilt.

Woman   Why did you say that?

Man   You spoilt him.

Woman   That you broke his arm. Like a . . . twig. Why did you say that? You're so weird. You're like a like a fucking . . .

Man   Maybe it's the coke we take together.

Woman   Like a fucking retard.

Man   Or the violent films I show him . . .

Woman   I'll tell social services. They'll stop you seeing him.

Man   You won't stop me seeing my son.

Woman   You said you broke his arm.

Man   I was joking, you / thick bitch.

Woman   You said you take coke . . .

Man   Coca-Cola. I was taking the piss out of you.

Woman   I love him. I don't want you near him. You don't know –

Man   I would do anything for him.

Woman   You won't even take him to a toy shop.

Man   He's spoilt. You spoilt him. You changed him.

Woman   Maybe he isn't even yours.

Man   What?

Woman   Around the time he was conceived, I was having an affair. Maybe he's not yours.

Man   We never stopped fucking till I left.

Woman   Yes, I was fucking someone else. And you. Both. He was bigger.

Man   Was it Karl?

Woman   No. Someone else.

Man   Fucking slapper.

The **Woman** *hits the* **Man.**

Woman   Your breath still smells bad. Can you leave? I don't want you looking after him again. I'm calling our solicitor. You better do the same, if you can afford it.

She faces the **Child.**

Woman   I do love you and so does Dad.

The **Child** *thinks about this.*

Child   But Dad's a wanker, isn't he?

Woman   Yes.

I'm afraid he is.

But . . .

Child   What?

Man   Hi.

Other Woman   I'm sorry.

Man   Hi.

Other Woman   Do I know you?

Man   No. But . . . can I buy you . . . ?

Can I buy you . . . ?

Can I buy you a drink?

Other Woman   . . .

Man   . . .

Older Woman   Love . . .

Other Woman   If you want.

Man   Thanks.

Older Woman   Love –

Woman   No.

Older Woman   Love . . .

Woman   No.

I haven't got the time.

Child   What?

Woman   Your dad. The person you call Dad. It might be that he isn't really. That Dad is actually someone else.

Child   Really?

Woman   Maybe. We'll have to do some tests. But would you like that? If he wasn't your dad any more?

Child   Yeah. It would be much better. Would my new real dad take me to Hamleys on Saturdays?

Woman   He might.

Child   Would he love you?

Woman   I'm with Karl.

Child   Does Karl love you?

Woman   Yes. Of course.

Child   He gets angry with you sometimes.

Woman   Sometimes we get angry with people we love, but –

Child   You get angry with me.

Woman   I'm sorry about that. I shouldn't. How's your arm?

Child   It's got a bruise on it now. Can we go to Starbucks? I want a muffin.

Older Woman   Love . . .

Woman   That means it's getting better. Starbucks? Not now, Mum.

Man   There.

Other Woman   Thanks.

Man   So, what do you do?

Other Woman   I've got a boyfriend. Thanks.

Man   I . . .

Other Woman   You were trying to chat me up, right?

Man   Yes. I suppose so.

Other Woman   I've got a boyfriend. So don't bother. Thanks for the drink.

She laughs.

Older Woman   Love . . .

Child   Mum.

Woman   What?

Child   Granny.

Woman   I know. I know. What?

*The **Older Woman** has urinated on herself.*

Woman   Oh. Mum. You're a fucking pain.

*The **Woman** starts to mop up the urine.*

Older Woman   Love . . . Sorry.

Woman   Why didn't you call someone?

Older Woman   I did.

Child   Can we go to Starbucks?

Woman   I should hire someone.

Older Woman   I hate all this.

Woman   Maybe a home then.

Older Woman   Don't be like that.

Child   Mum.

Woman   I'm coming. God, Mum, there's enough of it, isn't there?

Older Woman   You're horrible to me.

Woman   I'm joking.

Older Woman   You think this is funny?

Woman   The only way I can get through it. It's this, or not coming at all. Sorry.

Older Woman   Can't you show me the tiniest bit of love?

Woman   Not when I'm wiping you up, no. It fucking mings.

Older Woman   Don't use language like that.

Woman   Just shut up for a minute, will you?

Older Woman   Don't tell me to / shut up.

Woman   Calm down, or you'll shit yourself.

The **Older Woman** *reaches out and hits the* **Woman***. The* **Woman** *hits her back, but not as hard.*

Young Woman   Hello.

Man   Sorry. Excuse me.

Young Woman   DVD?

Man   What?

Young Woman   Cheap DVDs. New films.

Man   New?

Child   Mum.

Young Woman   Not available in the shops. Very cheap.

Child   I want to go to Starbucks.

Man   What've you got? It's for my son.

Woman   I've got to go.

Older Woman   I'm sorry. Do come back. Sorry, love. Sorry.

Woman   I find it difficult.

Older Woman   I know. I'm a pain. You don't have to come.

Woman   Yeah, but I do, don't I?

Older Woman   I suppose you do, yes.

I appreciate it though.

Where do you have to go?

Woman   I promised I'd take him to Starbucks. He likes the muffins.

Older Woman   That's nice. Does he want to come and visit me?

Woman   He doesn't like the smell.

Older Woman   Does he talk about me?

Woman   When he was younger, he used to talk about you all the time.

Older Woman   And now?

Woman   I think he's forgotten.

Older Woman   You should bring him to visit.

Woman   I'll try . . .

Older Woman   Good.

Woman   But we're busy. Wait till Christmas, maybe.

Man   Do you want to watch a film?

Child   I'm tired.

Man   I bought you a film. It's new.

Child   I'm tired.

What?

Man   *American Pie: The Wedding.*

Child   That's not new.

Man   Have you seen it?

Child   Is it a fifteen?

Man   Um. Yeah.

Child   I'll watch it later.

Man   No. Wait. It's an eighteen.

Child   Let me see it.

Man   All right. I'll put it on now.

The video comes on.

Child   This is shit. It's just a video camera in a cinema. It's a bootleg.

Man   Wait. It'll get better.

Child   No. No. This is shit.

I want to go home now.

Man   How's your arm?

Child   Like you care. You're not my dad, anyway.

Man   What?

Child   Mum told me. You're not my dad. I won't have to come and see you any more soon.

Man   Mum's wrong. I am your dad.

Child   No you're not. You're a wanker.

Man   Don't swear like that.

Child   You can't tell me what to do.

Man   Mum's lying to you. She wants you to hate me.

Child   Can I go home now?

Man   No. It's not four o'clock. We've still got a couple of hours.

Child   I want to go home.

Man   No.

Child   Let me go, you wanker.

The **Child** *starts attacking the* **Man**. *The* **Man** *doesn't respond. The* **Child** *stops and takes a step back.*

Man   I'll get the car.

Another Woman   Excuse me.

Man Yes.

Another Woman Does this train go to Victoria?

Man Um . . .

Another Woman Is it a Circle Line train?

Man Um . . . Yes . . . I think so.

Another Woman Right.

Another Man Yes, it is.

Another Woman Thank you.

Man I . . .

Another Woman . . .

Man I . . .

Another Woman I'm sorry?

Man Do you . . . ?

Another Woman Are you all right?

Man No.

Another Man Jesus.

Another Woman . . .

Man I want you to tell me something.

Woman What?

Man Did you really have an affair?

Woman Of course. Why do you think I wanted the test done?

Man Because you might have slept with someone. That doesn't mean you had an affair.

Woman This was nine years ago.

But it turns out you are his father. It doesn't matter.

Man   But this isn't about him now. I just want to know the truth.

Woman   Why?

Man   It matters to me.

Woman   Why?

Man   Whether, even though you fucked someone else, I was still the man you were emotionally faithful to.

Woman   Emotionally faithful?

Man   ...

Woman   Emotionally faithful?

Man   Okay ...

Woman   Are you with anyone at the moment?

Man   No.

Woman   Is this why you want to know? Because deep down you hope that underneath all this shit, and you letting me down, and me kicking you out, and my new husband, and our son who hates you, you hope that somewhere under all that I secretly still harbour a love for you that will never die.

Man   Yes. Exactly that.

Woman   And you hope that because right now you feel alone and unwanted by anyone, including your own son.

Man   Yes.

Woman   It was a fully operational affair. Sexually, emotionally and utterly unfaithful to you. I had finally realised that you were not the person I hoped you were. That you were, in fact, something less.

Man   But we still made love. You carried on with me through that.

Woman   I was desperate that we might find something to hold on to, but there wasn't. Not even a child could keep us together.

Man   No.

Woman   You know, even now, I still shudder at the thought that one day my son might remind me of you.

Man   Has he?

Woman   Not yet. Thank God.

Man   Why do you do this to me when you know I'm a good person?

Woman   That's not enough. You lack confidence. You are innocent. Stunted. You refuse to understand money, or responsibility. You are still a boy. You may be good or whatever but I want someone who knows when to buy me flowers, who pays bills for me, who isn't afraid of a spliff or outdoor sex, and I want someone who has a very clean car.

Man   I don't think you're happy.

Woman   I am. I just wish that you didn't exist.

Man   You want me dead.

Woman   I just wish that you were . . . erased.

Man   Erased.

Woman   That our son never needed you.

Man   Do you think he will?

Woman   Not if I can help it. We're starting fresh proceedings against you. That's what I wanted to say.

Man   On what grounds?

Woman   Abuse and neglect. His arm is still bruised. Either you did it, or you failed to stop it happening. Whatever, it doesn't look good for you.

Man   I can't afford a new solicitor.

Woman   I know.

Man

Woman

Man   Of course you do.

Woman   Is it worth it? Give him up. We don't need your money.

Man   He's my son.

Woman   No. He's nothing like you. He's another man's son now. You are just an unreliable irritant.

Man   Oh, fuck off.

Woman   Make sure you open your post.

Man   Yeah.

Mum?

Mother   Yes

Man   Why did you and Dad die?

Mother   It happens.

Man   Do you miss me?

Father   Of course. We always miss you.

Mother   We watch what you do.

Man   And? What do you think?

Mum?

What should I . . .

Have you ever seen a calf being taken away from the cow, so that the cow will give milk?

Older Woman   No.

Man   It rages. The farmer tries to fend it off with a cattle prod but it endures electricity tearing its body apart to get to its child. It breaks the pen, it screams and bleeds and scrabbles around. It takes hours for it to stop.

Older Woman   All so we can drink milk.

Man   Yeah.

Older Woman   Cows are normally so . . . placid.

Man   Well, I'm like that. I won't let him go.

Older Woman   Is this why you've come to see me?

Man   She's trying to take him away.

Older Woman   Why?

Man   She says I abused him. Apparently he hurt his arm when he was out with me.

Older Woman   How?

Man   I don't know.

Older Woman   How can you not know?

Man   I didn't see . . .

Older Woman   Anyway, she doesn't listen to me. There's nothing I can do.

Man   You always said you liked me.

Older Woman   I thought you were good for her.

Man   I used to love Christmas at your house.

Older Woman   It was nice, wasn't it? It was such a shame when you two . . .

Man   Do you think she misses me?

Older Woman   I'm sure she must. Somewhere. There must be something about you she'll never find in anyone else. You're a nice man, aren't you?

Man   How can I stop her?

Older Woman   I don't know. She's not happy. But if he hurt his arm –

Man   I don't think that was with me.

Older Woman   You're nice, but you're not reliable, are you? Maybe you shouldn't really be looking after a young boy by yourself. Even for an afternoon.

Man   They swear at him.

Older Woman   I know. But –

Man   Have you met Karl?

Older Woman   Yes.

Man   What do you think?

Older Woman   He's very rich, isn't he?

Man   Is he a good man?

Older Woman   I don't know what he is.

Man   Is he a good influence on my son?

Older Woman   From what I can tell, he looks after them both extremely well. You know they're getting a new house?

Man   Yes.

Older Woman   In Notting Hill.

Man   Yes.

Older Woman   It's got a roof terrace.

Man   . . .

Older Woman   He gives them everything they need.

Man   But is he a good man?

Older Woman   He has money. That's good. He loves them both. That's good. As for being a good man . . .

Man   Morals.

Older Woman   Listen. There's no point having morals if you keep letting people down. If you can't afford to carry out the decisions you make.

Man   I try.

Older Woman   That's not enough.

Man   Will you say something to her? Will you help me?

Older Woman   I don't want to get involved. It won't make any difference anyway.

Man   Please.

Older Woman   I'm sorry.

Man   I'm desperate.

Older Woman   No.

Man   . . .

Older Woman   Can you leave now?

Man   I'll help you in return. I'll come and visit and help you to stay. You won't have to go into a home.

Older Woman   She wouldn't like you coming here.

Man   What can I do?

Older Woman   Nothing, nothing. You shouldn't have come to me. It's not right. This isn't my business. Leave me alone.

Man   It is to do with you. It's your grandson. Don't you care?

Older Woman   Look. I want you to leave now.

Man   I won't give up.

Older Woman   Can you leave my house? Please. Now.

Man   Don't you understand?

Older Woman   Get out.

Man   Look –

Older Woman   You're frightening me.

Man   I'm not frightening you. I'm trying to make you understand. You would never have given up your daughter. I'm just doing what is natural.

Older Woman   Stand further away. I can believe you abused him.

Man   What?

Older Woman   I can believe it. Waving your arms around.

Man   No.

Older Woman   Maybe you are a violent man.

Man   No.

Older Woman   She was right to leave you. I don't know you at all. Get out.

She hits the **Man**. *She goes to do it again. He grabs her arm.*

Older Woman   I'll scream.

Man   Do you *want* to move out of here? To be sat in a home? In your own shit, until someone comes to change you? One of those people you see just sat there waiting to die?

I can look after you. Keep you here at home. Keep you happy. I promise. If you help me first. I'll look after you. I promise.

I'm your only option.

Do you understand?

Older Woman   Hello.

Child   Hello.

Older Woman   I'm really glad you came to visit me.

Child   Yeah.

Older Woman   It can get a bit lonely here all by myself.

Child   Yeah.

Older Woman   What are you up to?

Child   What do you mean?

Older Woman   Well . . . at school.

Child   Um . . . not much. Gavin's got a projector. We play games.

Older Woman   What's a projector?

Child   I want one.

Older Woman   What is it?

Child   Will you buy me one?

Older Woman   I don't know what it is.

Child   It projects stuff. Onto the wall.

Older Woman   I see.

Child   Will you buy me one?

Older Woman   You'll have to ask your mother.

Child   What's that smell?

Older Woman   I don't know.

Child   I only smell it here. Smells like a toilet.

Older Woman   It's rude to mention it.

Child   What is it? Have you wet yourself?

Older Woman   . . .

Child   . . .

Older Woman   Yes.

Child   . . .

Older Woman   If you ask these things you must expect an honest answer.

Child   That's gross.

Older Woman   That's what it's like being old.

Child   What's wrong with you?

Older Woman   My bladder won't hold in the urine.

Child   Sick.

Older Woman   Yes. I'm ill. Getting worse, too.

Child   Are you going to die?

Older Woman   Yes.

Child   When?

Older Woman   Soon.

Child   Now?

Older Woman   Maybe. Soon.

Child   I don't understand.

Older Woman   Love.

Woman   Hang on.

Child   Mum.

Woman   What?

Child   I don't get it.

Older Woman   Love.

Woman   No. Mum. No. Mum.

Older Woman   Love.

Woman   What did you tell him?

Older Woman   The truth. Where is he?

Woman   He's at a friend's house now. He didn't want to come again. You scared him last time.

Older Woman   How are you getting on?

Woman   Fine.

Older Woman   Do you see his father much?

Woman   Every Saturday.

Older Woman   It's important a boy sees his father, isn't it?

Woman   Not when his father is a dangerous twat, no.

Older Woman   You shouldn't talk like that.

Woman   Please get over it, Mum. Watch some television. This is the twenty-first century. This is how we speak.

Older Woman   He may have his flaws but, well, he is the boy's . . .

Woman   Two weeks ago, when my son came back, he had a bruise on his arm.

Older Woman   Well, you don't know –

Woman   It's still there. It isn't going away.

Older Woman   You don't know –

Woman   I know enough. I've seen it. Why do you think I kicked him out?

Older Woman   I just think you shouldn't try to stop him seeing his own son.

Woman   How did you know I wanted to?

Older Woman   I . . .

Woman   How did you know that?

Older Woman   . . .

Woman   Listen to me. How did you know?

Older Woman   I –

Woman   Stay out of my life.

Older Woman   I guessed that you would.

Woman   No.

Older Woman   . . .

Woman   From him?

Older Woman

Woman   Has he spoken to you? Visited you here?

Older Woman   He –

Woman   Fucking –

Older Woman   He was worried.

Woman   What did he tell you?

Older Woman   He just wants to keep in contact. He wanted me to have a word.

Woman   Why would you do that?

Older Woman   I –

Woman   Did you tell him I don't give a shit what you think? Why would you even try?

Older Woman   I just thought –

Woman   I fucking hate you / for what you used to do to me.

Older Woman   Don't swear.

Woman   Don't you dare tell me how to be a parent. You were useless. What you did to me.

Older Woman   I looked after you.

Woman You scared me. I used to hope Dad would get drunk because it might mean he stood up for himself. You made him small. When he died –

Older Woman I don't –

Woman When he died, I bet his last breath was a sigh of relief that you had finally shut the fuck up.

Older Woman

Woman

Young Woman Hello.

Man Hello.

Young Woman Looking for company?

Man Yes.

Some company.

Young Woman If you pay me. I don't care.

Man Oh. Right. No. Sorry.

Older Woman I still don't think that you should ruin your son's life for your own personal reasons.

Woman I don't want you near him any more.

Older Woman Don't say that.

Woman You could only do bad things to us.

Older Woman No. Please.

No.

I had to do it.

I had to try. He threatened me.

Woman He . . .

Older Woman He threatened me. Held my arm tightly. Said if I didn't help him, he would put me in a home.

Woman   He can't do that.

Older Woman   I was confused.

He made me.

Woman   Write this down. I need this.

Older Woman   Yes.

Man   She's fucking lying. I didn't do anything like that.

Woman   You went round to her house.

Man   Yes.

Woman   You wanted her to talk me into stopping proceedings.

Man   Yes.

Woman   Did you touch her?

Man   . . .

Woman   Did you touch her?

Man   Jesus.

Woman   Did you hold her arm?!

Man   She hit me and I restrained her.

Woman   She's in a fucking wheelchair.

Man   She got upset.

Woman   Why?

Man   She thought . . . I don't know.

Woman   Did you threaten her?

Man   I offered to help her.

Woman   She's scared of you.

Man   I didn't want to upset her.

Woman   This will count against you. She will tell them what you did.

Man   Please. You know me. You know I wouldn't hurt anyone. I just want to see my son.

Woman

Man   I don't know what to do.

Woman   Start again. Somewhere else. Without us.

Man   No.

Young Woman   What shall I do?

Man   Just sit with me.

Young Woman   Okay.

Man   . . .

. . .

. . .

Just having you here makes me feel dirty. Sorry.

Young Woman   Doesn't bother me.

Man   Are you happy? Doing . . . what you do?

Young Woman   Selling DVDs?

Man   No. I mean. This.

Young Woman   Of course not.

Man   Do you have a boyfriend?

Young Woman   Yes.

Man   Does he hit you?

Young Woman   No.

Man   Do you take drugs together?

Young Woman   Sometimes.

Man   Does he love you?

Young Woman   Very much.

Man   Why do you do this then?

Young Woman   Our son is a baby. We have to live.

Man   What's your son's name?

Young Woman   Nikolai.

Man   Nikolai. You must love him very much.
To do this.

Young Woman   Of course. I would die for him.

Man   Of course you would.

Young Woman   . . .

Man   Of course . . .

Young Woman   . . .

Man   Actually . . .

Young Woman   . . .

Man   . . .

Young Woman   Yes?

Man   . . .

Young Woman   . . .

Man   . . . can I have a blow job, please?

Young Woman   Of course.

She goes to give him a blow job.

After a few moments, she looks up at him.
Something's wrong.

Woman   Where is he?

Child   Where are we going?

Where are we going?

Woman   Where is he?

Child   Where are we going?

Man   Be quiet.

Child   Where are we going?

Woman   Where's he gone?

Older Woman   What?

Man   I said shut up.

Woman   It's gone four o'clock.

Child   Where are we going?

Man   We're not going back home today.

Child   What?

Woman   Where is he?

Man   We're not going back.

Child   Does Mum know?

Man   No.

Child   I want to go home.

Man   You can't.

Child   I want to. You let me.

Man   You can't.

Child   Let me go, you wanker.

Man   Don't swear.

Child   Let me go. Now.

*The **Man** goes to the **Child** and ties his hands behind his back.*

Child   Ow.

It hurts.

Woman   Hello?

Man   He's fine. He's with me.

Woman   What the fuck are you doing?

Man   He's staying with me.

Woman   Bring him back.

Man   I can't. He'll be safe.

Woman   You bring him back, or I'll fucking castrate you. /
I'll take an axe to your skull.

Man   You made me do this.

Child   Mum.

Woman   Is that him?

Man   Yes.

Woman   Where are you?

Man   You know why I had to do this, don't you?

Woman   You're not clever enough. We'll find you.

Man   Do you want to say goodbye to him?

Woman   . . .

. . .

Yes.

Child   Hello.

Woman   I'm coming to get you.

Child   Dad's tied my hands up.

Woman   Your dad's being a wanker, but I'm coming to get you soon. Don't worry.

Child   All right. I love you, Mummy.

Woman   I love you too.

Child   Goodbye.

Woman   Don't say that.

Don't . . .

Hello?

Hello?

Child   Where are we?

Man   I can't tell you that.

Child   Are we in Britain?

Man   I can't tell you. I'm sorry.

Child   I'm bored. I haven't been outside for ages.

Man   It'll be a while yet.

Child   You go out.

Man   I go to get food.

Child   I think Mum will find me.

Man   What makes you think that?

Child   She's clever.

Man   So am I.

Child   You're stupid.

Man   No. How do you know that?

Child   What?

Man   What makes you think I'm stupid?

Child   You are.

Man   No. You've been told that I'm stupid. Mum told you that. Didn't she?

Child   Yeah.

Man   You see.

Child   Because you are.

Man   No.

Child   You're thick. I've seen you in shops. On the Tube. You don't know stuff. People look at you like you're special or something.

Man   Don't say things like that. It's horrible.

Child   So Mum'll find you because she's cleverer than you.

Man   We'll see.

Child   I miss her.

Man   I'm sorry.

Child   I've never missed you.

Man   You've never really known me.

Child   I've been out with you every week of my life. I think I do.

Man   There's loads of stuff you don't know about me.

Child   Like what?

Man   I got a first in philosophy from Bristol University.

I lived in America for two years.

I can make kites.

I used to be the best in my street at arcade games.

You probably don't even know what they are, do you?

Child

Man   I was in the rugby A-team at school.

I used to own a motorbike –

Child   I knew some of that already.

Man   But not all of it.

Child   No. But I don't really care.

Man   Don't you want to get to know me?

Child   No.

I don't think I like you.

Man   What do you like?

Child   I don't know.

Man   Come on.

Child   Having fun.

Man   When do you have fun?

Child   With my friends at school.

Man   What do you do with them?

Child   Stuff.

Man   What else?

Child   When we went to the wrestling.

Man   Did Karl take you?

Child   Yeah.

Man   What did you like about that?

Child   It's cool.

Man   Okay.

Child   We was shouting at them, and one comes over to us, and says he's going to rip Dad's head off cos he said he was pussy.

Man   Dad.

Child   . . .

Man

Child   Yeah.

Man   You call him 'Dad'.

Child   Yeah. He wanted me to.

Man   . . .

Child   Well, he is really, isn't he?

Man   No. He's not.

Child   Yeah, he is. Really. I mean, like you are, but . . . most of the time you're not there so –

Man   It's different now.

Child   No. Mum'll find us. Or Dad will. He'll find you and if he doesn't kill you, you'll get sent to prison.

Man   Would you care?

Child   If he killed you?

No.

Man   I think you would a bit.

Child   No.

Man   Do you remember when we went out and had fun?

Child   No. I've forgotten.

Man   Do you remember going down the station and watching the trains? Counting the carriages. You used to love that.

Child   No. I hated it. It was shit.

Man   That's not true.

Child   Trains? God.

Man   And we used to have races in the park. Who could get from tree to tree first.

Child   I know.

Man   You liked it.

Child   It was all right.

Man   Yeah. Remember?

Child   It was all right. It wasn't that good. I was a kid.

Man   Maybe we can have fun again, now?

Child   No.

Man   Somewhere in you, you still love me.

Child   Shut up. No.

Woman   I miss you.

Child   I miss you too, Mum.

Man   It'll pass. It'll get better.

Woman   I don't think we'll find them.

Older Woman   I'm sorry for what I did.

Woman   I'm so scared.

Older Woman   You can talk to me.

Woman   I don't want to.

Older Woman   He'll look after him.

Woman   He'll try. But I'm scared what will happen when he fails.

Older Woman   He loves him.

Woman   That's not enough. You used to tell me you loved me.

Older Woman   I do.

Woman   See?

Most people really have no idea.

Man   I remember the night you were born. Your mother was all sweaty and tired. She was beautiful. We sat on the bed, with you in our arms. We named you, and I planned our future together. Maybe a brother or sister to come. A bigger house. Holidays. Grandchildren. She fell asleep, so did you, and I watched you both all night. I thought I had become someone different that night. I was a father, a grown-up. A man. I would protect you both for ever. I would always make sure you were safe. Both of you. Of course it turns out now she had already been sleeping with someone else. It turns out that maybe she was just a slut all along.

Woman   I'm dreaming of you.

Man   Are you?

Woman   Not you.

Child   Mum.

Woman   You.

Child   I'm dreaming of playing on the Xbox with you.

Woman   Me too.

Child   Are you?

Woman   Who's winning?

Child   Me.

Woman   Of course.

Child   You're a bit rubbish.

Man   I wish I did that with you.

Woman   . . .

Child   . . .

Man   Don't you two remember the good times?

Woman   There were a few.

Child   When we went to that theme park.

Man   Don't they count for anything?

Woman   No.

Child   I don't want to be here.

Man   Well, I'm starting something new.

Woman   I suppose you are.

Child   Mum.

Man   Are you awake?

Child   I want Mum. I want to go home.

Man   I'll look after you.

Child   No. It's not the same. What about my friends?

Man   You'll make new ones.

Child   No.

My arm.

Man   Is it still . . . ?

Child   It's gone black.

Man   Let me have a look.

Child   It's getting worse. It really hurts.

Man   Did you go to a doctor?

Child   He said it was a sprain.

Man   Sprains don't go black.

Child   What's wrong with me?

Man   I don't know.

Child   I should go to hospital.

Man   We can't. You can't leave the house.

Child   Don't you care?

Man   Of course . . . but . . .

Child   I might die.

Man   If I let you go now, I'll never see you again. Ever.

Child   What if I die?

Man   That won't happen.

Child   How do you know?

Man   We'll give it a couple of days.

Child   Then what?

Man   We'll give it a couple of days.

Child   Karl will be after you by now.

Man   I'm scared.

Child   He'll find you.

Man   Will he?

Child   Yes. Why don't you stop now? Give yourself up.

Man   No.

Child   You wouldn't go to prison.

Man   Yes I would, and they would never let me see you again.

Child   Why do you want to see me? / I'm horrible to you.

Man   You're my son.

Why are you so horrible to me?

Child   You left us.

Man   Your mum kicked me out. I wanted to stay.

Child   You're not very good. I want a dad that's strong. And rich.

Man   Are those things really important to you?

Child   Yeah.

You don't even like football.

Man   No.

Child   So who would take me?

Man   Who do you support?

Child   You don't even know.

Man   I wanted you to read books. / To like art.

Child   I don't like books. They're gay.

I'm good at art.

Man   Are you?

Child   Yeah. I showed you my picture. Don't you remember?

Man   Yes. Now I do. It was great.

Child   I got an A.

Man   I bet.

Child   Yeah.

Woman   It won't be long before someone sees him. His photo was on the news.

Older Woman   It's sad.

Woman   Karl's out now. He says he'll find him before the police.

Older Woman   What will he do if he finds him?

Woman   I don't care. I want my son back.

Older Woman   Are you all right, love?

Woman   No.

Older Woman   Come here.

Woman   No.

Older Woman   I'll hug you.

Woman   It's too late for you to start that now.

Older Woman   Maybe I've changed.

Woman   . . .

Older Woman   It's not too late.

Give me a chance.

Give me a fucking chance.

Woman   God.

Mum.

God.

Older Woman   You see, love.

I have changed.

I've been watching fucking television.

Child   We're in Scotland.

Man   What makes you think that?

Child   I heard someone go past, first thing this morning.

They had a Scottish accent.

Man   Maybe.

Child   What's that?

Man   A bandage for your arm.

Child   It's worse.

Man   We'll give it another day.

Child   I'll shout all night for help.

Man   No one will hear you. Put this on.

Child   I just want it to stop.

Man   Swallow this. It'll help the pain.

Woman   What about his arm?

Another Woman   I know him. I know that man. He looked . . .

Another Man   Jesus.

Another Woman   Lonely.

Man   Does that feel better?

Child   Yes. Thank you. Thanks, Dad.

The **Man** *kisses the* **Child** *on the forehead.*

Man   I'm so sorry about all this. I really am.

Child   I know.

Man   Is there a bit of you that loves me? Somewhere?

Child   . . .

Man   Or at least feels sorry for me.

Child   I do. I do feel sorry for you.

Maybe I love you. I don't know.

I wouldn't want to never see you again.

I do remember the trains.

I didn't enjoy it. Even then. I found it boring.

But I do remember it.

And I remember how much you liked it.

And at the time that made me happy.

The door of the room opens and **Karl** *walks in, from outside.*

Karl   So it is you.

Surprise.

Man   Stay in the other room.

Child   No.

Karl   What did your mum tell you when you were young?

Be kind?

Polite?

Well?

Well?

What did she tell you?

Man   She told me to be good.

Karl   Yeah.

Sit down.

Good.

Because we need to have a talk about –

Man   I'm not letting him go.

Karl   Um.

Sit down.

Good.

Because we need to talk, don't we?

When I was young and I did something wrong, my dad used to hit me round the back of the head. That was a good lesson. It taught me about consequences. We know all about consequences, don't we?

Child   Yeah.

Karl   That you have to take responsibility for what you do.

Do you agree?

Man   How did you find me?

Karl   Do you agree?

Man   Yes.

Karl   Good. I went to your flat the night you left. Just pushed open your door cos the lock's not working. You should fix that. I checked your computer. And I found that it still had on it all the holiday homes in Scotland you'd been trying to book. So that narrowed it down.

Man   What about the police?

Karl   I took your computer with me.

I wanted to find you first. But they won't be long now.

Man   Is she with you?

Karl   No.

Man   Does she know you're here?

Karl   Not yet.

Man   What do you want, then?

You're not taking him away.

Karl   Yes.

But that's not what we're going to talk about now.

Man   No. He's staying with me.

Karl   We're going to talk about how you make it up to my wife. And me and my son.

Child   Dad . . .

Karl   My son.

Man   He's not.

Child   Dad.

Man   Stop it.

Karl   His arm's black.

Man   . . .

Karl   You left his arm to rot.

Man   No.

Karl   You left his arm to rot.

You are a lame cunt.

Aren't you?

Man   Shut up.

Karl   So what are you going to do? To make amends.

Man   . . .

Karl   You're going tell him that you hope his arm gets better. Then you're going to say goodbye to my son.

Man   No.

Karl   You will. Or I'll tear your arm off with my hands.

Man   No.

Karl   Say goodbye.

Man   No. Come here.

Karl   Stay there. Say goodbye.

Man   Fuck you.

Karl   Don't swear in front of him.

Man   Get out.

Now.

Karl *grabs his arm, and twists it.*

Karl   Say goodbye.

Say goodbye.

Say goodbye.

Child   Dad . . .

Karl   Say goodbye.

Say goodbye.

Say goodbye.

Child   Dad.

Karl   Go to the car.

Child   No. Dad. Stop it.

Karl   Get into the car now.

Child   Stop. Fucking stop.

He breaks up the two men.

It's not right.

Karl   Your mum's been crying. She's probably crying right now.

Child   Yeah. But I don't like it.

Karl   Go outside. Get in the car. I'll be there in a minute.

Child   . . .

Karl   It's all right. We're just going to talk.

I thought you liked wrestling.

Child   . . .

Karl   Little pussy, aren't you?

Child   No.

Karl   Go and get in the car, then.

Child   Okay.

Karl   You not going to say goodbye?

Child   Goodbye, Dad.

Man   I'll see you in a minute.

Child   He's going to kill you now, I think.

Man   I'll see you in a minute.

Child   Goodbye, Dad.

Man

Karl   Little pussy.

Man   Don't call him that.

Karl   I'm doing him a favour. If he learns how life works now, he will be happy. He will be a success.

Man

Karl

Man   So what now?

Karl   When the police get here I'll say you refused to let him go.

I did what I had to.

Stand up.

The **Man** *stands.*

Karl   Come here.

If you don't I'll make it worse.

Karl *hits the* **Man.**

The **Man** *falls to the ground.*

Karl   Stand up.

Come here.

The **Man** *stands. Walks towards* **Karl.**

Karl *hits him hard.*

The **Man** *falls to the ground.*

Karl   Stand up.

Come here.

The **Man** *stands. Walks towards* **Karl.**

Karl *hits him hard.* **Karl** *laughs.*

Karl   Stand up.

Come here.

The **Man** *stands, just.*

Child   Dad. Stop it.

The **Man** *rages. He tears up the room. He tries to beat up* **Karl.** *He throws every object at him.* **Karl** *just stands, watching. Occasionally pushing him away.*

The **Man** *beats and beats at* **Karl.** *Destroys everything in the room. Eventually there is nothing left that he can do and he runs out of energy and sits on the floor.*

Child   Are you all right?

. . .

Dad?

Man   Yes.

Child   I told you he was tough.

Man   He likes wrestling.

Child   Yeah. I'm sorry he hit you.

Man   . . .

Child   Why did it take so long to fight back?

Man   I don't agree with it.

Child   You have to fight back, or you get beaten up.

Man   Sometimes it's best not to.

Child   And get messed up?

Man   Yeah.

Child   Doesn't work. Your nose looks broken.

Man   Maybe . . .

Child   Look.

Man   Yeah. Where is he?

Child   He's gone out. To make a phone call.

Man   I'm surprised he left you here with me.

Child   He's not scared of you.

Man   No.

Child   Are you going to do anything else? To keep me here?
Now.

Man   Like what?

Child   I don't know. Get a knife.

Kill him.

Man   Would you like that?

Child   No.

Man   Then why ask?

Child   I liked it when you were fighting him.

Man   Why?

Child   It was good.

Man   Were you proud of me?

Child   Yeah.

It was like you were a wrestler. Going mental.

Man   I'm not proud of it.

Child   Okay.

Karl   It's your mum. Want to talk to her?

Child   Mum?

Woman   Steven.

Oh my God.

The **Child** *starts crying.*

Woman   Oh my God.

Are you all right?

Are you all right?

Are you all right?

Child   My arm still hurts.

Woman   Karl's going to take you to a hospital now.

Listen to me. It's all right.

Oh God. Oh God. Oh God. Oh God.

What did he do to you?

Child   They had a fight.

Woman   I know.

Child   Dad, Karl, won easily.

Woman   Yes.

Child   But real Dad. He went mental too. It was good.

Karl   Come on.

Woman   Come here.

The **Child** *runs from the* **Man** *to the* **Woman.** **Karl** *joins them.*

Woman   You're safe.

Man   . . .

Child   Mum.

Woman   My child.

Child   Dad.

Woman   I know.

Man   Goodbye.

Bye.

Mum?

Mother   Yes.

Man   Why did you tell me all this?

Mother   All what?

Man   That it is better to be polite. To put others first. Not to be violent. To turn the other cheek. Not to treat people as rivals but as friends. To try to be moral and good, and not selfish.

To love.

Mother   Because it's right.

Man   No. It's not.

Look at me.

It's not how the world is.

Father   No. It's not.

But your mother and I are still agreed.

That it's right.

Man   But it doesn't work.

Does it?

Blackout.

Lucy Prebble

Enron

'The reasonable man adapts himself to the world;
the unreasonable one persists in trying to adapt
the world to himself. Therefore all progress
depends on the unreasonable man.'

George Bernard Shaw

*For my father.
An unreasonable man*

Lucy Prebble lives in London. Her first full-length play, *The Sugar Syndrome* (Royal Court Theatre, 2003) was awarded the George Devine Award and TMA Award for Best New Play in 2004. She also won the 2004 Critics' Circle Award for Most Promising Playwright. Her second play, *Enron* (Chichester Festival Theatre and Royal Court Theatre in a joint production with Headlong Theatre, 2009) was the winner of Best New Play at the 2009 TMA Theatre Awards. The play transferred to the West End in 2010. She created the TV series *Secret Diary of a Call Girl*, first broadcast on ITV2 in the UK in 2007 and on Showtime in the United States in 2008.

Author's Note

Though this play is inspired by the real events leading up to the Enron collapse, it should not be seen as an exact representation of events. It is the author's fiction, as changes have been made for dramatic effect.

For a thorough journalistic exploration of the facts I would direct the reader to Bethany McLean and Peter Elkind's *The Smartest Guys in the Room*, Loren Fox's *Enron: The Rise and Fall*, Kurt Eichenwald's *Conspiracy of Fools* and the website of the *Houston Chronicle* among many other sources. I would also highly recommend John Kenneth Galbraith's accounts of *The Great Crash 1929* for an insight into our financial follies, and also the works of Professor Niall Ferguson.

I would like to offer my great thanks to those who have taken the time to speak with me to aid my research.

Enron premiered in a Headlong Theatre, Chichester Festival Theatre and Royal Court production at the Minerva Theatre, Chichester, on 11 July 2009. The first performance in London was at the Royal Court Jerwood Theatre Downstairs, Sloane Square, London, on 17 September 2009. The cast was as follows:

News Reporter	Gillian Budd
Lehman Brother, **Trader**	Peter Caulfield
Security Officer, **Trader**	Howard Charles
Trader	Andrew Corbett
Claudia Roe	Amanda Drew
Congresswoman, Business Analyst, Irene Gant	Susannah Fellows
Arthur Andersen, **Trader**	Stephen Fewell
Lehman Brother, **Trader**	Tom Godwin
Andy Fastow	Tom Goodman-Hill
Lou Pai, Senator	Orion Lee
Hewitt, News Reporter, Prostitute	Eleanor Matsuura
Ken Lay (Enron Chairman / CEO)	Tim Pigott-Smith
Ramsay, **Trader**	Ashley Rolfe
Jeffrey Skilling	Samuel West
Daughter	Cleo Demetriou, Ellie Hopkins
Lawyer, **Trader**	Trevor White

All other parts played by members of the company.

Director Rupert Goold
Designer Anthony Ward
Lighting Designer Mark Henderson
Composer and Sound Designer Adam Cork
Video and Projection Designer Jon Driscoll
Choreographer Scott Ambler

Enron transferred to the Noël Coward Theatre, London, on 16 January 2010, and opened on Broadway at the Broadhurst Theatre on 27 April 2010, presented by Matthew Byam Shaw, Act, Caro Newling for Neal Street, Jeffrey Richards and Jeffrey Frankel.

Characters

Ken Lay, *Enron Chief Executive Officer (CEO)*
Jeffrey Skilling, *Enron President*
Andy Fastow, *Enron Chief Financial Officer (CFO)*
Claudia Roe, *Enron executive*
Skilling's Daughter
Arthur Andersen, *accountant*
Ramsay & Hewitt, *law firm (one male, one female)*
Sheryl Sloman, *analyst, Citigroup*
Lawyer
Irene Gant

Analysts, *J.P. Morgan*
Lehman Brothers
Lawyer
Reporter
Congresswoman
Security Officer
Senator
Court Officer
Police Officer
Employees/Market
Traders
The Board
Press
Raptors
Prostitute

Prologue

The eerie, mechanical sound of singing. It is the word 'WHY' from Enron commercials.

Three suited individuals enter, finding their way with white sticks. They have the heads of mice. Over which, the commercial's voice of:

Jeffrey Skilling (*voice-over*)   Enron Online will change the market. It is creating an open, transparent marketplace that replaces the dark, blind system that existed. It is real simple. If you want to do business, you push the button. We're trying to change the world.

The three mice-men have wandered across the stage, feeling their way with the sticks. Perhaps one turns and seems to stare at us.

A single bright light sharply illuminates the **Lawyer**.

Lawyer (*to us*)   I'm a lawyer and I'm one of the few who makes money when times are hard. When businesses fail, when unemployment rises, marriages break down and men jump to their deaths. Somebody. Divides up. The money. At times like this we are exposed to how the world really works. (I could explain to you how it works but I don't have the time and you don't have the money.) Every so often, someone comes along and tries to change that world. Can one man do that? We look at some and pray to God it isn't so. Then when things get desperate we find ourselves a great man, look up to him and demand he change things. Hypocrites. Within every great man there's a buried risk. The guy I know tried to change the world was the man behind the corporate crime that defined the end of the twentieth century and cast a shadow over this one. Now as a lawyer I choose my words carefully. So when we tell you his story, you should know it could never be *exactly* what happened. But we're going to put it together and sell it to you as the truth. And when you look at what happened here, and everything that came afterward, that seems about right. Here, in the beating heart of the economic world: America. In the heart of America, Texas. And in the heart of Texas, Houston. There was a company.

Act One

Scene One

A party in a small office at Enron. Present are: **Employees** *drinking champagne;* **Claudia Roe**, *a very attractive blonde woman of forty in a short skirt. She sticks close to the most powerful man in the room –* **Ken Lay**, *an easy, convivial man in his sixties, greeting and acknowledging every employee with practised southern hospitality;* **Andy Fastow**, *a nervy, lupine guy in his thirties, is circling with an unsettling grin.*

Fastow *is on the outskirts of the group of* **Employees**, *trying to ingratiate himself.*

Employee (*to* **Roe**)   I loved your speech, by the way.

Employee 2   Really great speech.

Roe   Oh, thank you so much.

Fastow   Quite a party.

Employee   I beg your pardon?

Lay   How you doing. Good to see you.

Lay *and* **Roe** *glide by this group, despite* **Fastow**'s *outstretched hand.*

Fastow (*one eye on* **Lay**)   Just. It's great news. About mark-to-market.

Employee 2   Oh, the accounting system.

Employee   We just came down for the champagne.

Employee 2   Tastes kind of sweet.

Roe   Should we expect a speech from you, sir?

Lay   No, Claudia, I don't think we need ourselves another speech right now. Informality. Colleagues enjoying themselves.

Fastow   Look, even Ken Lay's here.

Employee   Yeah.

Fastow   You think he plays golf?

Employee   I don't know!

Lay *magnanimously greets another couple of starstruck employees. He's like an avuncular politician.*

Fastow   Where's the guy who put this thing together?

Employee 2   What do you mean?

Fastow   Jeff Skilling.

Employee   No idea.

Fastow   The mark-to-market guy.

Employee 2   Never heard of him.

Fastow   Maybe he's not a big party guy.

Employee   Maybe you'd get on(!)

Fastow   Actually I always thought we would.

Lay   Have I met the mark-to-market guy?

Roe   Jeff Skilling. I don't know where he is.

Lay   I've only got a half-hour here. Make sure I shake his hand.

Outside the party, **Skilling** *straightens his suit, his hair. He looks like a bespectacled, overweight, balding accountant. He takes a deep breath.*

He enters the party and finds himself a drink for confidence.

Fastow   You can't get Lay away from Claws there. It's like she's his carer.

Employee   You should go talk to him!

Fastow   Yeah. You think I should?

Employee   I think you should.

Fastow   He's just a guy, I'm a guy.

Fastow   Yeah. This is how things happen!

Employee   You go, girl(!)

Roe (*noticing* **Skilling**)   There he is.

Roe *goes over to collect* **Skilling**.

Employee 2   You're a son of a bitch.

Employee   (Who is that guy?!)

Fastow *strides over to introduce himself to* **Lay**.

Roe   Jeff, come over – Ken Lay.

Skilling   'Hi, how are you.'

Roe (*sarcastic*)   'Hi, how are you.' Ken Lay.

Fastow   Hi there, Mr Lay.

Lay   Hi there, you're not Jeff Skilling, / by any chance –

Fastow   No sir, I wish I was, I'm Andy –

Lay   Andy, Andy Fastow.

Fastow   Yes sir!

Lay   I make a point of knowing people, son.

Roe *drags* **Skilling** *over to* **Lay**.

Roe   Ken –

Lay *slaps* **Skilling** *on the back*.

Lay   Here's the guy! Jeffrey 'mark-to-market' Skilling. You know Claudia. Our star abroad.

Skilling   I believe I may have seen her in *Vogue*.

Roe   That was cropped from a profile in *Forbes*.

Skilling   I'm surprised you find the time.

Roe   I'm surprised you read *Vogue*.

Lay   One of the fifty most powerful women, wasn't it?

Roe   I don't recall.

Skilling   Most powerful *women*?

Roe   Number fourteen.

Lay   That's the party I'd like to be at (!)

Skilling   I remember. There was a great bit on *Oprah* and her dogs.

Roe   We were talking mark-to-market.

Skilling   I think one of her dogs was at number twelve.

Fastow   I just wanted to say congratulations – mark-to-market, much more appropriate, much more transparent. Exactly the right thing.

Skilling   Thanks. Are you –

Fastow   Sorry. Andy, Andy Fastow, you hired me –

Roe   This new accounting system, Jeff, you think it's worth celebrating?

Skilling   You're not familiar with mark-to-market?

Roe   I'm not an accountant.

Lay   You settled for fourteenth most powerful woman in the world.

Fastow   Mark-to-market's the accounting system for all the big investment banks / on Wall Street.

Roe   Yes. But *we* are a gas and oil company.

Fastow   No, no, you see –

Skilling   We're an *energy* company. When you say 'gas and oil' people think . . . trapped wind and Arabs.

Lay (*gesturing to staff*)   I've been explaining mark-to-market but people get all tied up in knots.

Skilling   Seriously?

Lay   In what sense?

Skilling   There are people at this party who don't understand the *idea*?

Fastow   Mark-to-market lets us show the future / profits. / Hugely liberating –

Lay   / We know.

Skilling   / I know. A group of people have worked their asses off to get the SEC to understand and approve this –

Roe   And it's very much appreciated.

Skilling   Everyone gets mark-to-market here, right?

Fastow *exhales and glances at the group of employees who had teased him.*

Fastow   I've talked to some people, I don't know . . .

Skilling   I've got slides I can bring down.

Roe   No.

Skilling   It doesn't kill you? Everyone standing around celebrating their ignorance –

Roe   It's not a celebration of ignorance, Jeff, it's a party.

Skilling   These people are getting *paid*.

He takes it upon himself to clink his glass to get everyone's attention. It's a surprise. Any speech would be deemed to be **Lay***'s job.*

Skilling   Hi. Hi. Everybody. For those who don't know, I'm the reason you're here. I said I would only join this company if we started to use mark-to-market. What does that mean? Anybody? Well, it's a way for us to realise the profits we're *gonna* make *now*. If you have an idea, if you sign a deal, say that we're gonna provide someone with a supply of champagne for

the next few years at a set price, every month whatever –
Then that definite future income can be valued, at market
prices today, and written down as earnings the moment the
deal is signed. We don't have to wait for the grapes to be
grown and squashed and . . . however the hell you make
champagne. The market will recognise your idea and your
profit in that moment. And the company will pay you for it. If
you come up with something brilliant – you know, life is so
short. If you have a moment of genius, that will be rewarded
now. No one should be able to kick back in your job years
from now and take all the credit for the idea you had.

Fastow   They'll have to have their own ideas.

Skilling   Right. This guy gets it. Any questions? Anyone not
understand? OK, well. Have a party.

Skilling *turns and walks back to* **Lay,** **Roe** *and* **Fastow.**

Roe   Nicely done

Skilling *downs his drink.*

Skilling   I should have brought the fucking slides.

We see projections of the joys and stability of the 1990s.

*Bill Clinton, the break-up of the Soviet Union, Microsoft, the Internet and
the rise of the home computer and Intel,* Friends, *Nelson Mandela's election, images of Arnie in* Terminator 2.

An **Employee** *comes forward to speak to us.*

Employee 2 *(to us)*   The nineties. It's a time of little conflict
internationally, the fastest growing economy there has ever
been. And the fashions are pretty good too. There's a new
administration; a president who plays the saxophone. He's a
Democrat, but he understands the South.

It feels – genuinely – like the most exciting time to be doing
business in the history of the world. There's a feeling that the
people who are gonna change things aren't in parliaments or
palaces, but in corporate boardrooms all over the United
States of America.

Scene Two

AFTERPARTY

In a corporate boardroom, high up, **Skilling** *and* **Roe** *finish having clothed, quick sex.*

Roe   I've been thinking about mark-to-market.

Skilling   That's . . . concerning.

He is doing his trousers up. **Roe** *is pulling down her skirt and straightening herself.*

Roe   Essentially, we are deciding what our own future profits will be.

Skilling   No. The market is. You want to have this argument *now*?

Roe   All I said is, we get to decide the profits. Why would that be anything but a good thing?

Skilling   Right. But you're wrong.

Roe   Spiky.

Look at you! Look at your face!

Skilling   What?

Roe   You just changed is all.

Beat.

Roe   I'll bet you *were* a real serious kid. My oldest is like that.

Skilling   Not . . . really.

Roe   You know, I read that it's better to hire people who were bullied at school. Cos, you know, they want it more. They've got inbuilt competition.

Skilling   I wasn't bullied! I got things quicker. When you get things quicker, you begin to resent people who don't.

Roe   You thought you were special.

Skilling   No, hey, I was drunk when I told you that stuff . . . I don't want to get on the couch about it.

Roe   Oooh! 'Whatever.'

Skilling   You know what, we accept that some people are prettier than other people and their lives are probably easier, and we accept that some people are funnier – but if you're smarter, you're supposed to walk around like you're shamed by it. Like everyone's viewpoint is equally valid. Well, it's not, some people are fucking idiots.

Roe (*laughs*)   Not here.

Skilling   No, not here. Exactly.

They look out of a window over Houston.

Skilling   I love a workplace at night. No banality.

Roe   Before the market opens. The world waiting.

Beat.

Skilling   We need to talk about a thing.

Roe   Ohh! Ken told you.

Beat.

Skilling (*lying*)   Yeah.

Roe   Yeah. I like how you bring it up *after* you screwed me . . .

Skilling   / What did he say to *you*?

Roe   I'm not gonna break that confidence. But if you think when I'm president, you're getting special favours –

Skilling   Wait, Rich is leaving?!

Roe   Shit.

Skilling   You're getting *President*?

Roe   You said you knew!

Skilling   No!

Roe   You are a real son of a . . . I can't / believe –

Skilling   I was gonna say Susan and I have separated.

Beat.

Roe   Oh my God!

Skilling   Rich is leaving Enron?

Roe   Do I need to feel guilty?

Skilling   Has Lay *offered* you the job?

Roe   I can't be the cause of a marriage break up –

Skilling   I can't believe he's going.

Roe   We've only had sex three times.

Skilling   Rich is leaving (!) And it's four times.

Roe   Yes, Rich is leaving. And I had sex with you three times.

Skilling   That is wrong, but –

Roe   One, South America. Two, after the SEC announce- / ment. Three –

Skilling   / You forgot the plane.

Beat.

Roe   How are you defining sex?

Skilling   Sex. Penetration.

Roe   We didn't have penetrative sex on the Enron jet! We fooled around. I went down on you.

Skilling   That's penetration! I was penetrating your –

Roe   Oh my God, well if you want to throw that in . . . !

Skilling   I don't want to throw anything in (!) It doesn't matter, nothing will be penetrated any more.

Roe   When did Susan leave?

Skilling   Has he offered you the job?

Roe   That's none of your business. When did your wife leave?

Skilling   *I* left. She *left*. But I – *left*.

Roe   I hope I'm irrelevant.

Skilling   You are entirely irrelevant.

Roe   Good.

Beat.

Skilling   Will I have to call you Madam President?

Roe   Come on, how old are you?!

Skilling   I'm forty-two.

Roe   Yeah.

Skilling   Oh God.

Roe   Stop it. You're Harvard, you're McKinsey, you're running a whole division. You're just having a mid-life / (crisis).

Skilling   It's not that.

I just, don't think this is the world I want to live in.

Roe   Don't talk that way.

Skilling   I don't mean . . .

I've just been thinking. Waking up at night with all these ideas. Ideas for here.

You know, maybe every extraordinary thing that's ever happened was conceived by a man alone in a room at four in the morning.

Roe   I think most acts of depravity too.

Look, don't get all . . . I'm sure you've got ideas. I'll talk to Ken –

Skilling   He doesn't get me. I didn't grow up on a farm.

Roe *smiles.*

Roe   And you're a godless atheist.

Skilling   I'd like to be the other thing. Be nice.

Roe   It is nice.

She picks up her underwear and puts it in her handbag.

You gonna go home?

Skilling *shakes his head.*

Skilling   I'm going back to work.

She eyes him.

Roe   As an addendum, can I just say, previously you had an incentive equal, I believe, to mine for not disclosing this. I'd like to stress that this and the other three occasions, or four if you're gonna be a high-school girl about it, are not to be discussed or recounted at any future date. And it will not be happening again.

Skilling   Wow.

Roe   You got a Kleenex? I appear to be running.

Skilling *gets a tissue out of his pocket.* **Roe** *takes it and gently wipes all the way up her inner leg, wiping off the ejaculate that has run down her thigh.*

She tosses the Kleenex away deliberately casually and confidently strides from the office.

Scene Three

KEN LAY'S OFFICE, 1996

Bill Clinton (*on screen*)   I did not have sexual relations with that woman, Miss Lewinsky. I never told anybody to lie. Not a single time. Never.

In another office, **Ken Lay** *sits with* **Roe** *and* **Skilling** *sitting before him.*

Lay   When was Enron born? Was it in 1901 when the first Texas oilfield was discovered and Houston became the original oil town? Was it 1938 when Congress passed the Natural Gas Act regulating the energy industry, or in the eighties when Reagan freed it again?

Roe   I would –

Lay   Most folk'd say in 1985 when I oversaw the merger between Houston Natural Gas and Internorth to become head of a new unnamed company.

Skilling   Sure, that would be –

Lay   In the past folks thought the basic unit of society would be the state, or the church or, Lord help us, the political party. But we now know it's the company. And the family. And those things should be the same. A place where a group of like-minded individuals work for the betterment of themselves and for those they love. I believe in God, I believe in democracy and I believe in the company.

Now I think it's right for Rich to be leaving, I think it's the right decision. It does put me in the position of needing myself a president.

Skilling   Yes.

Roe   I imagine you'd want to indicate that Enron is not an old-fashioned, macho place to work.

Skilling   'Macho'. That's subtle.

Lay   Where is our company going? I wonder which of you knows.

Pause. **Lay** *leans back.*

The competitors look at each other.

Beat.

Roe   Ken, before he talks over me here I wanna say –

Skilling   I want to build a trading floor –

Roe   He doesn't have the skills to manage / people effectively –

Skilling   / A different sort of company. Hire the best graduates, if they're not top two per cent we don't want 'em. Make Wall Street look like Sesame Street.

Roe   / Jeff has trouble relating to others. He doesn't remember names. He called a client stupid.

Skilling   What client?

Roe   Fan Bridglen.

Skilling   I have no idea who that is.

Roe *makes a 'see?' gesture*

Skilling   You're a politician, Claud. I've never claimed to be.

Lay   Some of my best friends are politicians.

You wanna build a trading floor?

Skilling   Yes sir.

Lay   For trading?

Skilling   Ask me what I want to trade.

Lay   What were you gonna say, Claudia?

Roe   My vision. *The* international energy company. Enron: delivering gas and oil to the world.

Skilling *(spits it)*   That's a parochial vision.

Roe   *The world* is?

Jeff, sometimes I wonder if you have anger issues.

Skilling   Fuck you.

Beat.

Ask me. What. I would trade.

Lay What do you see us trading, Jeff?

Skilling Energy.

Roe Brilliant (!)

Skilling Sure, we make it. We transport it. We sell it. Why don't we *trade* it? You gotta pull back and look at this thing from above. Why do we even have to deliver the gas at all?

Roe Well, we're a gas company, Jeff.

Skilling If we got a customer wants a steady supply of natural gas and we don't have a pipeline near them, what do we do?

Lay We buy the gas off someone who does have a pipeline there and we charge the customer a little more than we pay for it.

Skilling So let's always do that. Buy from someone, sell it on. In. Out. Without ever having to deliver the gas or maintain the pipeline. We're just dealing in the numbers.

Roe We should be focusing on building more plants.

Skilling God, if you could hear yourself. 'Build more fucking powerplants.' No imagination, go crazy – What about wind farms or hydro . . . ?!

Roe *Wind farms?!* I'm sorry, I thought I was the only woman in the room.

Skilling We don't need the hard stuff.

Roe India, Africa – huge power requirements in the future –

Skilling That will take *years*! You really want to pay for people to go build pipelines along disputed borders, tribes with AK47s? You want that fucking *mess* – ?

Roe I think in the most volatile areas in the world it might be worth controlling their energy supply, yes.

Skilling Scratching around in the dirt. I'm not talking about pushing on an industry already in place. I'm trying to tell you . . . Ken, you've seen some changes in business since you started.

Lay   Sure. I'm as old as the plains.

Skilling   Well, it's time to evolve again. We *have to. America doesn't have the natural resources any more.* Not really. And that's good, that's fine. We have intellectual capital, and the best of it in the world. Look at the societies that *do* have the raw materials, how modern do they feel, really? Then take a landlocked, barren country like Switzerland. What do they do? They invent banking.

We should be coming up with new ideas. About everything. Employ the smartest people we can find. And have 'em free to look at whatever they want, free from the old assumptions about what this company is.

Roe   Sounds like hippy talk to me.

Skilling   I'm not gonna patronise you by pretending you believe what you just said.

Lay   You got one idea about trading.

Skilling   I got plenty of ideas. Mark-to-market, energy trading, that's just the beginning.

Roe   I can push through natural gas deals we already have experience of. You want power? Enron. India? Enron. South America? Enron.

Skilling   Countries are meaningless.

It's all going to be virtual. Oil and land run out.

Roe   In which case, don't you think it's worth being the only people in the world with power plants?!

Skilling   There is a whole, glistening, clean industry above what you're talking about that no one's even thought of yet.

Roe   Except you (!)

Silence.

Lay   You see, I'm like Claudia. I like holding things. In our father's day, a man worked and he saw himself in his work. If he made a table, he saw himself in the table he made. It was part of him, and he of it. I *am* oil and pipelines.

Skilling   My father was a valve salesman. I didn't want to grow up to sell valves. Tiny pieces of something bigger he never saw. There is a dignity to holding something, Ken. But your daddy was a baptist preacher. There's a dignity to giving people something they *can't* touch.

Roe   Suddenly you have a 'calling'. Well, I find it distasteful.

Skilling   I don't want to work for you. I feel I gotta say if Claudia takes this job I won't be staying.

Lay *considers the younger man and his presumption.*

Lay (*to* **Skilling**)   I think you should step out.

Skilling *tries to maintain his dignity and leaves.* **Lay** *takes* **Roe***'s hand.*

Lay (*to* **Roe**)   You know, you were always my favourite. But I'm offering Jeff the job.

As **Roe***'s dreams are shattered,* **Skilling***'s dreams are made real.*

The transformation of Enron. From discreet, regular offices, **Skilling** *and* **Lay** *oversee it becoming an open-plan, free, shiny expanse.*

It should feel like a physical liberation; a clearing of clutter.

Lay (*to us*)   Henry Ford. There's a man folk think revolutionised things. He did not. He took people out of the equation. Of which I do not approve. No, the man who ought to be remembered is Alfred P. Sloane – Head of General Motors and a great philanthropist. There was a time when the cost of the automobile meant that most Americans could never afford one. And General Motors felt there must be a way to open up that market. Over at Ford, Henry didn't care. Ford felt that only a man who'd saved every single cent for a car deserved one. And if he had not the money, he should not have the car. Never mind that meant the automobile was only available to the very rich. Now Alfred P. Sloane said, well hang on a minute, if a man will pledge to pay the full amount of the car in instalments, over time, we will provide him with one. And when we do, he will use that car to travel to a place of work, where he will make more money than he might otherwise, thus he will use that very car in his effort to make good on his promise. And in such a way the common man was given access to the automobile. And in such a way General Motors overtook Ford as the most successful and profitable company in America. And in such a way, the world is changed.

Today I am pleased to announce the appointment of Jeffrey Skilling to the post of President of the Enron corporation.

Skilling *and* **Lay** *shake hands.*

Skilling *looks down at the Enron he envisioned beneath him: glass, reflective surfaces, futuristic design, open spaces, a huge trading floor.*

Scene Four

AN ORGY OF SPECULATION

Skilling   Let's trade.

Magical music.

Above us somewhere there is a twinkle of gold. And then another of silver somewhere else. And then more – commodities like stars in the sky.

The sound of singing, each their own different song. It builds to an atonal babble of commodity prices and bids. It's a musical cacophony of the trading floor. Over time, the voices all conjoin to meet in a pure, single note. It is beautiful.

Voices (*sung*)
   Gold. Up twenty-five.

The gold glints somewhere in the auditorium.

The voices and notes become an atonal mess again. Eventually blending to everyone singing a single note and price.

Voices (*sung*)
Aluminum. Down one.

A shimmer from aluminum.

And again the clamour builds up before finding a commodity value in one distinct harmony.

Voices (*sung*)
Natural gas. Up five seventy-one.

Voices (*sung*)
Orange juice. Down fourteen.

They split again into babble.

Voices (*sung*)
Pork belly. Up seven twenty-four.

This empty, beautiful purity in **Skilling**'s *head is interrupted by the reality of the* **Traders**' *arrival.*

The **Traders** *flood the stage. The stock price rises.*

The chaos, the physicality, the aggression and shouting of a trading floor. This simmers to doing deals, buzzing on phones and computers making money. Overlap is fine.

A melee of sound and trading and speculation into –

Trader 5   I'm waiting on a call from Louisiana. Are you in play?

Trader 3   Speculation confirmed.

Trader 6   Spread's widened.

Trader 3   Another bid. What's the market doing?

Trader 5   What's the market doing?

Trader 7   Crude is up.

Trader 5 Gimme price.

Trader 7 Twenty-three.

Trader 1 Yes!

Trader 4 If market closes below twenty-one, this guy's fucked.

Trader 1 I really am.

Trader 2 You're fucked.

Trader 1 I lose a million.

Trader 6 Hey, it's *at* twenty-three –

Trader 2 *For now* . . .

Trader 5 That's off the back of upgraded / carbon price forecasts.

Trader 1 / Carbon price forecasts. Jesus Christ.

Trader 7 Dropping!

Trader 1 Oh fuck. I'm gonna lose a million dollars. Fuck.

Trader 3 Hey, market's not closed yet.

Trader 5 There goes your bonus.

Trader 1 Bonus ain't shit. I just don't want Jeff Skilling up my ass.

Trader 6 Chill, dude. Skilling gets it. He's a fucking trader, man.

Trader 3 You've drunk the Kool-Aid.

Trader 5 Tell him about last week.

Trader 6 Oh yeah. You were in Dallas.

Trader 4 Is this the shit with me?

Trader 6 Look at this kid, twenty-six years old – hey, you tell it.

Trader 4   So I had a big loss.

Trader 1   How much?

Trader 6   Tell him.

Trader 4   I got down twenty million / dollars.

Trader 8   Twenty million.

Trader 4   In one day.

Trader 5 *whistles the loss.*

Trader 4   It's not a good day.

Trader 5   And it's the day Jeff's coming down to visit the floor.

Trader 4   And I'm the skunk at the lawn party.

Trader 2   He's pacing and crying around the place.

Trader 4   It was twenty million dollars!'

Trader 6   'It was twenty million dollars!'

Trader 5   Any Wall Street bank'd push him off the roof then check his teeth for gold.

Trader 2   We thought it was hilarious.

Trader 4   You did. I remember that.

Trader 5   And Skilling's heard about the loss.

Trader 2   Sure he has.

Trader 4   There's nothing Skilling don't know. And he comes in, he makes a bee-line for my desk and everybody watches.

Trader 2   He goes over and he puts his arm round this fuck, in front of everybody and he says, what does he say?

Trader 4   He says, 'Only people prepared to lose are ever gonna win.' And he slaps me on the back and he leaves.

Trader 5   Slaps him on the back.

Trader 4   And he leaves!

Trader 2   True story.

Trader 4   And that's Jeffrey fucking Skilling.

Trader 2   Hey, anyone invited to Mexico here?

Trader 5   For what?

Trader 2   One of Skilling's death weekends, man! Rolling jeeps and motorcycles and wotnot. Someone's gonna fuckin die /

Trader 5   That is the coolest thing.

Trader 4   Dan Rice was on fire and shit / the last time.

Trader 2   And Fastow gets to go. Lapdog motherfucker.

Trader 7   Going up!

Trader 4   You seen that double-breasted douchebag? Thinks he's Sinatra.

Trader 2   What the fuck Skilling see in the guy?

Trader 3   We're going into electricity, a whole new market and you get Fastow to run it, I mean, really, *Fastow?*

Suddenly, **Fastow** *enters, all smooth self-importance. All the* **Traders** *react mockingly.*

Trader 5   Oh jeez, here it is.

Fastow   Yeah, hi. You gotta help with some figures. The electricity retail market.

Trader 3   You're kidding right? We're closing deals here.

Fastow   I'm here on behalf of Jeff Skilling.

One of the **Traders** *makes a 'whoo' noise.*

Trader 2   We don't have shit on your retail markets. We're traders.

Fastow   Just get me whatever numbers you've got on electricity suppliers you trade with, that's your fucking job.

Trader 2   No, that's your fucking job and you're asking *me* to do it. Skilling gets that, right?

Fastow *goes for* **Trader 2**, *physically. He gets right in his face, aggressively.*

Trader 5   Crude down six.

Trader 1   Fuck, man!

Fastow   I don't have time for you to be whoever the fuck you are!

Trader 3   We don't have other companies' figures lying around, Andy. You gotta call 'em up.

Fastow   Don't tell me what I got to do.

Trader 2   Is this guy serious?

Fastow *touches him.*

Fastow   I'm very serious.

Trader 3   Whoa whoa whoa.

Trader 2   Come on then, motherfucker, you wanna play with the big boys?

Trader 2 *shoves* **Fastow**, *who squares right up to him, fearless.*

Trader 3   Come on, Fastow, you'll get destroyed.

He moves in to break it up.

Fastow *is pulled away.*

Trader 1   Oh God, crude's falling.

Trader 5   You're gonna take it in the ass.

Fastow   I want that recorded.

Trader 3   I gotta fine you for that.

Trader 2   Fuck, Clem.

Trader 3   That was physical on the floor.

Trader 2   But it's Fastow!

Trader 3   I gotta take two hundred.

Fastow *watches, pleased.* **Trader 2** *reaches into his pockets and doles out a whole heap of bills on the floor.*

Trader 2   Take *five* hundred. Cos I'm gonna finish.

Trader 2 *swings around and hits* **Fastow**, *who, not expecting this, scrambles out of the way into other* **Traders**, *who all take a pop at him. Other* **Traders** *mock and physically berate him. One shows him his penis.*

Fastow   (That's illegal.)

As **Fastow** *beats a hasty retreat he tries to maintain some dignity.*

Fastow   I'll remember that when I'm CFO.

He exits.

Trader 2   Did everybody see that?

Trader 4   Big hat, no cattle. Motherfucka.

Trader 3 (*genuinely staggered*)   Is it me or did that guy just come in here and say, tell me how to sell electricity?

Trader 5   I think he did.

Trader 3   Unbelievable. Market closing!

The bell rings for end of trading.

Trader 1   This is it, this is it!

Trader 4   What's the price?

Trader 5   Someone call it!

Improvisation of trading at its highest pitch.

Market closes.

Trader 4   Boom!

Trader 1   COME ON!

Trader 1 *is delighted, sweating, filled with testosterone and joy.*

Trader 4   You're one lucky fucking cock-sucking cash-loving son of a bitch.

Trader 1 (*to us*)   I wish you knew. You're right. You were right. It's there in a number right in front of you and no one can dispute it. There's just you and the guy on the other end, and who can move faster and who can move smarter. But it's not just up here, there's something . . . primal. You never felt more alive in your life. Can tell by the movement of a guy across the floor what way things are going. You hear everybody and also you hear one voice. Closest thing there is to hunting. Closest thing there is to sex. For a man, that is.

Lights of commodity prices over the faces of all the **Traders***, a sea of figures.*

Alan Greenspan (*on screen*)   (Clearly, sustained low inflation implies less uncertainty about the future, and lower risk premiums imply higher prices of stocks and other earning assets. But how do we know when irrational exuberance has unduly escalated asset values . . .) irrational exuberance . . . irrational exuberance . . .

Scene Five

TRIMMING THE FAT

The sound of motorbikes revving, screeching brakes, the hum of manly pursuits.

Split scene.

Below: Enron gym. **Skilling** *is on a running machine, in sports clothes. He's pushing himself and relishing the physical challenge.*

Above: **Ken Lay**'s *office.* **Lay** *and* **Roe** *are meeting.*

Below: **Fastow** *enters the gym with trepidation in a suit.*

Skilling   Andy Fastow.

Fastow   You want me to go wait somewhere?

Skilling   This is the meeting. Get on.

He gestures to the running machine beside him. **Fastow**, *nervous, takes off his shoes and jacket and gets on the machine.*

Skilling *immediately ups it to a run for* **Fastow**.

Fastow   I'm sorry I screwed up Electricity.

Skilling   Yeah, you have. You know I was supposed to announce it on the tour today?

Fastow   Yeah. I tried, I really –

Skilling   I heard you got aggravated on some trader?

Fastow   I –

Skilling   They'll do that to ya.

Fastow   I won't be mocked.

Skilling   Is that right?

He can't help smiling a little. He ups **Fastow**'s *speed.* **Fastow** *tries to keep up.*

Skilling   You ever read those business books, *How to Win Friends and . . . The Seven Secrets of Highly Effective People* and shit like that –

Fastow   Yeah, I –

Skilling   Don't. It's bullshit. Read Dawkins, *The Selfish Gene*?

Fastow   I don't know it –

Skilling   Read Darwin.

Fastow   Am I getting fired, Jeff?

Skilling   By rights you should be out. I got this company running on Darwinian principles.

He ups **Fastow**'s *speed again.*

Fastow *redoubles his efforts.*

Fastow   Please don't fire me!

Skilling   Charles Darwin showed how an idea can change the world. A single beautiful idea changed the way we look at everything.

Fastow   That we're just animals?

Skilling   No. We're more. Because now we understand our own nature. And we can use that.

Fastow   Use it for what?

Skilling   For business. Business *is* nature.

Fastow   Like self-interest and competition?

Skilling   Exactly. Money and sex motivate people, Andy. And money is the one that gets their hand off their dick and into work.

Above:

Roe   I don't know if I can work under this regime, Ken.

Lay   Come on now, Claudia.

Roe   I mean it.

Lay   I don't like this fighting. This is a family!

Roe   Well, families fight! And Jeff doesn't listen to anyone.

Lay   He could learn something from you in charm, I'll give you that.

Roe   How am I supposed to head a division where ten per cent of my people are cut every time we have an evaluation?!

Lay   It's the bottom ten per cent.

Roe   Who don't get replaced! Or get replaced with really smart twenty-year-olds with no idea what's going on!

Lay It's a strategy! Gimme a break, Claudia, you gotta be nice to me today. It's my birthday.

Roe It is? Well, happy birthday, Ken.

Lay Fact I got a card from an old friend's son.

He passes it to **Roe**.

Roe 'Happy birthday, Kenny Boy! Now you're really old! Call me sometime. From *W*.'

Lay He ain't got the manners of his daddy. But I think we got a shot at the White House with him. Stick around, it's gonna get interesting.

Below:

Fastow I'm gonna have a heart attack.

Skilling That's cos you're weak.

Fastow I'm sorry I fucked up electricity!

Skilling What did you say?

Fastow I'm sorry I fucked up electricity!

Skilling I can't hear you!

Fastow I'm sorry!

Skilling *presses the stop button on* **Fastow**'s *running machine, hurling the younger man from his treadmill.*

Fastow *regains his balance and composure as* **Skilling** *calmly slows his own speed.*

Skilling Never apologise, Andy.

He gets off his machine.

Fact is, it's not all your fault.

An exhausted **Fastow** *agrees physically while he pants.*

Skilling   Electricity's an industry with no competition, no natural selection. We're never gonna make real money till it gets deregulated.

Fastow   Yes! Deregulate electricity and that market's ours.

Skilling   That's what I'm looking for. It's a political decision though. Ken's dealing with it.

Fastow   That's great. So I can keep my job?

Beat.

Skilling   Are you smart, Andy?

Fastow   Yeah, I am.

Skilling   I'm fucking smart. And I like guys with spikes. I didn't know you had any till I heard about you taking on a pack of traders. Now that takes a special kind of stupid. But also balls. You started in finance?

Fastow   Yeah.

Skilling   Let's get you back there. I know your background, you're an abstracts man. Securitisation, Risk assessment. I never met anyone less suited to retail in my life. Let's get you down in finance. Where you can keep away from people.

Fastow   Thank you. Yeah. I won't let you down.

Above:

Roe   I won't let you down.

Lay   What is it you want?

Roe   I want to build a power plant in India.

Lay   India? Nobody's in India.

Roe   You wanna be the first? Jeff won't go for it, he doesn't even think outside the States. One power plant.

Lay   'One power plant!'

Roe   It's India, Ken. The size of it. Don't you want some skin in that game?

Beat.

Lay   Okay, let's get you your power plant.

Roe   I knew I could come to you.

Lay   I understand your concerns about Jeff. But look, we got the stock analysts coming in today to rate the company. Let's see what Jeff Skilling means for the share price.

*As **Lay** says 'share price' the share price is revealed; a figurative representation of the company's worth, represented by light somewhere on stage.*

*An **Analyst** enters and speaks to us.*

Analyst (*to us*)   An analyst rates a company's stock to the outside world. We're go-betweens. The first port of call for someone looking to invest their money. Where's safe? Where's profitable? We'll rate a company at 'Buy', 'Sell' or 'Hold'. Why trust what we think? Well. We know the world, we're from the world. We're employed by the biggest investment banks and brokerage firms so we know how it works. You need access to hear the rumours, to get the skinny. It takes years to get access, to build up knowledge. A company needs customers and good press maybe, but if it really wants to thrive? It's us they need to impress.

*The analysts are **Sheryl Sloman** of Citigroup, **J.P. Morgan** and **Deutsche Bank**. All follow **Skilling**, enraptured.*

*As he walks around the space, various **Employees** approach **Skilling** with contracts for him to approve and sign. He smoothly signs though barely looks at them, treating them like autographs.*

Skilling   Ladies and Gentlemen, Enron is a new kind of company. You want to see the next big thing? It's in the minds of one of these people. We're not just an energy company, we're a powerhouse for ideas. No other company lets people work as freely and creatively as we do. If you hire only the most brilliant people you can create new industries, new economies and reinvent the old ones. Electricity will be deregulated, it has to be, and when it is, Enron will be right there, expanding our vision. The league we're in? We're not the Houston Oilers, we're not even the Dallas Cowboys. We're the whole damn NFL.

The **Analysts** *line up and face the audience.*

Skilling   Now, let's see Citigroup.

Citigroup Analyst, *after a drum roll, reveals her verdict:*

Citigroup Analyst   Strong buy!

The stock goes up.

Skilling   And J.P. Morgan.

J.P. Morgan Analyst   Strong buy!

The stock goes up.

Skilling   And finally . . . Deutsche Bank!

Deutsche Bank (*in German*)   Strong buy!

The stock goes up.

It's reached half of its full height. **Skilling** *looks genuinely touched by this.*

The **Analysts** *become a barbershop quartet and sing.*

Analysts (*singing*)

E-N-R-O-N, E-N-R-O-N, E-N-R-O-N, E-N-R-O-N.
If your company bank accounts need filling
He's available, and willing
To see to it that you make a killing!
Skilling, Skilling, Skilling, Skilling, Skilling,
Be boo doo wop wop ba doo!

The **Analysts** *parade off.*

Skilling   Thank you for recognising our work and I'm happy –

He notices the stock price rise.

I'm so excited –

He sees it rise again.

I'm a little sad?

It drops very slightly.

Ha! I'm Enron.

He's delighted by his power and effect. Grinning at the recognition and level of belief.

Lay *comes down and approaches his protégé.*

Lay   I got something for you, golden boy.

He hands **Skilling** *a fifty-dollar bill.*

Skilling   What, are you tipping me, Ken?

Lay   I'm handing out fifty-dollar bills to every employee I see. My money. This is the first time we've hit a fifty-dollar share price.

Skilling   Is it right you're using the jet later?

Lay   Yeah. Going to visit the kids.

Skilling   The company jet?

Lay   Time with the family. That's important.

Skilling   Just thought we were getting you out to Washington?

Lay   I'm stopping off in Washington. Bill and I are playing a little golf. I'll pretend I don't see him switching the balls in the rough.

Skilling   But deregulation's on that agenda?

Lay   Relax, will ya? These things take time.

Skilling   OK, well, enjoy your kids.

Scene Six

TIME IS MONEY

A memory.

Daughter (*voice-over*)   One, two, three, four, five, six . . . seven, six . . .

Skilling   You can do this. Seven . . .

Skilling*'s* **Daughter** *appears somewhere high up, not close to him.*

Daughter   Show me the money!

Skilling (*amused*)   God, I can't believe your mother let you watch that.

Daughter   Show me the money!

Skilling   OK, once more, but you count with me this time.

He gets a stack of one-dollar bills out of his pocket and begins counting them out ostentatiously, as a familiar game.

One, two, three, four, five, six, seven . . . come on! / Seven . . .

Daughter   Seven, eight, nine, ten!

Skilling   Good girl. Eleven, twelve . . . How long you think before I've counted out a million dollars?

Daughter   Um.

She doesn't know, she fidgets.

Skilling   One dollar bill a second. No stopping, how long before I counted out a million dollars? One, two – how long before a million? Dollar every second – guess.

She makes a noise, enjoying the attention of her dad but not comprehending.

It would take Daddy, at one dollar a second, eleven days to count out a million dollars. Eleven days! No sleeping.

Daughter   Again!

Skilling   What d'you mean, again? OK, one, two, three, four . . . how long would it take for Daddy to count out a *billion* dollars?

Daughter   No!

Skilling   Yeah, there's such a thing, a *billion* dollars! One, two three, four – I'm gonna do it now –

Daughter   No!

Skilling   OK. I'll work it out instead.

He calculates in his head.

Counting a billion dollars would take me . . . thirty-two years?!

He scowls, checks.

Yeah, around thirty-two years.

*His **Daughter** fades into the dark.*

Daughter (*voice-over*)   One, two, three, four, five, six, seven . . .

The counting continues into:

*Physical sequence. The company at work. The **Traders** dance. As they do they create a round table. **Skilling** holds meetings around it. People come and go. Meetings end and begin. The table is removed. Fast, ordered, fluidity. Numbers fly through the air. The stock price throbs, but never alters much, gradually edging up in comforting, rhythmic pulses. **Lay** plays golf somewhere in bright sunlight. Time passes. Days and nights. Gradually a slowing. Computer lights over faces. A calm.*

*Eventually, **Claudia Roe** makes her way through the building to **Skilling**'s office.*

Scene Seven

SKILLING'S OFFICE

Skilling *is watching the financial news.*

Roe   I've been trying to avoid you.

Skilling   Well. This is my office.

Roe   Yeah. Maybe it was the wrong place to come.

Skilling *turns the sound down on the television.*

Skilling   You probably want Ken's office. It's just down the hall.

Roe   Come on.

Skilling   Have you seen the stock price today?

Roe   I see it every day. I see it in the elevator, I see it on the walls. I see it on my desk.

Skilling *nods.*

Roe   I said to people, wait, just wait, the shine'll wear off, the bubble's gonna burst folks. And . . . a year goes by, two. But I keep saying it because, if I stop, it's bound to happen and the worst thing would be to not be able to say I told you so.

Skilling   Well, I'm sure you've got more class than that.

Roe   I don't. I don't think you do either. Go on, you can say it.

She waits for him to say it.

Skilling   It's not about that.

Roe   Oh come on! I know what you guys call my division on your biking weekends in Mexico.

Skilling   That's traders. I don't call it that.

Roe   Tits Industries. It's not even clever. At least it used to be . . . what did it used to be?

Skilling   I don't know.

Roe   You know.

Skilling   Skank of America.

She nods. Beat.

Roe   Anyways. I came by to say an old friend of mine from college emailed. He's a professor at Harvard now. He used to drink his own urine for a dare by the way. Now he's a professor. Still. He asked if I could put him in touch with you. They want to use Enron as one of the business models they teach.

Skilling   At Harvard?

Roe   Yeah.

Skilling   Really?

Roe   He said I must be proud.

Skilling   Give him my number.

Roe   I did. Just don't ask him for the stories about *me*.

Skilling   I heard about your party for the opening of the plant at Dabhol.

Roe   It was a great party.

Skilling   You hired an elephant.

Roe   Shame you couldn't make it.

Skilling   I don't have time to jet off to your consolation prize in India. I'm running a company here.

Roe   Ouch.

Beat.

Skilling   You know the whole thing was a coward's way of getting things done.

Roe I had to go to Ken. You wouldn't have. Every time I look at my assets there's less of 'em. You're selling everything I have!

Skilling That's not true.

Roe It is! I'm running a division which isn't expanding, it's not even contracting, it's having its *balls* cut off.

Skilling That's business!

Roe It's *your* business.

Skilling Damn right it is!

Roe I'm fighting to survive here!

Skilling Either I'm running this company or Ken is.

Roe You should tell *him* that.

Skilling I do! He just . . . nods and . . . gives me a cigar!

Roe It's his company.

Skilling It's the shareholders' company.

Beat.

Roe You need smart people around. To disagree with you.

Skilling I don't know if Ken is the smartest guy ever to run a company or the dumbest motherfucker in the world.

Roe I meant me. You need me around to disagree with you.

Skilling Do I?

Roe Yeah. You look good, by the way.

Skilling I . . . You mean I lost weight.

Roe Sure, but. You know three guys in my division got Laseks on their eyes after you. Can't find a soul in the building with glasses now. Everyone's copying Daddy.

Skilling It works.

Roe It's not dangerous?

Skilling Well, I don't know, Claud, I guess. It's lasers in your eyes.

She uses this as an excuse to look into his eyes.

She's deliberately close to his face. She puts her hands on his face.

Roe Have you ever failed at anything, Jeffrey Skilling?

Beat.

Skilling Don't. I don't think that's / (a very good idea).

Roe I'm not.

Beat. **Skilling** *closes his eyes. He leans in.*

Just then, over her shoulder, **Skilling** *spots a massive graphic flash up on the screen showing the financial news – 'ENRON!'*

Skilling *spins around. Once he sees what she's referring to, he's just as excited as* **Roe***. They both scrabble for the volume control. One gets there first and turns it up.*

Business Anchor By close of market today, energy darling Enron's stock rose twenty-six per cent in a single day to a new high of $67.25. That's staggering isn't it, Elise?

Analyst It sure is, Gayle. That's why we're naming them our Must Buy of the Week!

Business Anchor It's astounding, their ambition and creativity –

Analyst Yeah, yeah – they're unstoppable. They're the light of the new economy. I mean, I'd rate them, right now, at being worth sixty billion dollars.

Business Anchor Well, that's great news for their investors. So Jeffrey Skilling over at Enron's certainly doing something right!

Analyst He sure is!

Skilling *reacts to his name.*

Business Anchor   Now let's go over to Francine for a tale of two very different cities . . .

Roe   Sixty billion dollars! How can we be worth sixty billion dollars?!

Skilling   If someone's prepared to pay that for us then / that's what we're worth –

Roe   But that's huge! That's fantastic!

Skilling   Sixty billion dollars. That's nearly two thousand years.

Beat.

Roe   What?

Skilling   Forget it.

Fuck. How is that possible?!

Roe   Hey, we're announcing profits all the time, and you seem to know where that money's coming from. Everyone's behind you! And I'm just saying that includes me.

Skilling   Yeah.

She makes to leave.

Roe   Oh, and I don't know if you heard. You know your guy in finance, with the suit and the hair?

Skilling   Andy Fastow?

Roe   He's had a baby. Little boy. Named him Jeffrey.

Scene Eight

AN UNHOLY PARTNERSHIP

Below, darkly, **Fastow***'s lair: a dingy place at the bottom of Enron.* **Fastow** *flits happily between complex piles of paperwork, records and maybe screens.*

Fastow (*to us*)   I don't know if you're big fans of hedging.
I can't see how you wouldn't be. A hedge is just a way of
protecting yourself from risk. You literally hedge your bets. If
you got a lot of money in airlines, for example, you might
think, hey, this is all going really well, lots of people fly – my
investment is safe and going up. But what happens if there's a
huge airplane crash, maybe people die, oh no, folk get scared
of flying and your stocks plunge. Well, the smart guy hedges
his airline investment with – maybe – an investment in a car
rental company. When air travel frightens people, they want
to feel in control, they'll drive interstate. So when your airline
shares go (*noise and motion of plane crashing*), your car rental
shares go (*noise and motion of car brooming upwards*). So you never
lose money. Whoop . . . whoop. (*He repeats the same gestures again,
of a plane crashing, then the car brooming upwards. And then the upward
car again. A beat. The crashing plane.*) With enough imagination
you don't ever have to lose anything. When I write down
everything that can possibly go wrong, as a formula. A
formula I control. Nothing seems scary any more.

He goes back to his calculations.

Skilling *enters.*

Skilling   Andy. Andy, you had a baby.

Fastow (*delighted*)   Yeah.

Skilling   Congratulations, fella. You got a picture?

Fastow   In my wallet.

Skilling   OK.

Fastow *starts looking for his wallet.*

Fastow   Oh man, it's down the hall. Shall I – ?

Skilling   I don't (mind) –

Fastow   You really wanna –

Skilling   Do it next time.

Beat.

Fastow   He's called Jeffrey.

Skilling   Wow. Great name(!)

Fastow   Hey, who's done more for me in this world, you know?

Beat.

Skilling   You know what I was doing when my daughter was born?

Fastow   What?

Skilling   I was on the phone from the hospital negotiating my deal. To come work here.

Pause.

Fastow   You get a good deal?

Skilling *makes a so-so gesture and sound.*

Fastow   You know when you have a baby and it gets handed to you for the first time? I had this incredible, indescribable feeling – this defining realisation that in my life, from this point on – So. Many. Things could go. Wrong.

Skilling   I guess.

Fastow   And I say that as a man who knows how to manage risk. Risk is just the fear of losing something. Risk is life, basically.

Beat.

Skilling   These. What are these?

He is looking at papers covered in complex scrawlings. Maybe they're half-screwed up.

Fastow (*proud*)   Oh, these are the Raptors.

Skilling   Raptors?

Fastow   Financial models I'm –

Skilling   Are these hedges?

Fastow   Not as you'd normally understand them. But they're a way of managing risk. I'm playing with them. Just in my own time, just for . . .

Skilling   For fun?!

Fastow (*finds all three*)   Raptor One, Raptor Two, Raptor Three . . .

Skilling   Raptors.

Fastow   Like in *Jurassic Park*.

Skilling   You're thirty-seven years old.

Fastow   It's actually really well done.

Skilling   So these are protecting you against losses in investments?

Fastow   Yeah. Like, you know, with hedging how – say you've got a lot of money in airlines –

Skilling   I know about your planes and cars thing, Andy, I've heard you at parties –

Fastow   OK, well, I've been seeing if there's a way of making a model that acts like the car rental company, without actually having to give my money to the car rental company.

Casually intrigued, **Skilling** *looks through them all.*

Skilling   A little theoretical.

Fastow   Well, that's the thing. A theoretical car rental company hedges your airline investment just as good as a real one does. On the books.

Skilling   Well, sure, unless planes fall.

Fastow   Yeah, but they almost certainly won't. It's crazy to have all this money flying out the door for things that probably won't happen. This model locks in the high value of your first investment. You own that, that's real.

Skilling   These are interesting.

Fastow   Yeah . . . ?

Skilling   I could do with more guys like you.

Fastow *beams.*

Skilling *is having some pain.*

Fastow   You OK?

Skilling   These shoes . . . they're not broken in.

Fastow   What size are you? You want mine?

Skilling   No, Andy, I don't want your shoes. Thanks.

Fastow   You like 'em? They're Italian.

Skilling   Yeah I, jeez, I don't know. They're fucking shoes.

Pause.

Fastow   Great news about the stock price.

Nothing.

Skilling   You want to get a beer?

Fastow (*excited*)   I got a beer.

He opens up a tiny fridge that's been installed somewhere in his office / lair.

Skilling   You got a refrigerator?

Fastow   Yeah, I just asked 'em. I called up and said. Came down same day. Put it in.

Skilling   Who did?

Fastow   We did.

Skilling Wow.

Fastow It's a long way up to the . . . thing.

They open and drink two beers.

Skilling I got a problem, Andy. We got great stock price. We're declaring huge profits using mark-to-market. Correctly. But those *actual* profits aren't coming through yet. So.

Fastow There's losses.

Skilling That's right. We've got the best business plan, the highest share price, the smartest graduates. Trouble is. Right now. We're not making any money.

Long pause.

Fastow How bad?

Skilling You with me?

Fastow Always.

Skilling I can't find. Any area. Right now. Except trading. And there, day to day, we may lose as much as we make.

Pause.

Fastow Wow(!)

Skilling Yeah(!)

Fastow You're not kidding?

Skilling I am not kidding. I don't know what I'm gonna do. I don't mind taking losses. But I can't report taking losses right now. The gap between the perception and the reality is . . .

He has one hand up at neck level indicating the high perception and the other he puts lower to indicate the reality.

Skilling I don't know what I'm going to do.

His arms droop despondently. **Fastow** *dives in to hold the perception hand up.*

Fastow   Wait, you got a perception here, a reality here. You just need something for this to lean on while we bring this up.

Fastow *brings* **Skilling***'s lower hand up to meet his higher hand.*

Beat.

Skilling *shakes off the foolish physical intimacy.*

Skilling   If those Washington fucks would just deregulate electricity like Clinton promised, we'd *have* those profits!

Fastow   Hey. Fuck it. Two guys in a room. You want my help?

Beat.

Skilling   What you got?

Fastow   How you doing with a Chief Financial Officer?

Skilling   I haven't found him yet.

Fastow   You considered everybody?

Skilling   Everybody with / experience of –

Fastow   You considered me?

Skilling   For CFO . . . ? One of the most powerful positions in / any corporation . . . ?

Fastow   Yeah.

Skilling   You're not a people person, Andy.

Fastow   You really care about that?

Beat.

Skilling   Two guys in a room.

Fastow   You ever had an affair? When you were married.

Skilling   None of your fucking business.

Fastow   That's a yes.

Skilling   Is this something you've heard?

Fastow   No, OK, wait, that's wrong. You like porn?

Skilling   Do I – ? I don't have time to take a *shit*

Fastow   I think porn could save every marriage in this country. As internet porn goes up, divorce rates gonna go way down –

He makes gesture of one thing going up as the other goes down.

That's the industry to get into, I'll say that . . .

Skilling   Find the point.

Fastow   I want to give Enron a mistress.

Skilling (*beat*)   That's why I like you, Andy. You're fucking nuts.

Fastow   Having something off the books, even if it's Jenna Jameson in an unmarked folder, your *virtual* mistress – she supports your marriage, strengthens it. We can do the same for a company.

Skilling   Explain.

Fastow   For those occasions we need to . . . 'offload'. We create a company that exists purely to fulfil Enron's needs.

Skilling   Example.

Fastow   We could push debt, we could push those losses into this other entity, *sell it* to this entity. So we make money *and* move a loss off the books, wait for it to turn to profit –

Skilling   Then move it back. Why doesn't everyone do this?

Fastow   How would we know if they did?

Skilling   Andy!

Fastow   I mean it! This is an area where we're expected to be creative. The regulations *encourage* it.

Skilling This isn't one of your theoretical models. A whole investment fund with money enough to buy bad assets off Enron? Who would do that? Who would invest?

Fastow Maybe nobody has to invest. We can make the company ourselves. I could use these raptor models. To make a sort of shadow company. A virtual Enron.

Skilling We can't do business with ourselves –

Fastow Of course not. But. The rules state, if we're gonna do business with another entity, it has to be *independent from us*.

Skilling Exactly.

Fastow But. Here's the kicker. To qualify as independent it just means *three per cent* of its capital has to come from independent sources.

Skilling Only three per cent?

Fastow Yeah, so ninety-seven per cent of a whole shadow company could just be . . . Enron stock.

Skilling So Enron can do business with a company that's ninety-seven per cent Enron?

Fastow Sure.

Skilling Still gotta find that three per cent.

Fastow *is excitedy scoping out the room they are standing in.*

Fastow Maybe. Look, say this entity, let's call it . . . LJM. If this room is LJM – it's filled with Enron stock, now we own that, we don't have to pay for and it's worth a great deal. But we need three per cent of it to be real. The equivalent of this desk.

He walks around clearing the area to make the three per cent clear.

Fastow What if this three per cent is a smaller entity, designed the same way, which itself is made up of Enron stock –

Skilling   Except for three per cent.

Fastow   Yes, wait.

Fastow *opens a drawer in the desk and takes out a shoebox that had housed his new Italian shoes. He places it on the desk.*

Here. And this three per cent is an even smaller entity . . .

He opens up the shoebox.

Skilling   Made up of Enron stock . . .

Fastow   Except for three per cent!

Out of the shoebox he produces a matchbox.

Skilling   On and on.

Fastow   Until for all this to be real, for this huge shadow company to exist, all we actually need . . .

He opens the matchbox and takes out a tiny red, glowing box.

He holds it up. The men are bathed in it like some totem from an Indiana Jones film.

Fastow   Is this . . .

Skilling   And how much is that?

Fastow   Chump change. Few million.

Skilling   If that's a few million . . . ?

Fastow   Imagine what the whole structure is worth, what it could do for Enron.

Skilling   It's made entirely of Enron stock . . .

Fastow (*brandishing tiny box*)   Aaah, not entirely, this is what keeps it independent.

Skilling   But we can use it to *support* Enron stock, making sure it doesn't fall . . .

Fastow   Yup –

Skilling   The same stock that it's made of . . . ?

Fastow   Yes.

Beat.

Skilling   That's fucking brilliant.

Fastow   It is, isn't it?

Skilling   So this shadow company, what did you call it?

Fastow   LJM. After my wife and kids, Lea, Jeffrey and –

Skilling   This LJM can buy bad assets off Enron that are operating at a loss. And if anyone looks into it –

Fastow   It's just box after box after box. Russian dolls, until you get to . . .

The tiny box glows red and throbs.

Fastow   And who's gonna notice something as small as this? How's something this tiny ever gonna cause any trouble?

Skilling   Andy, you fucker! This is a whole new thing!

Fastow   And this is just a few million, hell, *I* could put that in.

Skilling   No, I don't like that.

Fastow   Oh. OK.

Skilling   Doesn't that feel a bit cheap? A special purpose entity financed by the CFO?

Fastow   The CFO?

Skilling   Why not? Come on, we'll get banks to put that in – Wall Street money.

Fastow *(slightly surprised)*   Yeah, but don't we check with our accountants?

Skilling   Sure.

Hey! Get me Arthur Andersen!

Arthur Andersen *appears to one side. He has a ventriloquist's dummy,* **Little Arthur**.

Arthur Andersen   As your accountant, we think this idea is –

A different voice from his mouth:

Little Arthur   – poor to very poor.

Arthur Andersen   This is due to –

Little Arthur   – conflict of interest.

Fastow (*to* **Skilling**)   Well, maybe we just need a more sympathetic accountant.

Beat.

Skilling (*to* **Arthur Andersen**)   We could always take our business elsewhere.

Arthur Andersen's *dummy's eyes flit wildly.*

Arthur Andersen   Arthur Andersen will –

Little Arthur   – approve –

Arthur Andersen   – approve the strategy –

Little Arthur   – if the lawyers approve.

Fastow   That's what we pay a million dollars a month for?

Skilling   Yeah, that's exactly what we pay a million dollars a month for.

I need the lawyers!

The law firm of **Ramsay** *and* **Hewitt** *appears to their other side: one male, one female. They appear as 'Justice'; blindfolded, with sword and scales.*

Ramsay   This is not a legal issue.

Hewitt   This is an accounting issue.

Skilling   The accountants say it's a legal issue.

Ramsay   Well, it was ever thus.

Hewitt   It's against your own code of conduct –

Ramsay   It's *their* code of conduct.

Hewitt   Oh yes. Quite right. Your board could waive it.

Ramsay   Ask your board.

Hewitt   It's really not our business.

Ramsay *and* **Hewitt**   We'll bill you later on today.

Skilling   I need the board.

And then, revealed on the level above **Skilling** *and* **Fastow***, the* **Board** *appear. The* **Board** *is made up of shadowy, dark, imposing figures with the heads of mice, and, in the centre,* **Ken Lay***.*

Skilling   The accountants and lawyers are OK with it if you're OK with it, Ken.

Lay   Oh, well in that case . . . One moment.

The **Board** *briefly consult.*

Lay   Who's gonna run this thing?

Fastow   I will. I mean, I want to.

Lay   And who are you?

Fastow (*to* **Skilling**)   You know you won't find anyone you can trust like you trust me.

Lay   Young Andy Fastow?

Skilling   He's our new Chief Financial Officer.

Fastow *is delighted at this.*

Lay   OK!

Arthur Andersen   OK?

Ramsay *and* **Hewitt**   OK?

Lay   OK?

Skilling   OK?

Little Arthur   OK.

Ramsay *and* **Hewitt**   OK.

Fastow   OK.

Lay   OK. Here's to LJM.

He signs papers in front of him.

The **Board***,* **Arthur Andersen** *and* **Hewitt** *and* **Ramsay** *disappear.* **Fastow** *and* **Skilling** *hug in the centre of the circle.*

Skilling   You've saved my fucking life.

Fastow   It's good, isn't it?

Skilling   All I have to do is keep the stock price up.

Fastow   Which makes LJM exist.

Skilling   Which makes Enron strong.

Fastow   Which keeps the stock price up.

Skilling   It's better than good. It's perfect.

Scene Nine

PARTY LIKE IT'S 1999

Flashes from cameras.

A media event becomes a party filled with **Employees***,* **Press** *and* **Analysts***. It's a financial love-in.*

Skilling *is being photographed for yet another magazine cover as the dynamic CEO changing the world. The* **Photographer** *is beneath him to make him look impressive, god-like.*

A **Reporter** *interviews him.*

Reporter   'World's Most Innovative Company', how does that feel?

Skilling   I'm just pleased we're giving shareholders value for money.

Reporter   I guess it's a work-hard, play-hard sort of environment?

Skilling   We're aggressive, we take risks, and that's why we're successful. Way I see it, if your executives aren't waking up at four in the morning, their heart beating out of their chest, they're not doing their job.

The **Reporter** *flirts a bit.*

Reporter   Sure. So, here we are at the end of a millennium! Can you let me know what the next big innovation's gonna be?

Skilling   Well, I was gonna wait to announce this later tonight, but I'll give you a sneak preview. Video On Demand. We've teamed up with Blockbuster and Enron's gonna be streaming movies directly into your home by this time next year.

Reporter   Oh my God!

The stock price goes up.

Skilling *is approached by* **Lay**.

Lay   Jeff, you know the Congresswoman?

Skilling   Hi, great to meet you.

Lay   Anne's been very useful for us up on the Hill.

Congresswoman   Such a creative atmosphere. I'm thrilled to meet you, you're the expert in energy trading, right?

Lay   That's like saying Alexander Graham Bell knew about telephones. You're meeting the guy who invented the concept.

Congresswoman   Well we're all just thrilled to be here. I don't know how you're doing it, but keep on doing it.

Split Scene.

Beneath:

Fastow's *lair is revealed. He is finishing constructing LJM, the huge construct that has been designed literally and metaphorically to 'support' the level above it, Enron.*

Fastow, *dressed in an even more dandyish fashion, is in his element.*

He takes calls on his phone. He's hugely in demand.

Hi you're talking to Andy Fastow, Chief Financial Officer to the stars. Hey Rex, you fuck, you know how many other divisions are begging for help with their numbers right now?! You're gonna have to hold. Lou baby, don't tell me 'bout your numbers now – hey, I know those targets were unhittable, I know that. But you gonna take those losses? I didn't think so!

Hold on, I got another one. Yeah yeah yeah, you love me. No I'm not going up to the party. I leave my office, the whole world falls apart, you know what I mean? Don't worry. Everything's developing nicely down here.

Above:

Lay   Where's our Chief Financial Officer?

Skilling   Still working, I guess.

Lay   No harm. He's hardly the life and soul –

Skilling   He's not a performer, he's got his own qualities.

Lay   Claudia thinks we should keep an eye on him.

Skilling   Oh for – seriously, Ken? You're listening to her!? She's jealous! This has all been built by me for Christ's sake. He's mine! All these ideas are mine!

Lay   It wasn't my intention –

Skilling   Broadband, electricity, energy trading, Video On Demand –

Concerned **Employees** *approach* **Skilling**.

Employee   Could we talk about Video On Demand?

Lay   Of course we can, sir, of course we can. Who doesn't want movies streamed direct into their homes?

Employee 2   I don't think it's possible for next year.

Skilling   Video On Demand?

Employee   I can't see how it's possible at all.

Lay   I don't like that talk. That's unsupportive.

Skilling   We've got our best people working on it.

Employee 2   Sir, that's us.

Employee   We're the ones working on it.

Skilling   Tell me what you need and you'll get it.

Employee   It's not that –

Employee 2   It's about what's physically possible. There's not bandwidth capacity for it.

Skilling   Bandwidth?

Employee 2   It's the sort of . . . lines that internet information travels / along –

Skilling   I know what the fuck bandwidth is. Buy as much as we need.

Employee   It doesn't work that way. There's a finite amount available.

Skilling   There's a finite amount?

Employee   Yeah.

Skilling   And people want it?

Employee   Yeah.

Skilling *slaps the employee on the back. He turns back to the press interview.*

Skilling   Here's the next big thing, people: trading bandwidth.

Reporter   *Trading bandwidth?*

Skilling (*turns to everyone*)   Yeah, it's a hell of an Enron idea. If you're not using your bandwidth capacity, we could sell it on. It's tradeable. But people don't think in those terms because it's a virtual commodity. Well, Enron *gets* virtual. We're changing business, we're changing people's lives, we're changing the world.

Lay *applauds. The* **Employees** *are congratulated and sheepishly proud. The stock goes up hugely. Reaction is ecstatic, like a religious cult.* **Skilling** *is messiah-like.*

A huge party: absurd, luxurious, delusional, the peak of bull-market excess. **Skilling** *shakes hands with everyone, is treated like a movie star.*

Just then, **Roe** *makes a grand entrance to the party. Never one to be outshone, she is on a Harley motorbike, dressed entirely in leather.*

Skilling   You've got to be kidding me.

She shows off the back on which is stitched 'ENRON'. Whoops of celebration. She removes the helmet, revealing herself, and shakes down her hair. Everyone loves it and all attention is lavished on her.

Skilling   This is what I'm talking about. Everything's the Claudia Roe show.

Lay   It's a very entertaining show!

Fireworks are starting to go off in the distance. The party reaches a peak of excitement as everyone goes upstairs to view them and celebratory opulence.

As everyone gets ushered out on to the balcony –

Below:

Fastow *hears/senses another presence in the lair of LJM.*

Above:

Roe *marshals guests into place for the countdown she will be leading.*

Below, during this:

Fastow *goes to seek out the source of the sound. Uncanny silence. He can sense someone . . . but where?*

Another movement from the opposite side. **Fastow** *swings around – what the . . . ?*

Above:

Roe *begins a countdown to welcome in the new millennium. Others eventually join in.*

Ten!

Nine!

Eight!

Seven!

Six!

Five!

Below, during this:

Out of the shadows, a **Raptor** *appears. It creeps forward, cocks its head and considers* **Fastow**. **Fastow** *stares back.*

Four!

Three!

Two!

One!

Above:

Roe *turns on the party's big event – the lighting up of a huge neon display welcoming in the new year: 2000.*

Below:

Fastow *turns slowly around to see the other two* **Raptors** *have also taken corporeal form and have crept into LJM.*

Fastow   Clever girls.

Blackout.

Act Two

Opening

Enron commercial with ethereal voices singing 'Why?'

Scene One

Fastow's *lair where LJM has been fully and complexly constructed, like a large, supportive web.*

Among the shadows there are strange movements going on. The **Raptors** *scuttle about. Not entirely human sounds. In the centre,* **Fastow**.

The tiny red box is safely put away, buried. We can see it throb. The **Raptors** *creep eerily around in the shadows.*

Skilling *enters. The* **Raptors** *hide.*

Skilling   Andy? Is everything right down here?

Fastow   Jeff! Everything's peachy.

Skilling   This place has got big.

Fastow   You won't believe the investment I got us. You wanted LJM to look official. Well, I've got fifteen million from J.P. Morgan, ten million Credit Suisse, five million from Merrill, everyone wants in with LJM –

Skilling   Everyone wants to invest in our shadow . . . ? Why?!

Two more figures emerge from the shadows: it is the **Lehman Brothers**.

Lehman Brothers   Hey, Mr Fastow!

Fastow   Oh, wait a second – it's the fucking Lehman Brothers. What do you guys want?

Lehman Brothers   We were wondering –

Fastow   I'm busy here, what the fuck d'you want?

Skilling   That's one of the biggest investment banks in the world. You can't talk to them that way!

Fastow   No, but that's the thing, Jeff. I can! They're all so desperate to be seen alongside Enron. And who's Enron's CFO? Check it out.

Lehman Brothers   We were in talks about doing some underwriting work for Enron.

Fastow   For Enron?

Lehman Brothers   Yeah, we were hoping you'd consider giving us the contract –

Fastow   Way I see it, if I give you a contract worth tens of millions of dollars, least you can do is invest in a side project I got going on. Course Enron could always take its business elsewhere –

Lehman Brothers   No, no, no, Andy, we heard. What you looking for?

Fastow   Let's start small, how 'bout ten million?

Lehman Brothers   Ten million! Everyone up at Enron OK with this, Jeff?

Skilling   What you asking me for?

Lehman Brothers   I mean, we assumed it was fine.

Skilling   You got a problem with LJM?

Lehman Brothers   Not at all.

Skilling   You got a problem with Andy?

Lehman Brothers   Well, he's got a certain –

Skilling   You do, you got a problem with me.

Lehman Brothers   No sir. Absolutely not. LJM's a real ground-breaking strategy.

The **Lehman Brothers** *give* **Fastow** *the money.*

Lehman Brothers   Nice doing business.

Fastow   Good job, fellas!

Skilling   Hey, Lehman Brothers!

The conjoined figures struggle to turn round in unison, both pulling in opposite directions. Eventually, they manage it.

Lehman Brothers   Yeeees?

Skilling   What's your analyst rating our stock at?

Lehman Brothers   Uh, Buy –

Skilling   Not Strong Buy?

Lehman Brothers   Not right . . . now.

Fastow   Let me.

Skilling *nods graciously.*

Fastow   If you rated us Strong Buy, more people would invest in Enron, right?

Lehman Brothers   I guess . . .

Fastow   And if more people invest in Enron, we can finance more projects, which makes Enron stronger and therefore –

Lehman Brothers   *Making* it a / Strong Buy . . .

Fastow   / A Strong Buy! See how it makes sense now?

Now, get the fuck out before I change my mind.

The **Lehman Brothers** *slink out.*

Skilling   I can't believe it. Everything upstairs is bullshit compared to this.

Fastow   I know! I think we've found the future of business . . . by accident.

Skilling   But where does all the debt go?

Sounds from the shadows.

What's that?

Fastow   Nothing.

Skilling   What is it?

Fastow   Don't worry about it.

Skilling   What the fuck is this?

Skilling *goes to explore. One of the* **Raptors** *approaches* **Skilling** *to check him out. It smells him cautiously.*

Fastow   The Raptors. You like 'em? They like you.

Skilling   That's where the debt goes?

Fastow   These sort of entities, we could never have them publicly at Enron, but LJM doesn't need to show its books. So we can . . . experiment here.

He feeds one of them a dollar bill.

Skilling   They're consuming our debt.

Fastow   Yes! And debt's just money. All money is debt.

Skilling   In . . . what . . . sense?

Fastow   If the bank gives you money, you owe *them*. You put money in the bank, they owe *you*.

All money is debt. It's just how you present it.

The **Raptors** *gain confidence at this and play with* **Skilling** *a little.*

Skilling   Go on.

Fastow   OK. Well, this one here, is dealing with Broadband. This one's taking care of Video On Demand while we set it up. And that one . . . that one's consuming all the fucking debt coming out of that rusting hulk of a power plant in Dabhol.

Skilling   That plant has no fucking power coming out of it. It's surrounded by *protesters*. When Claudia makes a deal it doesn't just lose money, *people march against it*.

Fastow   You gotta put a stop to all that.

Skilling   She thinks her balls are cut off, what about my balls?!

Fastow   A man's got a right to his balls.

Skilling   *This* is the future. Not Claudia and her gift from grampa. Ken's gotta accept it's my show!

Fastow   He has to.

Skilling   You think her numbers are right?

Fastow   Her division's numbers?

Skilling   Yeah. You think she's doing anything . . . untoward?

Fastow   I'd be surprised if there was *nothing* untoward. I mean, everybody . . . you know.

Beat.

You want me to take a look?

Skilling   If you have cause for concern.

Fastow   Well, sure, I mean. I can tell clever numbers. I'm the king of 'em!

Skilling *strokes a* **Raptor.**

Scene Two

THE PURGE

Roe (*to us*)   Something is happening to business. At the beginning of this century. Things have started to get divorced from the underlying realities. The best metaphor is this. Say we hold a competition here to determine who is the most beautiful woman in this room. Everyone gets a vote, the woman would be the one with the most votes and you'd win if you bet on her. Now the smart player wouldn't look at all the women and choose the one he finds most beautiful. No, the smart player would try and imagine what average opinion would state is the most beautiful woman, and vote for her. And there's a level above that, where the really smart person would assume that most other people are doing the same thing and so they would try and choose the woman that most other people would think was most other people's idea of the most beautiful woman. And there's even a level above that, and above that. And those are the values that determine prices, commodities and everybody's future. And who actually is the most beautiful woman in the room . . . is irrelevant.

One of the **Raptors** *runs towards* **Roe** *and chases her out of the building.*

After a moment, **Lay** *enters* **Skilling***'s office, looking pained.*

Skilling   Did you do it?

Lay   Still feel raw about that.

Skilling   I felt she had to hear it from you.

Lay   Can't recall what our thinking was there now.

Skilling   She wouldn't have taken it seriously from me.

Lay   I never did like letting people go.

You want to have a cigar?

Skilling   I'm good, thanks.

Lay *gives him one anyway.*

Lay   I was very disappointed in the things Claudia said in there. Didn't show a lot of class.

Skilling   Regarding what?

Lay I don't believe she had to go so far in trying to save her own skin.

Skilling I didn't want to have to bring those figures to your attention. I know they didn't look like much –

Lay Any deceit is deceit. If something's brought before me I have to act on it. Doesn't *have* to be brought to me, of course.

Skilling Sure.

Lay Now you made that decision and you brought it before me and a chain of events were put in place. Difficult to break that chain. You wanna pray with me, Jeffrey?

Pause.

Skilling Sure.

Lay *bows his head in prayer, his hands together. He closes his eyes.* **Skilling** *copies him.*

After a few moments, **Lay** *has not spoken.* **Skilling** *opens his eyes. He watches* **Lay***, not sure what to do.*

He watches **Lay***, fascinated.*

After a little while, **Lay** *stops his silent prayers and raises his head.* **Skilling** *immediately tries to bow his to make it look like he hadn't stopped.*

Lay Amen.

Skilling It's a privilege.

Lay Don't you worry, son.

You know how you tell the scout on a pioneer wagon?

Beat.

Lay He's the one with all the arrows sticking out of him.

Beat. **Lay** *touches* **Skilling** *on the shoulder. It's a paternal, almost saintly action, but takes* **Skilling** *by surprise.*

Lay   Listen, I know it's not been easy, having an old man on your back. You want to ride out, get the bit in your teeth and I'm all for that. I'm gonna take a step back. Place you can use me is on the board, on the Washington golf courses, charity luncheons. That's what I'm good at. You just carry on making us millions.

Skilling   We really gotta get deregulation moving –

Lay   I'm gonna have more talk with Junior. I got hope for him yet.

Skilling   But that's how we're gonna make our money. If he doesn't come through –

Lay   These things take time.

Beat.

Can't even smoke these indoors any more.

Skilling   You can do what you want, Ken.

Lay   Uh-uh. Can't even smoke indoors.

He drifts off. Pause. **Skilling** *picks up the cigar left him.*

Scene Three

ROOFTOP

Roe *is having a last cigarette outside on the rooftop/terrace of the Enron building.*

Skilling *comes out.*

Roe *has been crying. She hastily attempts to cover any sign of her tears.*

Skilling   You're not gonna jump are you, Claud?

Roe   Fuck you.

Skilling   I'll leave you alone.

Roe   Don't move. Don't you dare go anywhere.

Skilling   You can go and get any number of jobs –

Roe   I WANT TO WORK HERE!

Beat.

This is where I work!

Skilling   Not any more.

Roe   That man had faith in me for fifteen years. I've given my life to this company. You had him come in and talk to me like I'm some thieving kid in his store.

Skilling   I asked Ken because I thought it would be worse for me to fire you –

Roe   I was not fired. I resigned. You show me one part of my numbers done differently from anyone else here – you lied to get me out.

Skilling   I didn't have to lie. You're an amateur.

Roe   Oh, really?

Skilling   Did you tell him something I should know about . . . ?

Roe   There's rumours. Is it true Broadband and Electricity aren't bringing in any money? That Video On Demand doesn't even have the technology developed?

Skilling   Of course not. That would make all the profits we've declared on those things void.

Roe   Yes, it would.

Skilling   Why do people talk that way? We'll make those profits. It's like playing poker with these guys who get mad when you win on the last card, 'Why did you stay in? You're not playing properly!' It's *poker*, you idiot. Doesn't matter how you win – as long as you win! When electricity gets deregulated, the cashflow –

Roe   Oh, grow the fuck up. Electricity won't be deregulated! Ken's not gonna get that kid in the White House!

Skilling   We will.

Roe   I could have made India work! All your deals getting done all the time, bad deals. Sign it, book it, throw it over the fence. Doesn't matter if it's a bad deal, just get the deal done.

Skilling   You don't know anything.

Roe   I know you.

You know when you went to that college in Pennsylvania.

Skilling   I went to Harvard.

Roe (*shakes head*)   When your father showed you round his old college in Bethlehem, Pennsylvania. You told me about it our first night. You looked out that window, saw all those abandoned steel mills, for miles. All that dead industry. That gray sky.

Skilling   I left all that behind.

Roe   No. That's what you're creating now.

Skilling   Get out of my building.

Roe   You know what I'm gonna do? I'm gonna go home, to my beautiful children. And I'm gonna sell every single one of my shares.

She stubs her cigarette out. She leaves him.

His **Daughter** *blows bubbles somewhere on stage.*

Daughter   One, two, three, four, five -

Skilling   I have to check the stock price.

Daughter   Why?

Skilling   Because that's how Daddy knows how much he's worth.

Daughter   Why?

Skilling   Well, the market knows how many people believe in Daddy. That's important.

Daughter   Why?

Skilling   It's important because I want people to like me. I don't want them to go round saying bad things.

Daughter   Why?

Skilling   Because in business these things matter.

Daughter   Why?

Skilling   Because it's important to look strong. That's the first thing.

Daughter   Why?

Skilling   Because that's how you make money.

Daughter   Why?

Skilling   Because I want to provide for you.

Daughter   Why?

Beat.

Skilling   Because I love you. Now let Daddy go to work.

Skilling *turns to his* **Daughter** *but she has disappeared, leaving only bubbles in her wake.*

Scene Four

THE AMERICAN SPIRIT

Skilling *gives a speech to* **Employees**.

Skilling   Our stock is so strong. So strong that I think all employees should have the opportunity to benefit. I want to extend the stock option to everybody. From the mail room all the way up.

Employee   Why be paid in stock and not cash?

Skilling   Because if you're invested in the company you work for you are literally investing in yourself – it is an act of belief in yourself. Which you should all have. Because, I believe in you. So, grab that opportunity. Now, tonight's a big night for us. I hope you've all voted. I don't know if you know, but we got a local boy in the race(!)

Laughter. They are now looking up concentrating on an image of America on screens.

Election coverage:

The screen goes red.

INDIANA CALLED FOR BUSH.

+ 12.

They cheer.

Screen turns blue.

VERMONT CALLED FOR GORE.

+ 3.

They boo.

FLORIDA.

They inhale.

TOO CLOSE TO CALL.

Scene Five

ANDY'S LAIR OF LJM

Skilling *enters.* **Fastow** *is with the* **Raptors** *watching the election results roll in.*

Skilling   You got it on down here?

Fastow   Sure. We're having a party.

Fastow *turns round. He has a bottle of champagne. They all stare at the screen.*

An electoral map of the United States on screen:

ALABAMA: TOO CLOSE TO CALL.

Skilling   Alabama too close to call?! You gotta be fucking kidding me.

Fastow   Hey, it's early.

Skilling   I'm going crazy with this.

Fastow   Hey, they're calling my baby – !

It's blue.

NEW JERSEY: CALLED FOR GORE.

+ 15.

Fastow   Goddamn you, New Jersey. I love you, but you break my fucking heart. That's my cousins, there.

Beat.

Skilling   Now we got the big boys –

Fastow   Lone Star!

It's red.

TEXAS: CALLED FOR BUSH.

+ 32.

Fastow   Come on!

Skilling   Yeah but here goes the other side.

It's blue.

CALIFORNIA: CALLED FOR GORE.

+ 54.

Fastow   Surprise!

Skilling   It's all about Florida.

Beat.

FLORIDA: CALLED FOR GORE.

+ 25.

Fastow   No.

Beat.

Skilling   Fuck fuck fuck.

Fastow   What about Colorado, we might get Colorado.

Skilling   What the fuck we want with Colorado, eight fucking votes. This is chicken shit. Game's over.

Fastow   Hey, come on, we've had eight years of this shit, we'll have eight more –

Skilling   No, Andy, you don't know. Clinton's been real good to us. This guy . . . this guy scares me.

Fastow   Come on, man – scares you?! I've seen you nearly die on a quad bike just to see what it feels like to nearly die –

Skilling   That's it. We're done.

Fastow   Have a little faith.

Skilling   Faith?! Andy, you gotta understand. I don't have any cash. I can't operate. I have no money.

Fastow (*shock*)   You, personally?

I got money – I can –

Skilling   Not me *personally*, Andy, you prick. What, you think I'm some drinking, gambling-it-away prick can't find cash on my salary? What is it you think?!

Fastow   No, no, I . . . We'll get through this.

Skilling   Without someone friendly to us right now, we're dead.

He seems to be in pain – his stomach.

I haven't been sleeping. People need to get paid.

Fastow   Pay them in stock, with our stock price –

Skilling   Everyone *is* paid in stock. Already, *that's why it can't go down* –

Fastow   No, it can't. This whole set-up is founded on / the stock price –

Skilling   I know!

Fastow   Are you saying it's going down?

Skilling   I'm saying it *can't* go / down.

Fastow   That's what I'm saying.

Skilling   Well don't tell me what I already / know!

Fastow   I'm trying to make it work here!

Skilling   Well that's your fucking job, ain't it?

Beat.

Sorry.

Fastow   You need capital. You need cash. One, two, three?

Skilling   More like four –

Fastow   Four million I can find . . .

Skilling *stares at him.*

Skilling   Million?! No.

Beat.

Fastow   You need four *billion* dollars? Cash?!

Skilling   We're the world's most innovative company. How can we not find four/ billion dollars?!

Fastow   That's not what I do. This is all . . . this is *structured finance*. This is how it *looks* . . . I can't make real money just *appear*.

Skilling (*losing control*)   Then what good are you . . . ? What fucking good is any of this to me?! Then we're going down, Andy, / and it's your –

Fastow   Wait, look –

Screens go red.

RECOUNT: FLORIDA CALLED FOR BUSH.

Skilling   What does that mean?

Fastow   If you need actual capital . . .

Skilling   But they called it for Gore.

Fastow   If you need cash coming in the door, actual cash, then you need to sell something real . . .

Skilling   I've sold everything!

So, what, have we won?!

Fastow   Fox says yes!

Skilling   CNN says no.

Screens go blue.

FLORIDA RETRACTED FROM BUSH.

Fastow   No!

Skilling   What the fuck are they doing?

Fastow   Well, they gotta decide.

Skilling   What's going on out there?!

Fastow   Someone has to call this.

Skilling   What dumbass is running this thing?

Fastow   They can't do this. If there's one thing this country won't stand for it's ambiguity.

Flicking through channels.

Who's won? who's / won?!

Skilling   Who's won!?

Just then, **Lay** *enters, hanging up on a phone call. He is deliberately oblivious to the strange, exaggerated world of LJM. The* **Raptors** *scuttle away.*

Lay   Gentlemen. Guess who's just got off a call with the next President of the United States?

Skilling   Say we got a Texan in the White House.

Skilling *is clutching his stomach.*

Lay   Like father like son.

Skilling *falls to his knees with the relief.*

Lay   *And* we got ourselves a deregulated state to play with.

Fastow   *There's* your cash!

Skilling   A small state? Or . . .

Lay *grins.*

News Report   The state of California has announced it's going to be the first state to implement a deregulated electricity market.

Video footage of George W. Bush being sworn in as President of the United States.

Scene Six

TEXAS VS CALIFORNIA

The floor is flooded with **Traders***.*

During the following, **Traders** *are manipulating California's electricity market by moving energy around. It should be tremendous fun, extremely fast, physical and overlap is encouraged.*

Skilling (*addressed to the* **Traders**)   Gentlemen. We've finally got our chance to move out all across the country. This is about competition. A deregulated system means one thing and one thing only controls electricity. The *market*. The market is *supposed* to show the weakness of regulation. The free market is *there* to show regulators how wrong they're getting it. I'm setting you free in California, fellas, bring it on home.

Trader 3   California! Yes, people, an electricity market of such complexity, designed by people of such simplicity. Loopholes so big you could fuck a fat chick through 'em and neither of you touch the sides. Let's find arbitrage opportunities. Let's. Fucking. Play.

All right man, this is Clem up at Enron. We're buying as much electricity as we can and taking it out of the state.

Trader 4   Ricochet! Fat Boy! Burn Out! Death Star!

Trader 2   You want your power back? Fucking *pay*!

Trader 7   Wheeling electricity out of the state, push the prices up, get 'em high –

Trader 4   Sell it back when they're desperate!

Trader 5   The most beautiful thing about electricity –

All Traders   It cannot be stored!

Trader 4   Holy shit, price is up through a hundred!

They all look.

Trader 1   I've never seen prices like these –

Trader 5   Welcome to Californ–I–A!

Trader 6   We're making billions of dollars!

All Traders   For Enron!

Laughter.

News reports begin playing between and underneath the traders. They should overlap as appropriate.

News Report   California's power supply came up short today, and the lights went out. Rolling blackouts have hit the sixth largest economy in the world. For the first time in sixty-five years, the electric power market is in chaos. Electricity rates are climbing and California has gone into meltdown.

Trader 5   There's a fire on the core line!

Trader 2   More fires we have, more prices go up!

All Traders   Burn baby, burn!

Short physical sequence.

News Report   Another day, another death in the story of California's blackouts. The driver of a station wagon was killed early Friday when she collided with a transit bus at an Oakland intersection where the traffic lights were down.

This after surgeons were left without operating lights in San Pablo forcing patients to be airlifted to facilities out of state –

Laughter.

Skilling (*to camera crew*)   We are doing the right thing in California. I mean, people are saying we shouldn't trade electricity – do you really believe that? Let's, let's stop trading wheat. Let's stop trading – you know, we need automobiles to maintain the logistics system, so does that mean we can't trade steel? We are the good guys in California. We are on the side of angels.

Physical sequence.

News Report   Today, the governor of California, Gray Davis, declared a state of emergency after being forced to cut power for hundreds of thousands of people throughout the state.

Lay (*on phone*)   Kenneth Lay here for the Governor of California. Governor! I understand you're considering running for President. You think it's gonna help you any to have the sixth largest economy in the world go dark on your watch? Voters remember that sort of thing. So how 'bout paying the prices we're asking?

Well, I'm sorry to hear you say that, Governor.

He hangs up the phone.

Lay (*to* **Traders**)   Boys, step it up.

Trader 5   Come on!!

Physical sequence.

A climax of sound and activity is being reached. It builds and builds.

Trader 1   This is the largest single transfer of wealth I've ever seen!

Trader 7   We're like the Roman empire! We're going fucking down!

Trader 4   Let's rape this motherfucker!

Trader 5   Push it through the fucking roof!

Trader 1   Okay, okay!

Trader 2   / Do it, do it!

Everyone and everything is at fever pitch, yelling and encouraging.

A climax.

Skilling   You know the difference between the state of California and the Titanic? At least when the Titanic went down the lights were on.

Every light in the world seems to go out.

Utter darkness everywhere. For a shade longer than is comfortable.

And then . . .

Nothing but the light from a small doorway.

In front of the light of the doorway, a man comes into view. It is the short, homuncular figure of **Ken Lay**. *A suited man comes on stage and goes through the door, first shaking* **Lay**'s *hand.*

Lay   Hi, Mr Mayor, I'm sure we can get this under control.

Another suited man approaches the door. **Lay** *shakes hands with him.*

Thanks for coming out.

Another suited man right behind him shakes **Lay**'s *hand and goes in.*

Don't worry, I got the guy to fix this.

And then, another suited man approaches. He is huge and square and muscular in his suit. **Lay** *looks up at him, his face breaking into a grin. They shake hands. The man's broad back fills the doorway.*

Mr Schwarzenegger! I'm so glad you could make it. Now, let's go inside and talk about the future of California.

Arnold Schwarzenegger *steps into the meeting, followed by* **Lay**.

The door closes.

Scene Seven

SKILLING'S OFFICE

Skilling   I hate those guys. I hate those legislators and politicians – not because they restrict business and fuck up the markets, even though they do and it does. I hate government because I know those guys. I went to school with them. And let me tell you, the weakest, most ignorant, most drunken fucking incompetents went to work for the US government. Because they weren't smart enough for the private sector. And that's the truth. I got head-hunted. And those bottom-of-the-fucking-barrel, frat-party know-nothing fucks who never got the call design the regulations for an energy market they know nothing about. It's my job to find ways round that. Why should we respect ineptitude? Why should we look at the lazy

fucking regulations they've put in place by committee and go,
'Yeah, you suck at your jobs, fine, we'll ignore that and just
suck at ours too.' Who do you think is gonna win in the end?!
The greedy or the inept?! We're not perfect, but wait till you
see the other guys.

Skilling *is in a meeting with the* **Lawyer**.

Lawyer   Understood.

Skilling   So why the fuck are people picketing my house?!

Lawyer   There were deaths in California. If I'm gonna
represent you I need to know your level of involvement.

Skilling   I want you to represent me, not the company. I
didn't kill anyone.

Lawyer   There may be civil suits against *you*.

Skilling   This is crazy.

Lawyer   I can find other companies that were doing this
over there. But you're getting the bad press cos your guys gave
it a name.

Skilling   What do you mean?

Lawyer (*consults his papers*)   Ricochet. Fat Boy. Burn Out.
Death Star. All on record as your traders' names for their
strategies in California.

Skilling   Death Star?!

Lawyer   What I'm saying. 'Death Star' – makes it sound
like kids on a video game.

Skilling   That's a perception problem.

Lawyer   Jeff, sending a state into chaos is, you know, that's
not just a perception problem.

Skilling   Will this affect the stock price?

Lawyer   I'm a lawyer, not a stock analyst.

Skilling Cos that cannot happen.

Lawyer Maybe you should have thought of that before.

Skilling But we didn't do anything illegal in California.

Lawyer That's a matter of opinion.

Skilling I got a group of the smartest people in the world who can tell you why what they did was not illegal.

Lawyer If it wasn't illegal, it was stupid.

Skilling I don't think you understand how markets work.

Lawyer OK, well, let me put it to you this way, what do you think the chances are of other states deregulating after what happened in California?

Skilling You don't get to *choose*! You don't get to say, we like this much of free markets but not the whole thing. That's not free!

Lawyer I'm not interested in the economics.

Skilling So what are you interested in?

Lawyer Protecting you. There'll be a couple of guys in trading will take a fall, they'll get a little wire fraud –

Skilling Those guys deserve medals.

Lawyer There'll only be a bigger problem if there's anything else, any underlying . . .

The red box throbs from deep underneath.

Skilling Yeah. OK. But you can make this go away?

Lawyer I'm the best. You'd be paying for that. And that's why we'd win.

Skilling OK. OK.

A large Enron **Security Officer** *appears in* **Skilling***'s doorway.*

Skilling *looks dishevelled and highly strung.*

Security Officer You wanted me to take a look at something?

Skilling Yes, please. Yeah.

Lawyer I'll take care of it.

Skilling Thanks.

*The **Lawyer** leaves.*

Security Officer Sir.

Skilling Hey.

Sorry, this is a little – can you, can you sweep this office for . . . equipment or recording . . .

Security Officer You think you're being bugged, sir?

Skilling Maybe, something –

Security Officer That might be a matter for the FBI –

Skilling No, no, just take a look –

Security Officer You think it's the government, sir?

Skilling No –

Security Officer A rival company – ?

Skilling I don't know. I just got a feeling.

*The **Security Officer** checks around the office surfaces.*

Skilling How's things in Maintenance?

Security Officer I'm in Security, sir.

Skilling Sure.

Security Officer It's good.

Skilling You all got your 401Ks? You're all OK?

Security Officer Absolutely, sir. I got a daughter and I'd like her to go to college, do something real . . . Well, things become a lot easier with the stock options you've given us, that becomes a possibility.

Skilling   Yeah. Good.

Listen, can you hear, like a hiss like, you can tell something's on . . . ? Wait, maybe under . . .

He gets down on the floor. He eventually puts his ear near the floor.

Here.

The **Security Officer** *gets down on the floor too. He copies* **Skilling** *who puts his ear to floor. They listen, lying on the floor together.*

Skilling   There's a sort of, ticking sound.

They listen.

Security Officer   Might that be your watch, sir?

Skilling*'s head is leaning on his wrist with his watch on. He gets up, embarrassed.*

Skilling   It was earlier.

Security Officer   Could be something just needs rewiring, sometimes a static charge / (can build up).

Skilling   / Yeah.

Security Officer   Well, you let me know if you hear anything.

Skilling   Sure.

It's hot out, don't you think?

Security Officer   Real dry. The trees are bribing the dogs.

They laugh.

Skilling   Hey. You'll be straight. I've been thinking about our next venture. I've been thinking about taking Enron into weather.

Security Officer   Weather?

Skilling   Yeah, for investors or companies whose worth can be damaged by bad weather. We could carve out a market in protecting against that. Have people buy up shares in weather.

Security Officer   Like insurance?

Skilling   Sort of, yeah. We break up the risk, sell it off in parts like credit derivatives.

Security Officer   You're losing me, sir.

Skilling (*keen, looking for paper and pen*)   Sit down. I can explain it to you in minutes.

Security Officer   Sounds a little out of my –

Skilling   It's not, it makes total sense.

Security Officer   I just want to do my job.

Skilling   You don't want to hear what's next for the company?

Security Officer   You're telling me to –

Skilling   Sit down! You want to be a doorman the rest of your life? Sit down and listen!

Beat.

Security Officer   I'm a Security Officer, sir.

Skilling   Sure, I know.

Security Officer   I just got a shift I gotta do is all.

Skilling   I just wanted you to understand . . .

Security Officer   I'm fine. We trust you all up here, sir.

Skilling   Didn't mean to be wasting your time.

Security Officer   Nothing to it. I apologise.

Skilling   Very Enron, though. Dealing in weather?

Security Officer   Sure. It's your company, sir . . . You run it how you want it run.

Skilling *nods.*

Security Officer *leaves.*

Skilling's *intercom beeps.*

Skilling   Yes?

Secretary (*voice-over*)   Mr Skilling, there's a reporter on the line from *Fortune* magazine –

Skilling (*down phone*)   Jeff Skilling.

I can't answer those questions right now. I am not an accountant. Look, I don't think you understand the complexity of the way we operate here. If you print an article now without our side, I personally think that's unethical. Sure, I'll send someone out, at Enron's expense. He'll fly out and help you understand the questions you're asking.

Goddamn.

Scene Eight

ANDY'S LAIR

Skilling *enters* **Fastow**'s *shady lair, all anxiety.*

The **Raptors** *stay visible. Two have grown very bold now – fast and aggressive. One of them is weak and sickly, the other two flank it to protect it.*

Skilling *approaches to pet them and one of the strong* **Raptors** *is aggressive. He backs off. It follows him and pins him.* **Skilling** *is deeply unnerved by them.*

Skilling   Andy?!

No reply.

Andy!

Fastow *enters.*

He tazers a **Raptor** *to protect* **Skilling**. *It falls down, ultimately unharmed. The others back off.*

Fastow   Hey.

Skilling   What the fuck was that?!

Fastow   Something's spooked 'em.

Skilling   What's wrong with that one?

Fastow   It's sick. I don't know. Maybe I gave it too much.

Skilling   Too much what?

Fastow   Hmm? Oh, of the debt, Jeff.

Skilling   Will it spread?

Fastow   No. I don't know.

He tries to look at and comfort the injured **Raptor**.

Skilling   Well. That's a good reason. That's a good excuse, we're getting rid of them.

The **Raptors** *seem to hear him and snap around, maybe moving towards* **Fastow** *for support.*

Fastow   Jeff?!

Skilling   You heard me.

Fastow   We can't. They're consuming a billion dollars' worth of debt.

Skilling   Get rid of them.

Beat.

I need you to fly out to New York.

Fastow   What's in New York?

Skilling   A reporter. *Fortune* magazine. They're running an article on us.

Fastow   A reporter wants to talk to me!

Skilling   It's not a positive article.

Fastow   What do you mean, it's not a positive article?!

Skilling   They have *questions*.

Fastow   Fuck them! We don't have to –

Skilling   You got to go out there and explain how it works. How money flows through the business. That we're not a black box.

Fastow   But we *are* a black box, Jeff.

Skilling   We are not! We're a logistics company! With a ton of great ideas –

Fastow   I don't want to leave LJM.

Skilling   You're going and you're / (gonna) –

Fastow   Please don't make me go.

Skilling   You're Chief Financial Officer –

Fastow   Jeff, I'm at my best here.

Skilling (*violent*)   Be a fucking man! You're going to have to choose between LJM and Enron.

Fastow   I created LJM.

Skilling   I created *you*!

Andy, I love you. And I would do anything for you. But you're gonna have to choose.

Beat.

Fastow   What am I going to say?

Skilling   Look, if we disclose everything, there'll be panic, right?

Fastow   Right.

Skilling   So for everybody's good, they don't want trouble, we don't want trouble –

Fastow   What if they *do* want trouble? I mean, they're a *magazine*. What if they take a good look, what if they take a really close look and they come to the conclusion that everything's just hedged against our own stock –

Skilling   Andy, don't you dare say that in my – (presence).

Fastow   What if they look and they see that underneath there's nothing actually there –

Skilling   Nothing?! Twenty thousand employees taking home paychecks nothing? World's most innovative company? We *run* Texas, is that nothing? Then the whole fucking thing's nothing. Then the world's nothing.

Fastow   OK, OK! I'll go! I'll just take all the paperwork. Throw information at them. Bury them / in it.

Skilling   You go and you do that!

*As **Skilling** is at his most manic and the **Raptors** are circling, **Ken Lay** enters.*

*Lay is absolutely oblivious to the **Raptors**, the odd environment and the men's turmoil. He holds two scraps of material.*

Lay   Hey, Jeff! Here you are. Listen, I need your opinion. I don't know which of these for the cabin of the new jet.

He holds the choices up.

*Both men stare at him. The **Raptors** stare at him.*

Skilling (*slowly*)   Andy has to fly out to New York.

Fastow   There's a loss of confidence. I think. Going on.

Lay   So I'm hearing. I'll talk to Dick.

Skilling   That won't do it. Ken, this has all been across your desk, you know what's / going on.

Lay   Listen, if you boys are talking business –

Fastow   I mean, I was only doing what I was asked to do.

Skilling   And if the stock falls –

Lay   The stock is not going to fall. That is not going to happen. You're running this show, Jeff.

Skilling   We need to have a / conversation –

Lay (*threatening*)   I don't want to have a conversation! Once you bury a dead dog, you don't dig it up to smell it.

Now, which goddamn pattern?

Lay *doesn't look at the* **Raptors** *or anything except the material swatches and sometimes* **Skilling**.

Skilling, *desperately buying into the charade, points at one.* **Lay** *nods, satisfied and lowers the swatches.*

Lay   OK, listen up. This is a confidence thing. You're gonna have to make a call with the stock analysts to reassure the market. This is just a confidence thing.

Pause.

Lay   Now!

Skilling, *dead-eyed, gets ushered off by* **Lay**.

Fastow   So I'll just do . . . what you aked me to then, Jeff, yeah?

Lay *turns back, eyes the minion.*

Lay   Jeff's not here.

Fastow   I can – I'll take care of it, Mr Lay.

Lay   You don't belong to me, boy.

He leaves.

Left alone with his creations, **Fastow** *rallies himself to do his master's bidding. He eyes the* **Raptors**.

Fastow   I'm sorry, girls. I gotta take you off the books.

He destroys the **Raptors**.

Fastow I don't care what they say about the company. As long as they don't make me look bad.

He torches LJM.

Scene Nine

THE ASSHOLE

Skilling *climbs stairs like a man on his way to the gallows, unkempt and addled.*

He eyes the stock price.

Lay Everyone just needs a bit of faith restored. Stand straight, Jeffrey. You couldn't shave?

Skilling   I know. I'm fine. I'm Jeff Skilling. OK. OK.

As he goes up, he notices his presence pushing the stock price up a very little bit.

Lay Here we go.

*This spurs **Skilling** on.*

*As they go up, Enron **Analysts** and **Journalists** emerge from everywhere to listen to the conference call.*

Skilling Just an outstanding quarter, another outstanding quarter. We're growing real quick in earnings and revenue and we have the strongest position in every market we're in . . . You know, so I have no idea why our stock's as low as it is, fifty-four dollars, that's crazy! People are saying we're opaque, we're a black box, we're not. That's like calling Michael Jordan a black box just cos you don't know what he's gonna score each quarter! (*Pause.*) We are very optimistic.

*Silence. **Skilling** exhales.*

Lay You'll take questions now.

Skilling   I'll take questions now.

Pause.

Analyst   Hi. Richard Grubman here, hello.

Skilling   Mr Grubman.

Analyst (*slightly haughty*)   Hello. I don't really care about the earnings at this point. What I want to see is a balance sheet.

Skilling   We will have that done shortly. But until we put all that together, we just cannot give you that.

Analyst   I am trying to understand why that would be an unreasonable request.

Skilling   I'm not saying we can't tell you what the balances are. But we'll wait – at this point – to disclose those until all . . . the right accounting is put together.

Analyst   You're the only financial institution that cannot produce a balance sheet or a cashflow statement with their earnings.

Skilling   Well, you're . . . you – Well, uh, thank you very much. We appreciate it.

Analyst   Appreciate it?

Skilling   Asshole.

There is utter silence as everyone realises what he just said to an important stock analyst.

Then suddenly there is frenetic activity.

Business Anchor   Shockwaves were sent through the market today when Jeffrey Skilling referred to a senior stock analyst with a common but offensive term.

The **Analysts** *all get on their phones and BlackBerries to their banks and brokerage firms*

Analysts (*together, overlapping, merging into one*) You're never gonna guess what the fuck just happened – I think the big JS

is losing it here – You got shareprice on Enron? – Something's
going on down there – Called a Wall Street analyst an 'a-hole'
during a conference call – CEO's gone sorta postal – I'm
gonna recommend we hold – I don't know for now – I'm
hearin' stuff here I don't like – Enron, the energy company –
We gotta ask for the books – They're a black box – I wanna
sell – Are people selling? – Enron – OK, we're outta there –
Hold on Enron – Sell – Hold – Sell – Somebody selling –
Enron – Sell – Hold – OK – Selling – What's the market
doing? – Hold – Selling – Enron – Sell – Sell – Selling Enron,
Enron – 'Asshole, asshole, asshole.'

The **Analysts** *have taken themselves off, hurrying back to their
marketplace hubs, a sea change in the offing.*

*But their effects are already painfully clear on the stock price, which is
free-falling.*

A spotlight on **Skilling** *alone, unsupported. Just him and his
representation of his self-worth, the stock price.*

Skilling *approaches it desperately, trying to regain former glories.*

Skilling No! Please, come on. I'm happy, I'm . . . excited . . .

The stock price does not respond.

Come on, this is crazy.

Nothing.

IT'S ME! Everything will be fine, don't be idiotic!

The stock price drops slightly. **Skilling** *recoils with shock.*

No, no, no, sorry –

It drops further. He's terrified.

Jesus, no, stop. Oh God.

He goes to his phone. He dials a number he knows by heart. It rings.

Hi, sweetheart. It's your dad. Are you OK? Yeah, I'm sorry,
I know, it's four in the morning. Is your mom there?

Beat.

OK, well, this is important. I need you to tell her something. Are you awake? OK. Tell her to sell her shares. Sell her shares, All of them. I love you.

He turns to the stock price.

What do you want? You want me? Is that it? Is that what you want?!

He ends, his arms outstretched, crucifying himself before the market.

The blocks beneath where **Skilling** *was standing are removed by* **Analysts** *and* **Brokers** *as shares continue to be sold and the company weakens.*

A sour, tuneless version of the 'Enron' barbershop quartet from earlier plays.

Scene Ten

PRIVATE MEETING

Sheryl Sloman *and* **Ken Lay** *are in a meeting with* **Skilling**.

Sloman (*to* **Skilling**)   You're resigning?

Lay   We wanted to tell you first.

Sloman   When are you going public with this?

Lay   Later on today. We don't want the market getting the wrong idea. You've been a great cheerleader for us.

Sloman   I'm a professional stock analyst.

Let's not pretend. This is highly unusual. There should be a *year* leading up to this, a structured handover. Jeff, why are you resigning?

Pause.

Skilling (*teary*)   The company's in great shape, it couldn't be less to do with that. I . . . A company like this, it consumes your life. I've neglected my daughter. This is personal.

Lay   It's not cos of the stock.

Skilling   I'm doing this for the company. It'll go up when I announce. The market's decided. It wants me out.

Sloman   That's not true. People say, people say all over, 'I'm not long Enron, but I'm long Jeff Skilling.'

This seems to affect him deeply.

Skilling   You pour your life into something and, if it doesn't reflect back at you . . . I'm so tired.

I can't sleep.

Sloman   Are you worried about recent performance? Are there accounting issues?

Lay   There are no accounting / issues –

Sloman (*to* **Skilling**)   Is that why you can't sleep?

Skilling   I haven't slept since I was fourteen.

Sloman   People are talking about what's been going on here.

Lay   We're going to deal with all that.

Sloman   That *Fortune* article raised a lot of questions.

Lay   I can honestly say the company's in the best shape it's ever been.

Jeff?

Skilling   I should go.

Lay   Yeah, you go get ready to announce.

Skilling *leaves.*

Sloman   This is a blow for you.

Lay (*understating*)   I would have preferred he stay.

Sloman   Is Jeff sick, Ken?

Beat.

Lay   Depends what you mean by sick.

Sloman   I've always been a supporter of Enron Corporation. But, you know, the CEO leaving like this? That doesn't spin. You've got to hold this thing together.

Lay   Don't you worry about anything here. I'm a safe pair of hands.

With a reassuring squeeze of her arm, **Lay** *stalks off, leaving* **Sloman** *thoughtful.*

News Reporters   In breaking news, Enron's CEO has resigned. Now the market's left asking the question the company is famous for: WHY?

Act Three

Scene One

THE EARTHQUAKE HITS

Sloman (*to us*)   There's a strange thing goes on inside a bubble. It's hard to describe. People who are in it can't see outside of it, don't believe there is an outside. You get glazed over. I believed in Enron. Everybody did. I told people again and again to keep buying that stock and I kept rating it and supporting it and championing it like it was my own child. And people say, how could you? If you didn't understand how it worked. Well. You get on a plane, you don't understand exactly how it works, but you believe it'll fly. You know – and everyone else boarding that plane knows – it'll fly up into the air and take you to your destination, crazy as that may seem. And if you got out your seat, said 'I'm not flying, I don't know how it works,' you'd look crazy. Well, it's like that. Except. Imagine if the *belief* that the plane *could* fly was all that was keeping it in the air. It'd be fine. If everybody believed. If nobody got scared. As long as people didn't ask stupid questions. About what it is keeps planes in the air.

September 11th 2001.

They improvise their responses.

Eventually . . .

Ken Lay *comes out to give a speech.*

As the speech goes on, **Lay** *becomes surrounded by tiny pieces of shredded paper being blown all over him, all over the stage. He keeps trying to carry on regardless. The shredding represents the huge destruction of documents going on at Enron and Arthur Andersen.*

Lay   Well, I'm delighted to be back in charge. In more normal circumstances, I'd have a few words to say about September the 11th. Just like America's under attack by terrorism, I think we're under attack, at Enron.

News Report   (With the world's markets still reeling from the recent tragic events, a formal investigation has been opened into energy trading giant Enron, deepening its share price crisis. The company has lost 60 per cent of its value since . . .)

Lay   I'm sorry Jeff did resign. Despite the rumours, the company is doing well both financially and operationally. When our very way of life is being threatened, we remain proud of who we are and what we do. This is not the time for doubt, not the time for our confidence to be shaken –

News Report   The terror attacks on New York and Washington have seen stock exchanges all over the world evacuated and all trading has ceased. Market confidence has dissolved today as Tokyo, London and then New York fell to record lows –

Lay   Truth is the great rock. Whether it will continue to be submerged by a wave – a wave of terror by those attacking us – will be determined by Enron employees. We will testify to the truth. We will let the light shine in. We won't let this cloud of lies cover all our good works and deeds.
Collapse.

News Report   Today saw the largest corporate bankruptcy in the history of the world as energy giant Enron fell. Over twenty thousand people are thought to have lost their jobs, health insurance and retirement plans. The company has collapsed after it was found to have disguised billions of dollars of debt, leading an outraged Senate to call for an immediate investigation.

Scene Two

CIRCLE OF BLAME

Detritus litters the stage. Order must be restored. Trials / hearings.

Senator These hearings are an attempt to investigate America's largest corporate bankruptcy. What happened, why did it happen and who is responsible for it happening?

Those responsible are present around the outskirts of the stage, maybe some sort of a circle: **Lay, Fastow, Ramsay** *and* **Hewitt, Arthur Andersen,** *the* **Board.** *But not Skilling.*

A light moves from player to player as they speak.

Member of the Board (*as a statement*) The Board is shocked and dismayed by events. We are not lawyers and had no idea Mr. Fastow was doing anything illegal.

Ramsay As a law firm, we had a responsibility to the law

Hewitt If illegal practises went on –

Ramsay After we signed off on LJM –

Hewitt That's entirely another matter –

Ramsay Another matter entirely.

Hewitt We explicitly –

Ramsay *and* **Hewitt** – avoided the illegal. We are not accountants.

Arthur Andersen I am an accountant. For my sins (!) These procedures were unusual.

Little Arthur They were not illegal.

Arthur Andersen Arthur Andersen are happy to provide all Enron-related documents.

Little Arthur Except for all the ones we shredded.

Arthur Andersen *wrestles his dummy into acquiescence.*

Fastow Mr Chairman, on the advice of my counsel, I respectfully decline to answer the questions put to me based on the protection afforded me under the United States

Lay   I have been instructed by my counsel not to testify based on my fifth-amendment constitutional rights.

Skilling *enters the hearing.*

Skilling   I will testify. I'll answer any question you got. I'll take a lie detector test right here, right now. This whole situations's been terrible for a lot of people, and I'm here to explain what happened. And how I can help.

Senator   With due respect, Mr Skilling, I'm not going to ask you to help. Let me put something to you: is it a matter of coincidence that a few months after you left Enron the company collapsed?

Skilling   When I left Enron corporation, on August 14th of the year 2001, I believed that the company was in – was in great shape.

Senator   Do you have personal worth of more than a hundred million dollars?

Skilling   I don't have the records with me.

Senator   Would that be surprising to you to learn that you had that?

Skilling   No that would – that would not be a surprise.

Senator   And how do you feel about the employees whose families have lost their life savings?

Skilling   Well, I guess –

Senator   You donated any of that money to employees?

Skilling   At this point . . . I have thirty-six separate lawsuits against me. It is my expectation that I will spend the next five to ten years of my life battling those lawsuits.

Senator   And you don't believe you've done anything wrong?

Skilling   The markets were . . . destroyed after September 11th. There were allegations of accounting problems, of accounting irregularities. In business terms, that's tantamount to yelling fire in a crowded theatre. It becomes a run on the bank.

Senator/Judge (*to us*)   Thank you, Mr Skilling.

A few bad apples have shamed American corporate culture here. But today is our day. . . . Day for the US Senate, the courts. And the people. And we will see that those millionaires with their private jets and luxury lifestyles are forced to explain to those of us with normal lives on the ground what misdeeds have been done. The American Government will not stand for corporate crime on this scale. I mean, on any scale.

Gavel bang three times.

Scene Three

TRIAL

Lawyer   Mr Fastow, you've spent a great deal of time today describing your actions as 'a hero of Enron'. Do you really view your behaviour as heroic?

Fastow   I think I said I was a hero and I believed I was a hero in the context of Enron's culture.

Lawyer   Were you a hero when you stole from Enron – yes or no?

Fastow   No, I was not.

Lawyer   You must be consumed by an insatiable greed. Is that fair to say?

Fastow   I believe I was extremely greedy and that I lost my moral compass. I've done terrible things that I very much regret.

Lawyer   That sounded awfully rehearsed, Mr Fastow.

Fastow   With respect, your questions sound pretty rehearsed too.

Lawyer   Are you smart, Mr Skilling?

Skilling   Yes.

Lawyer 2   Sure you are. So you knew and understood what Mr Fastow was doing at your company?

Fastow   We knew and understood that it was wrong.

Skilling   I knew and understood that it was legal.

Lawyer   Did you steal?

Fastow   We stole. We all benefited financially.

Skilling   I would never steal from Enron.

Lawyer   Did you profit personally, illegally from LJM?

Fastow   I did.

Skilling   I did not know that.

Lawyer 2   You did not want to know.

Lawyer   How much?

Fastow   It's difficult to say.

Lawyer   Try.

Fastow   Around forty five million dollars –

Lawyer   Forty five million (!)

And how much did Mr Skilling profit personally?

Skilling   None.

Fastow   None. Directly.

Lawyer   None! So doesn't it make sense that you'd protect yourself today? Say anything to get your boss convicted, maybe make arrangements with the federal government!

Lawyer 2   Objection!

Lawyer   He promoted you, supported you and trusted you, did not profit at all, yet was betrayed by you!

Lawyer 2   Mr Skilling, During the period of February '99 through June 2001, did you convert your stock worth sixty-six million dollars?

Skilling   That sounds –

Lawyer 2   All the time telling employees to invest?

Fastow   When you misrepresent the nature of your company –

Skilling   I believed in Enron.

Fastow   Then cash in your stock options, that is stealing –

Lawyer   We all know you know 'bout stealing' Mr Fastow –

Fastow   We committed crimes at Enron.

Lawyer   No, you committed crimes at Enron!

Lawyer 2   You thought the company was fine, everything was fine, with things in such great shape, why did you resign?

Skilling   I resigned because the market demanded it.

Lawyer 2   You left a sinking ship! Women and children first, right after Jeff!

Skilling   The company was worth what it was worth because of me.

Lawyer 2   Does that include the nothing it's worth now?

Beat.

Lawyer 2   Remind me, Mr Skilling, who hired Andy Fastow?

Skilling   I did.

Lawyer   But LJM was your idea?

Fastow   I was *asked* to look for loopholes.

Lawyer 2 And when you made him CFO, you knew the sort of man he was?

Skilling I didn't know him *well*.

Lawyer 2 He worshipped you, wanted to impress you –

Skilling I don't see how that's – (relevant) /

Lawyer 2 Andy Fastow came to you with LJM, with this insane idea, you knew that it was wrong, but you signed off!

Skilling We didn't do anything that every other company doesn't do! We did it more! We did it better! Show me one transaction the accountants and lawyers didn't sign off on!

Lawyer When the history books are written about what happened at Enron you know your name is going to be on that page. You want to make sure Mr Skilling's name is on that page also.

Fastow You know what I'd like written on that page? That I had the courage to admit I did something wrong.

Court Officer Andrew Fastow, you are found guilty on two counts of criminal conspiracy.

Court Officer Kenneth Lay you are found guilty on six counts of conspiracy and securities fraud.

Lay *and* **Fastow** *are cuffed.* **Skilling** *is cuffed.*

Court Officer Jeffrey Skilling you have been found guilty of nineteen separate counts of securities fraud, wire fraud and insider trading.

Scene Four

THE STREET

Skilling (I don't want to do it any more.)

A man walks past him, completely ignores his intoxication and walks on by.

(*Mumbled.*)   I'm Jeff. Fuck off. Jeff. Where's it now and aren't talking to you when you're not even here . . .

Unintelligible sounds.

Another man walks past him, **Skilling** *almost walks into him. The man makes a sound of disgust and walks on.*

Skilling *walks by a* **Woman** *working as a prostitute.*

Woman   Hey, baby, do you need anything?

Skilling   What?

Woman   I want to get to know you better.

Skilling   Why, what do you want?

Woman   I like you, do you want to go somewhere and talk about it?

Skilling   They probably . . . I don't know if I should. I'm out on bail . . .

Woman   Hey, aren't we all? You got a lotta money, honey?

Skilling   Who are you?

Woman   I'm your new best friend if you want me.

Skilling   Are you with *them*?

Woman   Wow. OK.

Skilling   Are you talking through her now? No. You think I'm . . . You're with the FBI. Are you recording this?

Woman   Screw this.

Skilling   Stop recording! Who else?

Woman   I'm not with the FBI, sweetheart.

Skilling   Where's the fucking thing? Where's the wire –

Woman   Fuck you.

Skilling   Stop lying . . .

Skilling *gropes at the* **Woman***'s chest, trying to expose the wire under her shirt. He tears at it. She screams.*

Woman   Asshole! I hope your dick falls off!

She stoirms off.

Skilling   Don't you see! This is my life!

Scene Five

SKILLING'S HOUSE, OCTOBER 2006

Daughter *watches an Enron commercial on television with no sound. Eventually –*

The **Lawyer** *lets himself into* **Skilling***'s house.*

Slowly, eerily, she rises to face him, stares at him.

She walks away from him, leaving the room.

Daughter (*offstage*)   Daddy!

Eventually **Skilling** *enters in his robe, drinking a Diet Coke and eating a Twinkie.*

Skilling   Hey.

Lawyer   You mind me having a key?

Beat.

Skilling   No.

Thanks for coming to the house.

Lawyer   Not a lot of choice.

Skilling   Are we going to talk about the appeal?

Lawyer   We can do that.

I want to talk about the sentence.

Skilling   Oh.

Lawyer   I can tell you the maximum, but that is the maximum.

If they want to make an example of you –

Skilling   Which they may do –

Lawyer   They absolutely do.

Skilling   Twenty.

Pause.

Lawyer   Yeah.

Skilling   Let's talk about the appeal.

Lawyer   That's what you're instructing me to do?

Beat.

Skilling   You believe me, don't you?

Beat.

Lawyer   I'm gonna be straight with you, I think we should appeal, I think that's our option. But there is further evidence coming to light all the time of alleged wrongdoing at the company –

Skilling   Not *my* wrongdoing.

Lawyer   Not your wrongdoing.

Skilling   Doing. *Doyng*. Wrong*doyng*!

Lawyer   Recordings and testimony from those involved, particularly traders –

Skilling   Oh those fucking guys –

Lawyer   Stating that they behaved in an amoral manner –

Skilling   Ha!

Lawyer   An appeal would only shed further light on –

Skilling   I told my daughter I was innocent. I believe I am innocent.

Lawyer   Neither of those things make you innocent.

Skilling   Being innocent makes me innocent though, right?

Lawyer   Jeff, they're going to imply that the traders at your company caused huge blackouts in California for months, maybe years. That you gamed the state –

Skilling   The state's regulations were a mess.

Lawyer   And you took advantage of that?

Beat.

Skilling   Took advantage of that. Are you kidding me? Took advantage of . . . ! That's what we do. In business, you buy something at one price, you sell it at a higher one and what's in between, that's your advantage. Which you *take*. That's how the world *works*. If you want an objective morality present in every contract, you're living in a dream. You know how difficult it is to get five people in a room to agree *anything*? The only way I can be sure I can *trust* a contract is cos every party's in it for themselves. So when you ask, 'Did we take *advantage* of that?' . . . you know what I hear? I hear, 'Do you make a living, do you breathe in and out, are you a man?' And I know that the only difference between me and the people judging me is they weren't smart enough to do what we did.

Lawyer   A lot of people lost everything.

Skilling   I get that! *I've* lost everything. This is my life! I'm a captain of fucking industry!

Lawyer   Well you wanna put some pants on, captain?

Beat.

Skilling   None of them fit.

Lawyer   There's another player in this still we should talk about. You were running that company but you reported to its chairman, Ken Lay. And he's gonna be getting the same advice Andy got –

Skilling   Andy broke my goddamn heart. Ken'll never go that way.

Lawyer   But you could.

Skilling   What? Blame Ken?

Lawyer   The man's sixty-four years old –

Skilling (*snorts*)   You're going with that! You're going with the guy's closer to death . . . ?

Lawyer   They want a name. They want a face.

Skilling   And then just go on like before . . .

Skilling's *home phone begins to ring. He makes to answer the phone.*

Lawyer   I need you to stop answering the phone. Stop answering questions. Your name needs to be 'no comment' until I tell you.

The **Lawyer** *answers the phone.*

Lawyer   Who is it?

Skilling   But that makes us look guilty.

Lawyer   I'm his lawyer.

The **Lawyer** *listens.*

Lawyer   OK. OK.

Skilling   You don't think that makes me look guilty?

Lawyer   I will.

The **Lawyer** *hangs up.*

Lawyer   Jeff. Jeff, Ken Lay died.

Skilling *tries to process the news.*

Skilling How?

Lawyer They didn't say.

Lawyer I'm sorry. I gotta find out what this means.

Skilling I know what it means. It's just me.

Scene Six

THE FUNERAL

We're outside. Before a funeral. It is sunny.

As **Skilling** *dresses for a funeral, guests in mourning black gather.* **Claudia Roe** *enters in mourning black, an ostentatious hat obscuring her face. He sees her.*

Skilling Claudia.

Skilling *is flanked by a* **Police Officer** *in a suit and dark glasses. The Secret Service presence is noticeable.*

Skilling Can you just give me a minute?

Police Officer We can stand over there.

Skilling Then could you do that, please?

He does.

Roe I didn't think they'd let you come.

Skilling Dispensation. For an hour.

Roe Only one officer with you?

Skilling What do you think I'm gonna do?

Roe You look awful.

Skilling You seen what they're saying about us? Democrats trying to win votes from poor people they've never met.

Roe Is it true, after it fell – the only part of the business with any worth at all was my division? The things you could hold?

Skilling   You got out!

Roe   Not by choice.

Skilling   Well, aren't you gonna thank me!?

Irene Gant, *a more mature woman, approaches* **Skilling**.

Irene Gant   Mr Skilling? My name's Irene Gant. And I worked for Enron for twenty-five years. I did everything you asked. I took all my savings and I invested them in the company I worked for. I've lost a hundred and fifty thousand dollars. I have no money to retire on. And I'm living at my sister's. I wanted you to know because I swore, if I ever saw you in person, well, I don't wanna say.

Skilling   What do you expect me to say to that?

Irene Gant   I want an answer from you –

Skilling   I don't have answers.

Irene Gant   I have lost everything!

Roe   This is not the place –

Irene Gant   Oh, am I embarrassing you?! I'm sorry. Am I embarrassing you?!

Security Officer *from earlier scene approaches the hubbub.*

Security Officer   There trouble here?

Skilling   No.

The **Security Officer** *glares at* **Skilling**. **Skilling** *recognises him.*

Skilling   I should go wait in the car.

Irene Gant   Won't even apologise.

She spits at him and leaves.

The men look at each other. The **Security Officer** *ushers* **Irene Gant** *back into the funeral throng.*

Roe   That guy's not here to stop you running. He's here to stop you getting hurt.

Skilling   Can I walk in with you?

Roe   I got to take care of myself here.

Beat.

Baptist church bells. **Roe** *leaves to enter the church alone.*

Skilling *is left alone watching the employees enter the church. He eventually turns to leave.*

Epilogue

During this chorus section, **Skilling** *changes into prison garb and hands in his possessions.*

Board   When Enron was declared bankrupt, it was over thirty billion dollars in debt.

Security Officer   Days before employees were told to leave, the latest round of bonus cheques was handed out to Enron executives, more than fifty-five million dollars.

Employee   That week, twenty thousand employees lost their jobs.

Senator   The financial practices pioneered at Enron are now widespread throughout the business world.

Business Analyst   Over the last year and a half, the US Government has pumped over ten trillion dollars into the financial system to try and keep it from collapse.

Sloman   Counting that amount at a dollar a second would take more than three hundred and twenty thousand years.

News Reporter   Andy Fastow received a reduced sentence of six years in minimum security in exchange for testifying against his former boss.

Lawyer   Jeffrey Skilling was sentenced to twenty-four years and four months in prison. That is the longest sentence for a corporate crime in history. His case is going to the Supreme Court.

Skilling (*to us*)   I'm not a bad man. I'm not an unusual man. I just wanted to change the world. And I think there'll come a time when everyone understands that. They'll realise they were banishing something of themselves along with me. I believe that.

I know it's hard to understand. How can something be worth a million dollars in the morning and nothing by the afternoon?

Same way a man goes from captain of all industry to a fraud sitting in jail. You want to look at something and know it has . . . a worth, a fundamental value? Bullshit. You're making the same mistake as any religious person. You wanna hold a mirror up to nature?

The huge crack along the wall of the building glows from behind and becomes the jagged line graph of the Dow Jones Index over the last century.

The line on the graph/crack glows.

Skilling (*to us*)   There's your mirror. Every dip, every crash, every bubble that's burst, that's you. Your brilliant stupidity. This one gave us the railroads. This one the internet. This one the slave trade. And if you wanna do anything about saving the environment or reaching other worlds, you'll need a bubble for that too. Everything I've ever done in my life worth anything has been done in a bubble; in a state of extreme hope and trust and stupidity. Would you have gotten married if you could see her face twenty years on turn to you through tears, saying, 'You never knew me at all'?

September the eleventh. 1929. Beginning of the Great Depression, and *Washington Post* prints Mark Twain: 'Don't part with your illusions. When they are gone you may still exist, but you have ceased to live.'

He points to spikes and dips on the graph.

All humanity is here. There's Greed, there's Fear, Joy, Faith, Hope . . .

And the greatest of these . . . is Money.

The sound of prison doors slamming.